I0131913

Mastering PostgreSQL 9.6

A comprehensive guide for PostgreSQL 9.6 developers and administrators

Hans-Jürgen Schönig

Packt>

BIRMINGHAM - MUMBAI

Mastering PostgreSQL 9.6

First published: May 2017

Production reference: 1250517

Published by Packt Publishing Ltd.
Livery Place
35 Livery Street
Birmingham
B3 2PB, UK.
ISBN 978-1-78355-535-2

www.packtpub.com

Credits

Author
Hans-Jürgen Schönig

Reviewer
Shaun Thomas

Commissioning Editor
Amey Varangaonkar

Acquisition Editor
Varsha Shetty

Content Development Editor
Aishwarya Pandere

Technical Editor
Dinesh Pawar

Copy Editor
Vikrant Phadkay

Project Coordinator
Nidhi Joshi

Proofreader
Safis Editing

Indexer
Aishwarya Gangawane

Production Coordinator
Arvindkumar Gupta

About the Author

Hans-Jürgen Schönig has 18 years of experience with PostgreSQL. He is the CEO of a PostgreSQL consulting and support company called Cybertec Schönig & Schönig GmbH (`www.postgresql-support.de`). It has successfully served countless customers around the globe.

Before founding Cybertec Schönig & Schönig GmbH in 2000, he worked as a database developer at a private research company that focused on the Austrian labor market, where he primarily worked on data mining and forecast models. He has also written several books about PostgreSQL.

About the Reviewer

Shaun Thomas has been working with PostgreSQL since late 2000. From 2011 and beyond, he's been a frequent presenter at the PostgresOpen conference on topics such as handling extreme throughput, high availability, monitoring, architecture, and automation. He contributed a few PostgreSQL extensions, as well as a tool for administering massive database clusters. On occasion, he's even been known to guest lecture at the local university. His goal is to help the community make PostgreSQL a bigger, better database for everyone to enjoy.

www.PacktPub.com

For support files and downloads related to your book, please visit www.PacktPub.com.

Did you know that Packt offers eBook versions of every book published, with PDF and ePub files available? You can upgrade to the eBook version at www.PacktPub.com and as a print book customer, you are entitled to a discount on the eBook copy. Get in touch with us at service@packtpub.com for more details.

At www.PacktPub.com, you can also read a collection of free technical articles, sign up for a range of free newsletters and receive exclusive discounts and offers on Packt books and eBooks.

⋀Mapt

https://www.packtpub.com/mapt

Get the most in-demand software skills with Mapt. Mapt gives you full access to all Packt books and video courses, as well as industry-leading tools to help you plan your personal development and advance your career.

Why subscribe?

- Fully searchable across every book published by Packt
- Copy and paste, print, and bookmark content
- On demand and accessible via a web browser

Customer Feedback

Thanks for purchasing this Packt book. At Packt, quality is at the heart of our editorial process. To help us improve, please leave us an honest review on this book's Amazon page at https://www.amazon.com/dp/1783555351.

If you'd like to join our team of regular reviewers, you can e-mail us at customerreviews@packtpub.com. We award our regular reviewers with free eBooks and videos in exchange for their valuable feedback. Help us be relentless in improving our products!

Table of Contents

Preface

PostgreSQL is an open source database management tool used for handling large datasets (big data) and as a JSON document database. It also has applications in the software and web domains. This book will enable you to build better PostgreSQL applications and administer databases more efficiently.

What this book covers

Chapter 1, *PostgreSQL Overview*, will give you an overview of PostgreSQL and its features. You will learn about new stuff and new functionality available in PostgreSQL.

Chapter 2, *Understanding Transactions and Locking*, will cover one of the most important aspects of any database system. Proper database work is usually not possible without the existence of transactions, and understanding transactions and locking is vital to performance as well as professional work.

Chapter 3, *Making Use of Indexes*, covers everything you need to know about indexes. Indexes are key to performance and are therefore an important cornerstone if you want good user experience and high throughput. All important aspects of indexing will be covered.

Chapter 4, *Handling Advanced SQL*, will introduce some of the most important concepts of modern SQL. You will learn about windowing functions as well as other important, more modern, elements of SQL.

Chapter 5, *Log Files and System Statistics*, will guide you through more administrative tasks, such as log file management and monitoring. You will learn how to inspect your servers and extract runtime information from PostgreSQL.

Chapter 6, *Optimizing for Good Query Performance*, will tell you everything you need to know about good PostgreSQL performance. The chapter will cover SQL tuning as well as information about memory management.

Chapter 7, *Writing Stored Procedures,* teaches you some more advanced topics related to server-side code. The most important server-side programming languages are covered and important aspects are pointed out.

Chapter 8, *Managing PostgreSQL Security,* has been designed to help you improve the security of your server. The chapter features everything from user management to row-level security. Information about encryption is also included.

Chapter 9, *Handling Backup and Recovery,* is all about backups and data recovery. You will learn to backup your data and it will enable you to restore things in case of disaster.

Chapter 10, *Making Sense of Backups and Replication,* is all about redundancy. You will learn to asynchronously and synchronously replicate PostgreSQL database systems. All modern features are covered as extensively as possible.

Chapter 11, *Deciding on Useful Extensions,* describes widely used modules that add additional functionality to PostgreSQL. You will learn about the most common extensions.

Chapter 12, *Troubleshooting PostgreSQL,* offers a systematic approach to fixing problems in PostgreSQL. It will enable you to spot common problems and approach them in an organized way.

Chapter 13, *Migrating to PostgreSQL,* is the final chapter of this book and shows you the way from commercial databases to PostgreSQL. The most important databases migrated these days will be covered.

What you need for this book

This book has been written for a broad audience. In order to follow the examples presented in this book, it makes sense to have at least some experience with SQL and maybe even PostgreSQL in general (although this is not a hard requirement). In general, it is a good idea to be familiar with the Unix command line.

Who this book is for

This book has explicitly been written for people who want to know more about PostgreSQL and who are not satisfied with basic information. The aim is to write a book that goes a bit deeper and explains the most important stuff in a clear and easy-to-understand way.

Conventions

In this book, you will find a number of text styles that distinguish between different kinds of information. Here are some examples of these styles and an explanation of their meaning.

Code words in text, database table names, folder names, filenames, file extensions, pathnames, dummy URLs, user input, and Twitter handles are shown as follows: "In this case, the \timing command will tell psql to show the runtime of a query."

Any command-line input or output is written as follows:

```
test=# CREATE TABLE t_test (id serial, name text);
CREATE TABLE
test=# INSERT INTO t_test (name) SELECT 'hans'
FROM generate_series(1, 2000000);
```

New terms and **important words** are shown in bold.

> Warnings or important notes appear in a box like this.

> Tips and tricks appear like this.

Reader feedback

Feedback from our readers is always welcome. Let us know what you think about this book—what you liked or disliked. Reader feedback is important for us as it helps us develop titles that you will really get the most out of.

To send us general feedback, simply e-mail feedback@packtpub.com, and mention the book's title in the subject of your message.

If there is a topic that you have expertise in and you are interested in either writing or contributing to a book, see our author guide at www.packtpub.com/authors.

Customer support

Now that you are the proud owner of a Packt book, we have a number of things to help you to get the most from your purchase.

Errata

Although we have taken every care to ensure the accuracy of our content, mistakes do happen. If you find a mistake in one of our books-maybe a mistake in the text or the code-we would be grateful if you could report this to us. By doing so, you can save other readers from frustration and help us improve subsequent versions of this book. If you find any errata, please report them by visiting http://www.packtpub.com/submit-errata, selecting your book, clicking on the **Errata Submission Form** link, and entering the details of your errata. Once your errata are verified, your submission will be accepted and the errata will be uploaded to our website or added to any list of existing errata under the Errata section of that title.

To view the previously submitted errata, go to https://www.packtpub.com/books/content/support and enter the name of the book in the search field. The required information will appear under the **Errata** section.

Piracy

Piracy of copyrighted material on the Internet is an ongoing problem across all media. At Packt, we take the protection of our copyright and licenses very seriously. If you come across any illegal copies of our works in any form on the Internet, please provide us with the location address or website name immediately so that we can pursue a remedy.

Please contact us at copyright@packtpub.com with a link to the suspected pirated material.

We appreciate your help in protecting our authors and our ability to bring you valuable content.

Questions

If you have a problem with any aspect of this book, you can contact us at questions@packtpub.com, and we will do our best to address the problem.

1
PostgreSQL Overview

PostgreSQL is one of the world's most advanced open source database systems and it has many features widely used by developers and system administrators alike. In this book, many of those cool features will be covered and discussed in great detail.

In this chapter, you will be introduced to PostgreSQL and the cool new features available in PostgreSQL 9.6 and beyond. All relevant new functionality will be covered in detail. Given the sheer number of changes made to the code and given the size of the PostgreSQL project, this list of features is of course not complete, so I tried to focus on the most important aspects relevant to most people.

The features outlined in this chapter will be split into the following categories:

- Database administration
- SQL and developer-related
- Backup, recovery, and replication
- Performance-related topics

What is new in PostgreSQL 9.6?

PostgreSQL 9.6 was released in late 2016 and is the last version that will still be following the old numbering scheme PostgreSQL has been using for more than a decade now. From PostgreSQL 10.0 onward, a new version numbering system will be in place. From 10.0 on, major releases will happen way more frequently.

Understanding new database administration functions

PostgreSQL 9.6 has many new features that can help the administrator to reduce work and make systems more robust.

One of those features is the `idle_in_transaction_session_timeout` function.

Killing idle sessions

In PostgreSQL, a session or a transaction can basically live almost forever. In some cases, this has been a problem because transactions were kept open for too long. Usually, this was due to a bug. The trouble is this: insanely long transactions can cause cleanup problems and table bloat can occur. The uncontrolled growth of a table (table bloat) naturally leads to performance problems and unhappy end users.

Starting with PostgreSQL 9.6, it is possible to limit the duration a database connection is allowed to spend inside a transaction without performing real work. Here is how it works:

```
test=# SET idle_in_transaction_session_timeout TO 2500;
SET
test=# BEGIN;
BEGIN
test=# SELECT 1;
 ?column?
----------
        1
(1 row)

test=# SELECT 1;
FATAL:  terminating connection due to idle-in-transaction timeout
```

Administrators and developers can set a timeout, which is 2.5 seconds in my example. As soon as a transaction is idle for too long, the connection will be terminated automatically by the server. Nasty side effects of long idle transactions can be prevented easily by adjusting this parameter.

Finding more detailed information in pg_stat_activity

The `pg_stat_activity` function is a system view that has been around for many years. It basically contains a list of active connections. In older versions of PostgreSQL, administrators could see that a query is waiting for somebody else—however, it was not possible to figure out why and for whom. This has changed in 9.6. Two columns have been added:

```
test=# \d pg_stat_activity
          View "pg_catalog.pg_stat_activity"
      Column        |          Type          | Modifiers
--------------------+------------------------+-----------
 . . .
 wait_event_type    | text                   |
 wait_event         | text                   |
 . . .
```

In addition to this extension, a new procedure has been added, which shows who caused whom to wait:

```
test=# SELECT * FROM pg_blocking_pids(4711);
 pg_blocking_pids
------------------
 {3435}
(1 row)
```

When the function is called, it will return a list of blocking PIDs.

Tracking vaccum progress

For many years, people have asked for a progress tracker for vacuum. Finally, PostgreSQL 9.6 makes this wish come true by introducing a new system view. Here is how it works:

```
postgres=# SELECT * FROM pg_stat_progress_vacuum ;

[ RECORD 1 ]+

pid | 29546
datid | 67535
datname | test
relid | 16402
phase | scanning heap
heap_blks_total | 6827
heap_blks_scanned | 77
heap_blks_vacuumed | 0
index_vacuum_count | 0
```

```
max_dead_tuples | 154
num_dead_tuples | 0
```

PostgreSQL will provide detailed information about ongoing vacuum processes so that people can track the progress of this vital operation.

Improving vacuum speed

PostgreSQL 9.6 not only provides you with deeper insights into what vacuum does at the moment, it will also speed up the process in general. From PostgreSQL 9.6 onward, PostgreSQL will keep track of all frozen pages and avoid vacuuming those pages.

Tables that are mostly read-only will massively benefit from this change, as vacuum load is drastically reduced.

Digging into new SQL and developer-related functions

One of the most promising new features of PostgreSQL is the ability to perform phrase searching. Up to 9.5 it was only possible to search for words—phrase searching was very hard to do. 9.6 nicely removes this limitation. Here is an example of how it works:

```
test=# SELECT phraseto_tsquery('Under pressure') @@
to_tsvector('Something was under some sort of pressure');

?column?

----------

f

(1 row)

test=# SELECT phraseto_tsquery('Under pressure') @@
to_tsvector('Under pressure by David Bowie hit number 1 again');

?column?

----------

t

(1 row)
```

The first query returns false because the words we are looking for do not occur in the desired order. In the second example, true is returned because there really is a proper match.

However, there is more: in 9.6 it is possible to check whether words show up in a certain order. In the following example, we want a word to be between united and nations:

```
test=# SELECT tsquery('united <2> nations') @@
to_tsvector('are we really united, happy nations?');

?column?

----------

t

(1 row)

test=# SELECT tsquery('united <2> nations') @@
to_tsvector('are we really at united nations?');

?column?

----------

f

(1 row)
```

The second example returns false as there is no word between united and nations.

Using new backup and replication functionality

PostgreSQL 9.6 has also seen improvements in the area of backup and recovery.

Streamlining wal_level and monitoring

The wal_level setting has always been a bit hard to understand for many people. Many were struggling with the difference between the archive and hot_standby settings. To remove this confusion altogether, both settings have been replaced with the easier-to-understand replica setting, which does the same as hot_standby.

In addition to that, the monitoring of replicated setups has been simplified. Prior to 9.6, there was only the `pg_stat_replication` view, which could be queried on the master to supervise the flow of data to the slave. Now it is also possible to monitor the flow of data on the slaves, by consulting the `pg_stat_wal_receiver` function. It is basically the slave-side mirror of the `pg_stat_replication` function and helps to determine the state of replication.

Using multiple synchronous standby servers

PostgreSQL has been able to perform synchronous replication for quite a while already. In PostgreSQL, it is possible to have more than just one synchronous server from 9.6 onward. Earlier, only one server had to acknowledge a commit. Now it is possible to have an entire group of servers that has to confirm a commit. This is especially important if you want to improve reliability in case of multi-node error.

The syntax to use this new feature is simple:

```
synchronous_standby_names = '3 (server1, server2, server3, server4)
```

However, there is more to synchronous replication in PostgreSQL 9.6. Previously, PostgreSQL ensured (`synchronous_commit = on`) that the transaction log has reached the slave. However, this did not mean that data was actually visible. Consider an example: somebody adds a user to the master, instantly connects to the slave, and checks for the user. While the transaction log was guaranteed to be on the slave, it was not necessarily guaranteed that the data inside the log was already visible to the end user (due to replication conflicts and so on). By setting `synchronous_commit = 'remote_apply'`, it is now possible to query the slave directly after a commit on the master, without having to worry that data might not be visible yet. The `remote_apply` value is slower than the `on` value but it allows to write more advanced applications.

Understanding performance-related features

Just like every release of PostgreSQL, there are numerous performance improvements, which can help to speedup applications. In this section, I want to focus on the most important and most powerful ones. Of course, there are many more small improvements than listed here.

Improving relation extensions

For many years PostgreSQL has extended a table (or an index) block by block. In the case of a single writer process, this was usually fine. However, in cases of high-concurrency writing, writing a block at a time was a source of contention and suboptimal performance. From 9.6 onward, PostgreSQL started to extend tables by multiple blocks at a time. The number of blocks added at a time is 20 times the number of waiting processes.

Checkpoint sorting and kernel interaction

When PostgreSQL writes changes to disk during a checkpoint, it now does so in a more orderly way to ensure that writes are more sequential than earlier. This is done by sorting blocks before sending them too. Random writes will be dramatically reduced this way, which in turn leads to higher throughput on most hardware.

Sorted checkpoints are not the only scalability thing to make it into 9.6. There are also new kernel write-back configuration options: what does this mean? In case of large caches, it could take quite a long time to write all changes out. This used to be especially nasty on systems with hundreds of gigabytes of memory because fairly intense I/O storms could happen. Of course, the operating system, level behavior of Linux could be changed using the `/proc/sys/vm/dirty_background_ratio` command. However, only a handful of consultants and system administrators actually knew how to do that and why. The `checkpoint_flush_after`, `bgwriter_flush_after`, and `backend_flush_after` functions can be used now to control the flush behavior. In general, the rule is to flush earlier. Still, as the feature is new, people are still gathering experience on how to use those settings in the most efficient way possible.

Using more advanced foreign data wrappers

Foreign data wrappers have been around for many years. Starting with PostgreSQL 9.6, the optimizer can use foreign tables way more efficiently. This includes join push down (joins can now already be performed remotely) and order push down (sorting can now happen remotely). Distributing data inside a cluster is now way more efficient due to faster remote operations.

Introducing parallel queries

Traditionally, a query had to run on a single CPU. While this was just fine in the OLTP world, it started to be a problem for analytical applications, which were bound to the speed provided by a single core. With PostgreSQL 9.6, parallel queries were introduced. Of course, implementing parallel queries was hard and so a lot of infrastructure has already been implemented over the years. All this infrastructure is now available to provide the end user with parallel sequential scans. The idea is to make many CPUs work on complicated WHERE conditions during a sequential scan. Version 9.6 also allowed for parallel aggregates and parallel joins. Of course, there is a lot of work left, but we are already looking at a major leap forward.

To control parallelism, there are two essential settings:

```
test=# SHOW max_worker_processes;
 max_worker_processes
----------------------
 8
(1 row)

test=# SHOW max_parallel_workers_per_gather ;
 max_parallel_workers_per_gather
---------------------------------
 2
(1 row)
```

The first one limits the overall number of worker processes available. The second one controls the number of workers allowed per gather node.

> **TIP**
>
> A gather node is a new thing you will see in an execution plan. It is in charge of unifying results coming from parallel subprocesses.

In addition to those fundamental settings, there are a couple of new optimizer parameters to adjust the cost of parallel queries.

Adding snapshot too old

Those of you using Oracle would be aware of the following error message: `snapshot too old`. In Oracle, this message indicates that a transaction has been too long, so it has to be aborted. In PostgreSQL, transactions can run almost infinitely. However, long transactions can still be a problem, so the `snapshot too old` error has been added as a feature to 9.6, which allows transactions to be aborted after a certain amount of time.

The idea behind that is to prevent table bloat and to make sure that end users are aware of the fact that they might be about to do something stupid.

Summary

In PostgreSQL 9.6 and 10.0, a lot of functionality has been added, which allows people to run even more professional applications even more faster and more efficiently. As far as PostgreSQL 10.0 is concerned, the exact new features are not fully defined yet; some things are already known and are outlined in this chapter.

2
Understanding Transactions and Locking

Locking is an important topic in any kind of database. It is not enough to understand just how it works to write proper or better applications; it is also essential from a performance point of view. Without properly handling locks, your applications might not only be slow, it might also be wrong and behave in an insane way. In my judgment, locking is key to performance and having a good overview will certainly help. Therefore, understanding locking and transaction is important for administrators and developers alike.

In this chapter, you will learn:

- Basic locking
- Transactions and transaction isolation
- Deadlocks
- Locking and foreign keys
- Explicit and implicit locking
- Advisory locks

At the end of the chapter, you will be able to understand and utilize PostgreSQL transactions in the most efficient way possible.

Working with PostgreSQL transactions

PostgreSQL provides you with a highly advanced transaction machinery that offers countless features to developers and administrators alike. In this section, it is time to look at the basic concept.

The first important thing to know is this: in PostgreSQL, everything is a transaction. If you send a simple query to the server, it is already a transaction. Here is an example:

```
test=# SELECT now(), now();
              now              |              now
-------------------------------+-------------------------------
 2016-08-30 12:03:27.84596+02  | 2016-08-30 12:03:27.84596+02
(1 row)
```

In this case, the SELECT statement will be a separate transaction. If the same command is executed again, different timestamps will be returned.

> Keep in mind that the now() function will return the transaction time. The SELECT statement will, therefore, always return two identical timestamps.

If more than one statement has to be part of the same transactions, the BEGIN clause must be used:

```
test=# h BEGIN
Command:      BEGIN
Description: start a transaction block
Syntax:
BEGIN [ WORK | TRANSACTION ] [ transaction_mode [, ...] ]

where transaction_mode is one of:

    ISOLATION LEVEL { SERIALIZABLE | REPEATABLE READ
    | READ COMMITTED | READ UNCOMMITTED }
    READ WRITE | READ ONLY
    [ NOT ] DEFERRABLE
```

The BEGIN clause will ensure that more than one command will be packed into a transaction. Here is how it works:

```
test=# BEGIN;
BEGIN
test=# SELECT now();
              now
-------------------------------
 2016-08-30 12:13:54.839277+02
(1 row)
test=# SELECT now();
              now
-------------------------------
 2016-08-30 12:13:54.839277+02
(1 row)
test=# COMMIT;
COMMIT
```

The important point here is that both timestamps will be identical. As mentioned earlier, we are talking about transaction time here.

To end the transaction, COMMIT can be used:

```
test=# h COMMIT
Command:      COMMIT
Description: commit the current transaction
Syntax:
COMMIT [ WORK | TRANSACTION ]
```

There are a couple of syntax elements here. You can just use COMMIT, COMMIT WORK, or COMMIT TRANSACTION. All three options have the same meaning. If this is not enough, there is more:

```
test=# h END
Command:      END
Description: commit the current transaction
Syntax:
END [ WORK | TRANSACTION ]
```

The END clause is the same as the COMMIT clause.

ROLLBACK is the counterpart of COMMIT. Instead of successfully ending a transaction, it will simply stop the transaction without ever making things visible to other transactions:

```
test=# h ROLLBACK
Command:      ROLLBACK
Description: abort the current transaction
Syntax:
ROLLBACK [ WORK | TRANSACTION ]
```

Some applications use ABORT instead of ROLLBACK. The meaning is the same.

Handling errors inside a transaction

It is not always the case that transactions are correct from beginning to end. However, in PostgreSQL, only error-free transactions can be committed. Here is what happens:

```
test=# BEGIN;
BEGIN
test=# SELECT 1;
 ?column?
-----------
        1
(1 row)

test=# SELECT 1 / 0;
ERROR:  division by zero
test=# SELECT 1;
ERROR:  current transaction is aborted, commands ignored until end of
transaction block
test=# COMMIT;
ROLLBACK
```

Note that the division by zero did not work out.

> In any proper database, an instruction like this will instantly error-out and make the statement fail.

It is important to point out that PostgreSQL will error-out, unlike MySQL, which does not seem to have a problem with a mathematically wrong result.

After an error has occurred, no more instructions will be accepted even if those instructions are semantically and syntactically correct. It is still possible to issue a COMMIT. However, PostgreSQL will roll back the transaction because it is the only thing at this point that can still be done.

Making use of savepoints

In professional applications, it can be pretty hard to write reasonably long transactions without ever encountering a single error. To solve the problem, users can utilize something called SAVEPOINT. As the name indicates, it is a safe place inside a transaction that the application can return to in the event things go terribly wrong. Here is an example:

```
test=# BEGIN;
BEGIN
test=# SELECT 1;
 ?column?
----------
        1
(1 row)

test=# SAVEPOINT a;
SAVEPOINT
test=# SELECT 2 / 0;
ERROR:  division by zero
test=# ROLLBACK TO SAVEPOINT a;
ROLLBACK
test=# SELECT 3;
 ?column?
----------
        3
(1 row)

test=# COMMIT;
COMMIT
```

After the first SELECT clause, I decided to create a SAVEPOINT to make sure that the application can always return to this point inside the transaction. As you can see, a SAVEPOINT has a name, which is referred to later.

After returning to a, the transaction can proceed normally. The code has jumped back before the error, so everything is fine.

The number of savepoints inside a transaction is practically unlimited. We have seen customers with over 250,000 savepoints in a single operation. PostgreSQL can easily handle that.

If you want to remove a savepoint from inside a transaction, there is RELEASE SAVEPOINT:

```
test=# h RELEASE SAVEPOINT
Command:     RELEASE SAVEPOINT
Description: destroy a previously defined savepoint
Syntax:
RELEASE [ SAVEPOINT ] savepoint_name
```

Many people ask, What will happen if you try to reach a savepoint after a transaction has ended? The answer is that the life of a savepoint ends as soon as the transaction ends. In other words, there is no way to return to a certain point in time after the transactions have been completed.

Transactional DDLs

PostgreSQL has a very nice feature that is unfortunately not present in many commercial database systems. In PostgreSQL, it is possible to run DDLs (commands that change the data structure) inside a transaction block. In a typical commercial system, a DDL will implicitly commit the current transaction. Not so in PostgreSQL.

Apart from some minor exceptions (DROP DATABASE, CREATE TABLESPACE/DROP TABLESPACE, and so on), all DDLs in PostgreSQL are transactional, which is a huge plus and a real benefit to end users.

Here is an example:

```
test=# d
No relations found.
test=# BEGIN;
BEGIN
test=# CREATE TABLE t_test (id int);
CREATE TABLE
test=# ALTER TABLE t_test ALTER COLUMN id TYPE int8;
ALTER TABLE
test=# d t_test
      Table "public.t_test"
 Column |  Type  | Modifiers
--------+--------+------------
 id     | bigint |

test=# ROLLBACK;
```

```
ROLLBACK
test=# d t_test
Did not find any relation named "t_test".
```

In this example, a table has been created and modified, and the entire transaction is aborted instantly. As you can see, there is no implicit COMMIT or any other strange behavior. PostgreSQL simply acts as expected.

Transactional DDLs are especially important if you want to deploy software. Just imagine running a CMS. If a new version is released, you'll want to upgrade. Running the old version would still be OK; running the new version is also OK but you really don't want a mixture of old and new. Therefore, deploying an upgrade in a single transaction is definitely highly beneficial as it makes upgrades an atomic operation.

> **TIP**
> psql allows you to include files using the i directive. It allows you to start a transaction, load various files, and execute them in a single transaction.

Understanding basic locking

In this section, you will learn about basic locking mechanisms. The goal is to make you understand how locking works in general and how to get simple applications right.

To show how things work, a simple table can be created. For demonstration purposes, I will add one row to the table:

```
test=# CREATE TABLE t_test (id int);
CREATE TABLE
test=# INSERT INTO t_test VALUES (1);
INSERT 0 1
```

The first important thing is that tables can be read concurrently. Many users reading the same data at the same time won't block each other. This allows PostgreSQL to handle thousands of users without problems.

> **TIP**
> Multiple users can read the same data at the same time without blocking each other.

The question now is: what happens if reads and writes occur at the same time? Here is an example:

Transaction 1	Transaction 2
`BEGIN;`	`BEGIN;`
`UPDATE t_test SET id = id + 1 RETURNING *;`	
User will see 1	`SELECT * FROM t_test;`
	User will see 1
`COMMIT;`	`COMMIT;`

Two transactions are opened. The first one will change a row. However, this is no problem as the second transaction can proceed. It will return the old row as it was before the `UPDATE`. This behavior is called **Multi-Version Concurrency Control** (**MVCC**).

Note that a transaction will see data only if it has been committed by the writing transaction. One transaction cannot inspect the changes made by an active connection.

> A transaction can see only those changes that have already been committed.

There is also a second important aspect: many commercial or open source databases are still (as of 2017) unable to handle concurrent reads and writes. In PostgreSQL, this is absolutely not a problem. Reads and writes can coexist.

> Writing transactions won't block reading transactions.

After the data has been committed, the table will contain 2.

What will happen if two people change data at the same time? Here is an example:

Transaction 1	Transaction 2
`BEGIN;`	`BEGIN;`
`UPDATE t_test SET id = id + 1 RETURNING *;`	
It will return 3	`UPDATE t_test SET id = id + 1 RETURNING *;`
	It will wait for transaction 1
`COMMIT;`	It will wait for transaction 1
	It will reread the row, find 3, set the value, and return 4
	`COMMIT;`

Suppose you want to count the number of hits on a website. If you run the code as outlined just now, no hit can be lost because PostgreSQL guarantees that one `UPDATE` is performed after the other.

> PostgreSQL will only lock rows affected by the `UPDATE`. So if you have 1,000 rows, you can theoretically run 1,000 concurrent changes on the same table.

It is also noteworthy that you can always run concurrent reads. Our two writes will not block reads.

Avoiding typical mistakes and explicit locking

In my life as a professional PostgreSQL consultant (`http://postgresql-support.de/`), I have seen a couple of mistakes that are made again and again. If there are constants in life, these typical mistakes are definitely some of the things that never change.

Here is my favorite:

Transaction 1	Transaction 2
BEGIN;	BEGIN;
SELECT max(id) FROM product;	SELECT max(id) FROM product;
User will see 17	User will see 17
User will decide to use 18	User will decide to use 18
INSERT INTO product ... VALUES (18, ...)	INSERT INTO product ... VALUES (18, ...)
COMMIT;	COMMIT;

In this case, there will be either a duplicate key violation or two identical entries. Neither variation of the problem is all that appealing.

One way to fix the problem is to use explicit table locking:

```
test=# h LOCK
Command:     LOCK
Description: lock a table
Syntax:
LOCK [ TABLE ] [ ONLY ] name [ * ] [, ...] [ IN lockmode MODE ] [ NOWAIT ]

where lockmode is one of:

    ACCESS SHARE | ROW SHARE | ROW EXCLUSIVE |
    SHARE UPDATE EXCLUSIVE| SHARE |
    SHARE ROW EXCLUSIVE | EXCLUSIVE | ACCESS EXCLUSIVE
```

As you can see, PostgreSQL offers eight types of locks to lock an entire table. In PostgreSQL, a lock can be as light as an ACCESS SHARE lock or as heavy as an ACCESS EXCLUSIVE lock. The following list shows what these locks do:

- ACCESS SHARE: This type of lock is taken by reads and conflicts only with ACCESS EXCLUSIVE, which is set by DROP TABLE and the like. Practically, this means that a SELECT cannot start if a table is about to be dropped. This also implies that DROP TABLE has to wait until a reading transaction is completed.

- ROW SHARE: PostgreSQL takes this kind of lock in the case of SELECT FOR UPDATE/SELECT FOR SHARE. It conflicts with EXCLUSIVE and ACCESS EXCLUSIVE.

- ROW EXCLUSIVE: This lock is taken by INSERT, UPDATE, and DELETE. It conflicts with SHARE, SHARE ROW EXCLUSIVE, EXCLUSIVE, and ACCESS EXCLUSIVE.
- SHARE UPDATE EXLUSIVE: This kind of lock is taken by CREATE INDEX CONCURRENTLY, ANALYZE, ALTER TABLE, VALIDATE, and some other flavors of ALTER TABLE as well as by VACUUM (not VACUUM FULL). It conflicts with the SHARE UPDATE EXCLUSIVE, SHARE, SHARE ROW EXCLUSIVE, EXCLUSIVE, and ACCESS EXCLUSIVE lock modes.
- SHARE: When an index is created, SHARE locks will be set. It conflicts with ROW EXCLUSIVE, SHARE UPDATE EXCLUSIVE, SHARE ROW EXCLUSIVE, EXCLUSIVE, and ACCESS EXCLUSIVE.
- SHARE ROW EXCLUSIVE: This one is set by CREATE TRIGGER and some forms of ALTER TABLE, and conflicts with everything but ACCESS SHARE.
- EXCLUSIVE: This type of lock is by far the most restrictive one. It protects against reads and writes alike. If this lock is taken by a transaction, nobody else can read or write to the table affected.

Given the PostgreSQL locking infrastructure, one solution to the max-problem outlined previously would be:

```
BEGIN;
LOCK TABLE product IN ACCESS EXCLUSIVE MODE;
INSERT INTO product SELECT max(id) + 1, ... FROM product;
COMMIT;
```

Keep in mind that this is a pretty nasty way of doing this kind of operation because nobody else can read or write to the table during your operation. Therefore, ACCESS EXCLUSIVE should be avoided at all costs.

Considering alternative solutions

However, there is an alternative solution to the problem. Consider the following example: you are asked to write an application generating invoice numbers. The tax office might require you to create invoice numbers without gaps and without duplicates. How would you do it? Of course, one solution would be a table lock. But you can really do better. Here is what I would do:

```
test=# CREATE TABLE t_invoice (id int PRIMARY KEY);
CREATE TABLE
test=# CREATE TABLE t_watermark (id int);
CREATE TABLE
test=# INSERT INTO t_watermark VALUES (0);
INSERT 0 1
```

```
test=# WITH x AS (UPDATE t_watermark SET id = id + 1 RETURNING *)
       INSERT INTO t_invoice
       SELECT * FROM x RETURNING *;
 id
----
  1
(1 row)
```

In this case, I introduced a table called `t_watermark`. It contains just one row. The `WITH` will be executed first. The row will be locked and incremented, and the new value will be returned. Only one person can do this at a time. The value returned by the CTE is then used in the invoice table. It is guaranteed to be unique. The beauty is that there is only a simple row lock on the watermark table; no reads will be blocked in the invoice table. Overall, this way is more scalable.

Making use of FOR SHARE and FOR UPDATE

Sometimes, data is selected from the database, then some processing happens in the application and finally some changes are made back on the database side. This is a classic example of `SELECT FOR UPDATE`.

Here is an example:

```
BEGIN;
SELECT * FROM invoice WHERE processed = false;
** application magic will happen here **
UPDATE invoice SET processed = true ...
COMMIT;
```

The problem here is that two people might select the same unprocessed data. Changes made to those processed rows will then be overwritten. In short, a race condition will occur.

To solve this problem, developers can make use of `SELECT FOR UPDATE`. Here is how it works:

```
BEGIN;
SELECT * FROM invoice WHERE processed = false FOR UPDATE;
** application magic will happen here **
UPDATE invoice SET processed = true ...
COMMIT;
```

The SELECT FOR UPDATE will lock rows just like an UPDATE would. This means that no changes can happen concurrently. All locks will be released on commit as usual.

If one SELECT FOR UPDATE is waiting for some other SELECT FOR UPDATE, one has to wait until the other one completes (COMMIT or ROLLBACK). If the first transaction does not want to end, for whatever reason, the second transaction might potentially wait forever. To avoid that, it is possible to use SELECT FOR UPDATE NOWAIT.

Here is how it works:

Transaction 1	Transaction 2
BEGIN;	BEGIN;
SELECT ... FROM tab WHERE ... FOR UPDATE NOWAIT;	
Some processing	SELECT ... FROM tab WHERE ... FOR UPDATE NOWAIT;
Some processing	ERROR: could not obtain lock on row in relation tab

If NOWAIT is not flexible enough for you, consider using lock_timeout. It will contain the amount of time you want to wait on locks. You can set this on a per-session level:

```
test=# SET lock_timeout TO 5000;
SET
```

In this, the value is set to 5 seconds.

While SELECT does basically no locking, SELECT FOR UPDATE can be pretty harsh. Just imagine the following business process: we want to fill up an airplane providing 200 seats. Many people want to book seats concurrently. In this case, the following might happen:

Transaction 1	Transaction 2
BEGIN;	BEGIN;
SELECT ... FROM flight LIMIT 1 FOR UPDATE;	
Waiting for user input	SELECT ... FROM flight LIMIT 1 FOR UPDATE;
Waiting for user input	It has to wait

The trouble is that only one seat can be booked at a time. There are potentially 200 seats available but everybody has to wait for the first person. While the first seat is blocked, nobody else can book a seat even if people don't care which seat they get in the end.

SELECT FOR UPDATE SKIP LOCKED will fix the problem. Let us create some sample data first:

```
test=# CREATE TABLE t_flight AS
    SELECT * FROM generate_series(1, 200) AS id;
SELECT 200
```

Now comes the magic:

Transaction 1	Transaction 2
BEGIN;	BEGIN;
SELECT * FROM t_flight LIMIT 2 FOR UPDATE SKIP LOCKED;	SELECT * FROM t_flight LIMIT 2 FOR UPDATE SKIP LOCKED;
It will return 1, 2	It will return 2, 3

If everybody wants to fetch two rows, we could serve 100 concurrent transactions at a time without having to worry about blocking transactions.

> **TIP**
>
> Keep in mind that *waiting* is the slowest form of execution. If only one CPU can be active at a time, it is pointless to buy ever bigger servers.

However, there is more. In some cases a FOR UPDATE can have unintended consequences. Most people are not aware of the fact that FOR UPDATE will have an impact on foreign keys. Let us assume we have two tables: one to store currencies and the other to store accounts:

```
CREATE TABLE t_currency (id int, name text, PRIMARY KEY (id));
INSERT INTO t_currency VALUES (1, 'EUR');
INSERT INTO t_currency VALUES (2, 'USD');

CREATE TABLE t_account ( id int, currency_id int REFERENCES t_currency (id)
ON UPDATE CASCADE ON DELETE CASCADE, balance numeric);
INSERT INTO t_account VALUES (1, 1, 100);
INSERT INTO t_account VALUES (2, 1, 200);
```

Now, we want to run `SELECT FOR UPDATE` on the account table:

Transaction 1	Transaction 2
`BEGIN;`	
`SELECT * FROM t_account FOR UPDATE;`	`BEGIN;`
Waiting for user to proceed	`UPDATE t_currency SET id = id * 10;`
Waiting for user to proceed	It will wait on transaction 1

Although there is a `SELECT FOR UPDATE` on accounts, the `UPDATE` on the currency table will block. This is necessary because otherwise there is a chance of breaking the foreign key constraint altogether. In a fairly complex data structure, you can therefore easily end up with contentions in an area where they are least expected (some highly important lookup tables).

On top of `FOR UPDATE`, there are `FOR SHARE`, `FOR NO KEY UPDATE`, and `FOR KEY SHARE`. The following listing describes what those modes actually mean:

- `FOR NO KEY UPDATE`: This one is pretty similar to `FOR UPDATE`. However, the lock is weaker and therefore it can coexist with `SELECT FOR SHARE`.
- `FOR SHARE`: `FOR UPDATE` is pretty strong and works on the assumption that you are definitely going to change rows. `FOR SHARE` is different because more than one transaction can hold a `FOR SHARE` lock at the same time.
- `FOR KEY SHARE`: This behaves similarly to `FOR SHARE`, except that the lock is weaker. It will block `FOR UPDATE` but will not block `FOR NO KEY UPDATE`.

The important thing here is to simply try things out and observe what happens. Improving locking behavior is really important as it can dramatically improve the scalability of your application.

Understanding transaction isolation levels

Up to now, you have seen how to handle locking as well as some basic concurrency. In this section, you will learn about transaction isolation. To me, this is one of the most neglected topics in modern software development. Only a small fraction of software developers are actually aware of this issue, which in turn leads to disgusting and mind-boggling bugs.

Here is an example of what can happen:

Transaction 1	Transaction 2
`BEGIN;`	
`SELECT sum(balance) FROM t_account;`	
User will see 300	`BEGIN;`
	`INSERT INTO t_account (balance) VALUES (100);`
	`COMMIT;`
`SELECT sum(balance) FROM t_account;`	
User will see 400	
`COMMIT;`	

Most users would actually expect the left transaction to always return 300 regardless of the second transaction. However, this is not true. By default, PostgreSQL runs in READ COMMITTED transaction isolation mode. This means that every statement inside a transaction will get a new snapshot of the data, which will be constant throughout the query.

An SQL statement will operate on the same snapshot and will ignore changes by concurrent transactions while it is running.

If you want to avoid that, you can use TRANSACTION ISOLATION LEVEL REPEATABLE READ. In this transaction isolation level, a transaction will use the same snapshot through the entire transactions. Here is what will happen:

Transaction 1	Transaction 2
BEGIN TRANSACTION ISOLATION LEVEL REPEATABLE READ;	
SELECT sum(balance) FROM t_account;	
User will see 300	BEGIN;
	INSERT INTO t_account (balance) VALUES (100);
	COMMIT;
SELECT sum(balance) FROM t_account;	SELECT sum(balance) FROM t_account;
User will see 300	User will see 400
COMMIT;	

As just outlined, the first transaction will freeze its snapshot of the data and provide us with constant results throughout the entire transaction. This feature is especially important if you want to run reports. The first and the last page of a report should always be consistent and operate on the same data. Therefore, repeatable read is key to consistent reports.

Note that isolation-related errors won't always pop up instantly. It can happen that trouble is noticed years after an application has been moved to production.

Repeatable read is not more expensive than read committed. There is no need to worry about performance penalties.

Considering SSI transactions

On top of read committed and repeatable read, PostgreSQL offers **serializable** (or **SSI**) transactions. So, in all, PostgreSQL supports three isolation levels. Note that read uncommitted (which still happens to be the default in some commercial databases) is not supported: if you try to start a read uncommitted transaction, PostgreSQL will silently map to read committed. However, back to serializable.

The idea behind serializable is simple; if a transaction is known to work correctly if there is only a single user, it will also work in the case of concurrency if this isolation level is chosen. However, users have to be prepared; transactions may fail (by design) and error-out. In addition to that, a performance penalty has to be paid.

If you want to know more about this isolation level, consider checking out `https://wiki.postgresql.org/wiki/Serializable`.

> Consider using serializable only when you have a decent understanding of what is going on inside the database engine.

Observing deadlocks and similar issues

Deadlocks are an important issue and can happen in every database I am aware of. Basically, a deadlock will happen if two transactions have to wait on each other.

In this section, you will see how this can happen. Let us suppose we have a table containing two rows:

```
CREATE TABLE t_deadlock (id int);
INSERT INTO t_deadlock VALUES (1), (2);
```

The next listing shows what can happen:

Transaction 1	Transaction 2
BEGIN;	BEGIN;
UPDATE t_deadlock SET id = id * 10 WHERE id = 1;	UPDATE t_deadlock SET id = id * 10 WHERE id = 2;
UPDATE t_deadlock SET id = id * 10 WHERE id = 2;	

Waiting on transaction 2	`UPDATE t_deadlock SET id = id * 10 WHERE` `id = 1;`
Waiting on transaction 2	Waiting on transaction 1
	Deadlock will be resolved after one second (`deadlock_timeout`)
`COMMIT;`	`ROLLBACK;`

As soon as the deadlock is detected, the following error message will show up:

```
ERROR:  deadlock detected
DETAIL:  Process 91521 waits for ShareLock on transaction 903; blocked by
process 77185.
Process 77185 waits for ShareLock on transaction 905; blocked by process
91521.
HINT:  See server log for query details.
CONTEXT:  while updating tuple (0,1) in relation "t_deadlock"
```

PostgreSQL is even kind enough to tell us which row has caused the conflict. In my
example, the root cause of all evil is tuple (0, 1). What you can see here is a ctid. It tells
us about the physical position of a row inside the table. In this example, it is the first row in
the first block (0).

It is even possible to query this row if it is still visible to your transaction:

```
test=# SELECT ctid, * FROM t_deadlock WHERE ctid = '(0, 1)';
 ctid  | id
-------+----
 (0,1) |  1
(1 row)
```

Keep in mind that this query might not return a row if it has already been deleted or
modified.

However, it isn't only the case that deadlocks that can lead to potentially failing transactions. It can also happen that transactions are not serialized for various reasons. The following example shows what can happen. To make the example work, I assume that you've still got two rows: `id = 1` and `id = 2`:

Transaction 1	Transaction 2
`BEGIN ISOLATION LEVEL REPEATABLE READ;`	
`SELECT * FROM t_deadlock;`	
Two rows will be returned	
	`DELETE FROM t_deadlock;`
`SELECT * FROM t_deadlock;`	
Two rows will be returned	
`DELETE FROM t_deadlock;`	
The transaction will error-out	
`ROLLBACK;` - we cannot `COMMIT` anymore	

In this example, two concurrent transactions are at work. As long as transaction 1 is just selecting data, everything is fine because PostgreSQL can easily preserve the illusion of static data. But what happens if the second transaction commits a `DELETE`? As long as there are only reads, there is still no problem. The trouble begins when transaction 1 tries to delete or modify data, which is at this point already really dead. The only solution here for PostgreSQL is to error-out:

```
test=# DELETE FROM t_deadlock;
ERROR:  could not serialize access due to concurrent update
```

Practically, this means that end users have to be prepared to handle erroneous transactions. If something goes wrong, properly written applications must be able to try again.

Utilizing advisory locks

PostgreSQL has a highly efficient and sophisticated transaction machinery that is capable of handling locks in a really fine grained and efficient way. Some years ago, some people came up with the idea of using this code to synchronize applications with each other. Thus, *advisory locks* were born.

When using advisory locks, it is important to mention that they won't go away on COMMIT as *normal* locks do. Therefore, it is really important to make sure that unlocking is done properly and in a totally reliable way.

If you decide to use an advisory lock, what you really lock is a *number*. So this is not about rows or data: it is really just a number. Here is how it works:

Session 1	Session 2
BEGIN;	
SELECT pg_advisory_lock(15);	
	SELECT pg_advisory_lock(15);
	It has to wait
COMMIT;	It still has to wait
SELECT pg_advisory_unlock(15);	It still waiting
	Lock is taken

The first transaction will lock 15. The second transaction has to wait until this number has been unlocked again. The second session will even wait after the first one has committed. This is highly important as you cannot rely on the fact that the end of the transaction will nicely and miraculously solve things for you.

If you want to unlock all locked numbers, PostgreSQL offers the pg_advisory_unlock_all() function to do exactly that:

```
test=# SELECT pg_advisory_unlock_all();
 pg_advisory_unlock_all
------------------------

(1 row)
```

Sometimes you might want to see if you can get a lock and error-out if it is not possible. To achieve that, PostgreSQL offers a couple of functions. If you use df *try*advisory*, PostgreSQL returns a list of all available functions.

Optimizing storage and managing cleanup

Transactions are an integral part of the PostgreSQL system. However, transactions come with a small price tag attached. As already shown in this chapter, it can happen that concurrent users will be presented with different data. Not everybody will get the same data returned by a query. In addition to that, DELETE and UPDATE are not allowed to actually overwrite data as ROLLBACK would not work. If you happen to be in the middle of a large DELETE operation, you cannot be sure whether you will be able to COMMIT or not. In addition to that, data is still visible while you do a DELETE, and sometimes data is even visible once your modification has long since finished.

Consequently, this means that cleanup has to happen asynchronously. A transaction can not clean up its own mess and COMMIT/ROLLBACK might be too early to take care of dead rows.

The solution to the problem is VACUUM:

```
test=# h VACUUM
Command:     VACUUM
Description: garbage-collect and optionally analyze a database
Syntax:
VACUUM [ ( { FULL | FREEZE | VERBOSE | ANALYZE } [, ...] ) ] [ table_name [
(column_name [, ...] ) ] ]
VACUUM [ FULL ] [ FREEZE ] [ VERBOSE ] [ table_name ]
VACUUM [ FULL ] [ FREEZE ] [ VERBOSE ] ANALYZE [ table_name [ (column_name
[, ...] ) ] ]
```

VACUUM will visit all pages that potentially contain modifications and find all the dead space. The free space found is then tracked by the **free space map** (**FSM**) of the relation.

Note that VACUUM will, in most cases, not shrink the size of a table. Instead, it will track and find free space inside existing storage files.

> **TIP**
>
> Tables will usually have the same size after a VACUUM. If there are no valid rows at the end of a table, file sizes can go down in some rare cases. This is not the rule but rather the exception.

What this means to end users will be outlined in the *Watching VACUUM at work* section of this chapter.

Configuring VACUUM and autovacuum

Back in the early days of PostgreSQL projects, people had to run VACUUM manually. Fortunately this is long gone. Nowadays administrators can rely on a tool called autovacuum, which is part of the PostgreSQL Server infrastructure. It automatically takes care of cleanup and works in the background. It wakes up once per minute (see autovacuum_naptime = 1 in postgresql.conf) and checks if there is work to do. If there is work, autovacuum will fork up to three worker processes (see autovacuum_max_workers in postgresql.conf).

The main question is: When does autovacuum trigger the creation of a worker process?

> Actually the autovacuum process does not fork processes itself. Instead it tells the main process to do so. This is done to avoid zombie processes in the case of failure and to improve robustness.

The answer to this question can again be found in postgresql.conf:

```
autovacuum_vacuum_threshold = 50
autovacuum_analyze_threshold = 50
autovacuum_vacuum_scale_factor = 0.2
autovacuum_analyze_scale_factor = 0.1
```

The autovacuum_vacuum_scale_factor tells PostgreSQL that a table is worth vacuuming if 20% of data has been changed. The trouble is that, if a table consists of one row, one change is already 100%. It makes absolutely no sense to fork a complete process to clean up just one row. Therefore autovacuum_vacuuum_threshold says that we need 20% and that 20% must be at least 50 rows. Otherwise, VACUUM won't kick in. The same mechanism is used when it comes to optimizer stats creation. 10% and at least 50 rows are needed to justify new optimizer stats. Ideally, autovacuum creates new statistics during a normal VACUUM to avoid unnecessary trips to the table.

Digging into transaction wraparound-related issues

There are two more settings in `postgresql.conf` that are quite important to understand:

```
autovacuum_freeze_max_age = 200000000
autovacuum_multixact_freeze_max_age = 400000000
```

To understand the overall problem, it is important to understand how PostgreSQL handles concurrency. The PostgreSQL transaction machinery is based on the comparison of transaction IDs and the states transactions are in.

An example: If I am transaction ID 4711 and if you happen to be 4712, I won't see you because you are still running. If I am transaction ID 4711 but you are transaction ID 3900, I will see you provided you have committed; and I will ignore you if you failed.

The trouble is as follows: transaction IDs are finite, not unlimited. At some point, they will start to wrap around. In reality, this means that transaction number 5 might actually be after transaction number 800,000,000. How does PostgreSQL know what was first? It does so by storing a watermark. At some point, those watermarks will be adjusted, and this is exactly when VACUUM starts to be relevant. By running VACUUM (or autovacuum), you can ensure that the watermark is adjusted in a way that there are always enough future transaction IDs left to work with.

> Not every transaction will increase the transaction ID counter. As long as a transaction is still reading, it will only have a virtual transaction ID. This ensures that transaction IDs are not burned too quickly.

`autovacuum_freeze_max_age` defines the maximum number of transactions (age) that a table's `pg_class.relfrozenxid` field can attain before a VACUUM operation is forced to prevent transaction ID wraparound within the table. This value is fairly low because it also has an impact on clog cleanup (the clog or commit log is a data structure that stores 2 bits per transaction, which indicate whether a transaction is running, aborted, committed, or still in a subtransaction).

The `autovacuum_multixact_freeze_max_age` configures the maximum age (in `multixacts`) that a table's `pg_class.relminmxid` field can attain before a VACUUM operation is forced to prevent `multixact` ID wraparound within the table. Freezing tuples is an important performance issue and there will be more about this process in `Chapter 6`, *Optimizing for Good Query Performance*, which is about query optimization.

A word on VACUUM FULL

Instead of normal VACUUM, you can also use VACUUM FULL. However, I really want to point out that VACUUM FULL actually locks the table and rewrites the entire relation. In the case of a small table, this might not be an issue. However, if your tables are large, the table lock can really kill you in minutes! VACUUM FULL blocks upcoming writes and therefore some people talking to your database might have the feeling that it is actually *down*. Hence, a lot of caution is advised.

To get rid of VACUUM FULL, I recommend that you check out pg_squeeze (http://www.cyb ertec.at/introducing-pg_squeeze-a-postgresql-extension-to-auto-rebuild-bloat ed-tables/), which can rewrite a table without blocking writes.

Watching VACUUM at work

After this introduction, it is time to see VACUUM in action. I have included this section here because my practical work as a PostgreSQL consultant and supporter (http://postgresql-support.de/) indicates that most people only have a very vague understanding of what happens on the storage side.

To stress this point again, in most cases, VACUUM will not shrink your tables; space is usually not returned to the filesystem.

Here is my example:

```
CREATE TABLE t_test (id int) WITH (autovacuum_enabled = off);

INSERT INTO t_test
    SELECT * FROM generate_series(1, 100000);
```

The idea is to create a simple table containing 100,000 rows. Note that it is possible to turn autovacuum off for specific tables. Usually, this is not a good idea for most applications. However, there are corner cases where autovacuum_enabled = off makes sense. Just consider a table whose life cycle is very short. It does not make sense to clean out tuples if the developer already knows that the entire table will be dropped within seconds. In data warehousing, this can be the case if you are using tables as staging areas. VACUUM is turned off in this example to ensure that nothing happens in the background; all you see is triggered by me and not by some process.

First of all the size of the table is checked:

```
test=# SELECT pg_size_pretty(pg_relation_size('t_test'));
 pg_size_pretty
----------------
 3544 kB
(1 row)
```

`pg_relation_size` returns the size of a table in bytes. `pg_size_pretty` will take this number and turn it into something human-readable.

Then all rows in the table will be updated:

```
test=# UPDATE t_test SET id = id + 1;
UPDATE 100000
```

What happens is highly important to understanding PostgreSQL; the database engine has to copy all the rows. Why that? First of all, we don't know whether the transaction will be successful, so the data cannot be overwritten. The second important aspect is that there a concurrent transaction might still be seeing the old version of the data.

> **TIP**
>
> The UPDATE operation will copy rows.

Logically, the size of the table will be larger after the change has been made:

```
test=# SELECT pg_size_pretty(pg_relation_size('t_test'));
 pg_size_pretty
----------------
 7080 kB
(1 row)
```

After the UPDATE, people might try to return space to the filesystem:

```
test=# VACUUM t_test;
VACUUM
```

As stated previously, VACUUM does not return space to the filesystem in most cases. Instead, it will allow space to be reused. The table, therefore, does not shrink at all:

```
test=# SELECT pg_size_pretty(pg_relation_size('t_test'));
 pg_size_pretty
----------------
 7080 kB
(1 row)
```

However, the next UPDATE will not make the table grow because it will eat the free space inside the table. Only a second UPDATE would make the table grow again, because all the space is gone, and so additional storage is needed:

```
test=# UPDATE t_test SET id = id + 1;
UPDATE 100000
test=# SELECT pg_size_pretty(pg_relation_size('t_test'));
 pg_size_pretty
-----------------
 7080 kB
(1 row)

test=# UPDATE t_test SET id = id + 1;
UPDATE 100000
test=# SELECT pg_size_pretty(pg_relation_size('t_test'));
 pg_size_pretty
-----------------
 10 MB
(1 row)
```

If I had to plump for one thing you should remember after reading this book, this is it. Understanding storage is the key to performance and administration in general.

Let us run some more queries:

```
VACUUM t_test;
UPDATE t_test SET id = id + 1;
VACUUM t_test;
```

Again the size is unchanged. Let us see what is inside the table:

```
test=# SELECT ctid, * FROM t_test ORDER BY ctid DESC;
ctid       |   id
-----------+--------
 (1327,46) |    112
 (1327,45) |    111
 (1327,44) |    110
. . .
 (884,20)  |  99798
 (884,19)  |  99797
 . . .
```

The `ctid` is the physical position of a row on disk. By using, `ORDER BY ctid DESC`, you will basically read the table backwards in physical order. Why should you care? The reason is that there are some very small values and some very big values at the end of the table. What happens if they are deleted?

```
test=# DELETE FROM t_test WHERE id > 99000 OR id < 1000;
DELETE 1999
test=# VACUUM t_test;
VACUUM
test=# SELECT pg_size_pretty(pg_relation_size('t_test'));
pg_size_pretty
----------------
 3504 kB
(1 row)
```

Although only 2% of the data has been deleted, the size of the table has gone down by two thirds. The reason is that if `VACUUM` only finds dead rows after a certain position in the table, it can return space to the filesystem. This is the only case in which you will actually see the table size go down. Of course, normal users have no control over the physical position of data on disk. Therefore, storage consumption will most likely stay somewhat the same unless all rows are deleted.

> Why are there so many small and big values at the end of the table anyway? After the table is initially populated with 100,000 rows, the last block is not completely full, so the first `UPDATE` will fill up the last block with changes. This naturally shuffles the end of the table a bit. In this carefully crafted example, this is the reason for the strange layout at the end of the table.

In real-world applications, the impact of this observation cannot be stressed enough. There is no performance tuning without really understanding storage.

Making use of snapshot too old

`VACUUM` is doing a good job and it will reclaim free space as needed. But when can `VACUUM` actually clean out rows and turn them into free space? The rule is this: if a row cannot be seen by anybody anymore, it can be reclaimed. In reality this means that everything that is no longer seen even by the oldest transaction can be considered to be really dead.

This also implies that really long transactions can postpone cleanup for quite some time. The logical consequence is table bloat. Tables will grow beyond proportion and performance will tend to go downhill.

Fortunately PostgreSQL 9.6 has a nice feature that allows the administrator to intelligently limit the duration of a transaction. Oracle administrators will be familiar with the `snapshot too old` error; since PostgreSQL 9.6, this error message is also available. But it is more of a feature than an unintended side-effect of bad configuration (which it actually is in Oracle).

To limit the lifetime of snapshots, you can make use of a setting in `postgresql.conf`:

```
old_snapshot_threshold = -1
        # 1min-60d; -1 disables; 0 is immediate
```

If this variable is set, transactions will fail after a certain amount of time. Note that this setting is on an instance level and it cannot be set inside a session. By limiting the size of a transaction, the risk of insanely long transactions will decrease drastically.

Summary

In this chapter, you learned about transactions, locking and its logical implications, and the general architecture the PostgreSQL transaction machinery can have for storage, concurrency, as well as administration. You saw how rows are locked and which features are present.

In the next chapter, you will learn one of the most important topics in database work: indexing. You will learn about the PostgreSQL query optimizer as well as various types of index and their behavior.

3
Making Use of Indexes

In the previous chapter, you learned about concurrency and locking. In this chapter, it is time to attack indexing head on. The importance of this topic cannot be stressed enough—indexing is (and will most likely stay as) one of the most important topics in the life of every database engineer.

After 17 years of professional, full-time PostgreSQL consulting and PostgreSQL 24x7 support, I can say one thing for sure. Bad indexing is the main source of bad performance. Of course, it is important to adjust memory parameters and all that. However, it is all in vain if indexes are not used properly. There is simply no replacement for a missing index.

Therefore, I have dedicated an entire chapter to indexing alone to give you as many insights as possible.

In this chapter, you will learn these topics:

- When does PostgreSQL use indexes?
- How does the optimizer handle things?
- What types of indexes are there and how do they work?
- Using your own indexing strategies

At the end of the chapter, you will be able to understand how indexes can be used beneficially in PostgreSQL.

Understanding simple queries and the cost model

In this section, we will get started with indexes. To show how things work, some test data is needed. The following code snippet shows how data can be created easily:

```
test=# CREATE TABLE t_test (id serial, name text);
CREATE TABLE
test=# INSERT INTO t_test (name) SELECT 'hans'
    FROM generate_series(1, 2000000);
INSERT 0 2000000
test=# INSERT INTO t_test (name) SELECT 'paul'
    FROM generate_series(1, 2000000);
INSERT 0 2000000
```

In the first line, a simple table is created. Two columns are used: an auto increment column, which just keeps creating numbers, and a column that will be filled with static values.

> **TIP**
>
> The generate_series function will generate numbers from 1 million to 2 million. So in this example, 2 million static values for hans and 2 million static values for paul are created.

In all, 4 million rows have been added:

```
test=# SELECT name, count(*) FROM t_test GROUP BY 1;
 name |  count
------+----------
 hans | 2000000
 paul | 2000000
(2 rows)
```

These 4 million rows have some nice properties. IDs are ascending and there are only two distinct names.

Let's run a simple query now:

```
test=# \timing
Timing is on.
test=# SELECT * FROM t_test WHERE id = 432332;
   id    | name
--------+------
 432332 | hans
(1 row)

Time: 119.318 ms
```

In this case, the \timing command will tell psql to show the runtime of a query. Note that this is not the real execution time on the server but the time measured by psql. In case of very short queries, network latency can be a substantial part of the total time, so this has to be taken into account.

Making use of EXPLAIN

In this example, reading 4 million rows has taken more than 100 milliseconds. From a performance point of view, it is a total disaster. To figure out what is going wrong, PostgreSQL offers the EXPLAIN command:

```
test=# \h EXPLAIN
Command:     EXPLAIN
Description: show the execution plan of a statement
Syntax:
EXPLAIN [ ( option [, ...] ) ] statement
EXPLAIN [ ANALYZE ] [ VERBOSE ] statement

where option can be one of:

    ANALYZE [ boolean ]
    VERBOSE [ boolean ]
    COSTS [ boolean ]
    BUFFERS [ boolean ]
    TIMING [ boolean ]
    FORMAT { TEXT | XML | JSON | YAML }
```

When you have the feeling that a query is not performing well, EXPLAIN will help you to reveal the real performance problem.

Here is how it works:

```
test=# EXPLAIN SELECT * FROM t_test WHERE id = 432332;
                              QUERY PLAN
-----------------------------------------------------------------
 Gather   (cost=1000.00..43463.92 rows=1 width=9)
   Workers Planned: 2
   ->  Parallel Seq Scan on t_test
         (cost=0.00..42463.82 rows=1 width=9)
         Filter: (id = 432332)
 (4 rows)
```

What you see in this listing is a so called *execution plan*. In PostgreSQL, an SQL statement will be executed in four stages. The following components are at work:

- The parser will check for syntax errors and for obvious problems
- The rewrite system take care of rules (views and other things)
- The optimizer will figure out how to execute a query in the most efficient way and work out a plan
- The plan provided by the optimizer will be used by the executor to finally create the result

The purpose of EXPLAIN is to see what the planner has come up with to run the query efficiently. In my example, PostgreSQL will use a parallel sequential scan. This means that two workers will cooperate and work on the filter condition together. The partial results are then united through a thing called *gather node*, which has been introduced in PostgreSQL 9.6 (it is part of the parallel query infrastructure). If you look at the plan more precisely, you will see how many rows PostgreSQL expects at each stage of the plan (in this example, rows = 1 that is, one row will be returned).

> **TIP**
>
> In PostgreSQL 9.6, the number of parallel workers will be determined by the size of the table. The larger an operation is, the more parallel workers PostgreSQL will fire up. For a very small table, parallelism is not used as it would create too much overhead.

Parallelism is not a must. It is always possible to reduce the number of parallel workers in pre-PostgreSQL 9.6 behavior by setting the following variable to 0:

```
test=# SET max_parallel_workers_per_gather TO 0;
SET
```

Note that this change has no side effect as it is only inside your session. Of course you can also decide the change in the `postgresql.conf` file, but I would not advise you to do that as you might lose quite a lot of performance provided by parallel queries.

Digging into the PostgreSQL cost model

If only one CPU is used, the execution plan will look like this:

```
test=# EXPLAIN SELECT * FROM t_test WHERE id = 432332;
                         QUERY PLAN
------------------------------------------------------------
 Seq Scan on t_test   (cost=0.00..71622.00 rows=1 width=9)
    Filter: (id = 432332)
(2 rows)
```

PostgreSQL will sequentially read (sequential scan) the entire table and apply the filter. It expects the operation to cost `71622` penalty points. Now what does that mean? Penalty points (or costs) are mostly an abstract concept. They are needed to compare different ways to execute the query. If a query can be executed by the executor in many different ways, PostgreSQL will decide on the execution plan promising the lowest cost possible. The question now is: how did PostgreSQL end up with `71622` points?

Here is how it works:

```
test=# SELECT pg_relation_size('t_test') / 8192.0;
      ?column?
--------------------
 21622.000000000000
(1 row)
```

The `pg_relation_size` function will return the size of the table in bytes. Given the example, you can see that the relation consists of `21622` blocks (8,000 each). According to the cost model PostgreSQL will add costs of one for each block it has to read sequentially.

The configuration parameter to influence that is:

```
test=# SHOW seq_page_cost;
 seq_page_cost
----------------
 1
(1 row)
```

However, reading a couple of blocks from disk is not everything we have to do. It is also necessary to apply the filter and to send those rows through the CPU. Two parameters are here to account for those costs:

```
test=# SHOW cpu_tuple_cost;
 cpu_tuple_cost
------------------
 0.01
(1 row)
test=# SHOW cpu_operator_cost;
 cpu_operator_cost
--------------------
 0.0025
(1 row)
```

This leads to the following calculation:

```
test=# SELECT 21622*1 + 4000000*0.01 + 4000000*0.0025;
 ?column?
-------------
 71622.0000
(1 row)
```

As you can see, this is exactly the number seen in the plan. Costs will consist of a CPU part and an I/O part, which will all be turned into a single number. The important thing here is that costs have nothing to do with real execution, so it is impossible to translate costs to milliseconds. The number the planner comes up with is really just an estimate.

Of course, there are some more parameters outlined in this brief example. PostgreSQL also has special parameters for index-related operations:

- `random_page_cost = 4`: If PostgreSQL uses an index, there is usually a lot of random I/O involved. On traditional spinning disks, random reads are much more important than sequential reads, so PostgreSQL will account for them accordingly. Note that on SSDs, the difference between random and sequential reads does not exist anymore, so it can make sense to set `random_page_cost = 1` in the `postgresql.conf` file.
- `cpu_index_tuple_cost = 0.005`: If indexes are used, PostgreSQL will also consider that there is some CPU cost invoiced.

If you are utilizing parallel queries, there are even more cost parameters:

`parallel_tuple_cost = 0.1`: This defines the cost of transferring one tuple from a parallel worker process to another process. It basically accounts for overhead of moving rows around inside the infrastructure.

`parallel_setup_cost = 1000.0`: This adjusts the costs of firing up a worker process. Of course, starting processes to run queries in parallel is not free, and so this parameter tries to model those costs associated with process management.

`min_parallel_relation_size = 8 MB`: This defines the minimum size of a table considered for parallel queries. The larger a table grows, the more CPUs PostgreSQL will use. The size of the table has to triple to allow for one more worker process.

Deploying simple indexes

Firing up more worker processes to scan ever larger tables is sometimes not the solution. Reading entire tables to find just a single row is usually not a good idea. Therefore, it makes sense to create indexes:

```
test=# CREATE INDEX idx_id ON t_test (id);
CREATE INDEX
test=# SELECT * FROM t_test WHERE id = 43242;
   id   | name
--------+------
 43242  | hans
(1 row)
Time: 0.259 ms
```

PostgreSQL uses Lehman-Yao's high concurrency B-tree for standard indexes. Along with some PostgreSQL specific optimizations, those trees provide end users with excellent performance. The most important thing is that Lehman-Yao allows you to run many operations (reading and writing) on the very same index at the same time, which helps to improve throughput dramatically.

However, indexes are not for free:

```
test=# \di+
                        List of relations
 Schema |  Name   | Type  | Owner | Table  | Size  | Description
--------+---------+-------+-------+--------+-------+-------------
 public | idx_id  | index | hs    | t_test | 86 MB |
(1 row)
```

As you can see, our index containing 4 million rows will eat up 86 MB of disk space. In addition to that, writes to the table will be slower because the index has to be kept in sync all the time.

Making use of sorted output

B-tree indexes are not only useful to find rows. They are also useful to feed sorted data to the next stage in the process:

```
test=# EXPLAIN SELECT * FROM  t_test ORDER BY id DESC LIMIT 10;
                         QUERY PLAN
--------------------------------------------------------------
 Limit   (cost=0.43..0.74 rows=10 width=9)
   ->  Index Scan Backward using idx_id on t_test
         (cost=0.43..125505.43 rows=4000000 width=9)
(2 rows)
```

In this case, the index already returns data in the right sort order and therefore there is no need to sort the entire set of data. Reading the last 10 rows of the index will be enough to answer this query. Practically, it means that it is possible to find the top N rows of a table in a fraction of a millisecond.

However, ORDER BY is not the only operation requiring sorted output. The min and max functions are also all about sorted output so an index can be used to speed up those two operations as well. Here is an example:

```
test=# explain SELECT min(id), max(id) FROM  t_test;
                         QUERY PLAN
--------------------------------------------------------------
 Result   (cost=0.93..0.94 rows=1 width=8)
   InitPlan 1 (returns $0)
     ->  Limit   (cost=0.43..0.46 rows=1 width=4)
           ->  Index Only Scan using idx_id on t_test
                   (cost=0.43..135505.43 rows=4000000 width=4)
                 Index Cond: (id IS NOT NULL)
   InitPlan 2 (returns $1)
     ->  Limit   (cost=0.43..0.46 rows=1 width=4)
           ->  Index Only Scan Backward using idx_id on t_test t_test_1
                   (cost=0.43..135505.43 rows=4000000 width=4)
                 Index Cond: (id IS NOT NULL)
(9 rows)
```

In PostgreSQL, an index (or a B-tree, to be more precise) can be read in normal order or backward. The thing now: a B-tree can be seen as a sorted list. So naturally the lowest value is at the beginning and the highest value is at the end. Therefore, min and max are perfect candidates for a speed up.

In SQL, many operations rely on sorted input; therefore, understanding those operations is essential because there are serious implications on the indexing side.

Using more than one index at a time

Up to now, you have seen that one index at a time has been used. However, in many real-world situations, this is, by far, not sufficient. There are cases demanding more logic in the database.

PostgreSQL allows the use of multiple indexes in a single query. Of course, this makes sense if many columns are queried at the same time. However, that's not always the case. It can also happen that a single index is used multiple times to process the very same column. Here is an example:

```
test=# explain SELECT * FROM  t_test WHERE id = 30 OR id = 50;
                        QUERY PLAN
-----------------------------------------------------------------
 Bitmap Heap Scan on t_test (cost=8.88..16.85 rows=2 width=9)
   Recheck Cond: ((id = 30) OR (id = 50))
   ->  BitmapOr  (cost=8.88..8.88 rows=2 width=0)
         ->  Bitmap Index Scan on idx_idv (cost=0.00..4.44 rows=1 width=0)
               Index Cond: (id = 30)
         ->  Bitmap Index Scan on idx_id (cost=0.00..4.44 rows=1 width=0)
               Index Cond: (id = 50)
(7 rows)
```

The point here is that the id column is needed twice. First the query looks for 30 and then for 50. As you can see, PostgreSQL will go for a so -called *bitmap scan*.

> A bitmap scan is not the same as a bitmap index, which people from an Oracle background might know. They are two totally distinct things and have nothing in common. Bitmap indexes are an index type in Oracle while bitmap scans are basically a scan method.

The idea behind a bitmap scan is that PostgreSQL will scan the first index, collecting a list of blocks containing the data. Then the next index will be scanned to again compile a list of blocks. This works for as many indexes as desired. In the case of OR, those lists will then be unified, leaving us with a large lists of blocks containing the data. Using this list, the table will be scanned to retrieve those blocks. The trouble now is that PostgreSQL has retrieved a lot more data than needed. In our case, the query will look for two rows; however, a couple of blocks might have been returned by the bitmap scan. Therefore, the executor will do a so called *recheck* to filter out those rows, which do not satisfy our conditions.

Bitmap scans will also work for AND conditions or a mixture of AND and OR. However, if PostgreSQL sees an AND condition it does not necessarily force itself into a bitmap scan. Let's suppose that we got a query looking for everybody living in Austria and a person with a certain ID. It really makes no sense to use two indexes here because after searching for the ID there is really not much data left. Scanning both indexes would be ways more expensive because there are 8 million people (including me) living in Austria, and reading so many rows to find just one person is pretty pointless from a performance standpoint. The good news is that the PostgreSQL optimizer will make all those decisions for you by comparing the costs of different options and potential indexes, so there is no need to worry.

Using bitmap scans effectively

The question naturally arising now is: when is a bitmap scan most beneficial and when is it chosen by the optimizer? From my point of view, there are really two use cases:

- Avoiding using the same block over and over again
- Combining relatively bad conditions

The first case it quite common. Suppose you are looking for everybody who speaks a certain language. For the sake of the example, we can assume that 10% of all people speak the required language. Scanning the index would mean that a block in the table has to be scanned all over again as many skilled speakers might be stored in the same block. By applying a bitmap scan, it is ensured that a specific block is only used once, which of course leads to better performance.

The second common use case is to use relatively weak criteria together. Let's suppose we are looking for everybody between 20 and 30 years of age owning a yellow shirt. Now, maybe 15% of all people are between 20 and 30 and maybe 15% of all people actually own a yellow shirt. Scanning a table sequentially is expensive, and so PostgreSQL might decide to choose two indexes because the final result might consist of just 1% of the data. Scanning both indexes might be cheaper than reading all of the data.

Using indexes in an intelligent way

So far, applying an index feels like the Holy Grail, which always improves performance magically. However, this is not the case. Indexes can also be pretty pointless in some cases.

Before digging into things more deeply, here is the data structure we are using for this example. Remember that there are only two distinct names and unique IDs:

```
test=# \d t_test
                Table "public.t_test"
 Column |  Type   |               Modifiers
--------+---------+---------------------------------------
 id     | integer | not null default nextval('t_test_id_seq'::regclass)
 name   | text    |
Indexes:
    "idx_id" btree (id)
```

At this point, one index has been defined, which covers the id column. In the next step, the name column will be queried. Before doing that, an index on name will be created:

```
test=# CREATE INDEX idx_name ON t_test (name);
CREATE INDEX
```

Now it is time to see if the index is used correctly:

```
test=# EXPLAIN SELECT * FROM  t_test WHERE name = 'hans2';
                         QUERY PLAN
-----------------------------------------------------------
 Index Scan using idx_name on t_test  (cost=0.43..4.45 rows=1 width=9)
   Index Cond: (name = 'hans2'::text)
(2 rows)
```

As expected, PostgreSQL will decide on using the index. Most users would expect that. But note that my query says hans2. Remember: hans2 does not exist in the table and the query plan perfectly reflects this. rows=1 indicates that the planner only expects a very small subset of data being returned by the query.

> **TIP**
>
> There is not a single row in the table, but PostgreSQL will never estimate zero rows because it would make subsequent estimations a lot harder.

Let us see what happens if we look for more data:

```
test=# EXPLAIN SELECT * FROM  t_test WHERE name = 'hans' OR name = 'paul';
                         QUERY PLAN
-----------------------------------------------------------
 Seq Scan on t_test  (cost=0.00..81622.00 rows=3000011 width=9)
   Filter: ((name = 'hans'::text) OR (name = 'paul'::text))
(2 rows)
```

In this case, PostgreSQL will go for a straight sequential scan. Why is that? Why is the system ignoring all indexes? The reason is simple: `hans` and `paul` make up the entire dataset because there are no other values. Therefore, PostgreSQL figures that the entire table has to be read anyway. There is no reason to read all of the index and the full table if reading just the table is sufficient.

In other words, PostgreSQL will not use an index just because there is one. PostgreSQL will use indexes when they make sense. If the number of rows is smaller, PostgreSQL will again consider bitmap scans and normal index scans:

```
test=# EXPLAIN SELECT * FROM  t_test WHERE name = 'hans2' OR name =
'paul2';
                          QUERY PLAN
-----------------------------------------------------------------
 Bitmap Heap Scan on t_test  (cost=8.88..12.89 rows=1 width=9)
   Recheck Cond: ((name = 'hans2'::text) OR (name = 'paul2'::text))
   ->  BitmapOr  (cost=8.88..8.88 rows=1 width=0)
       ->  Bitmap Index Scan on idx_name (cost=0.00..4.44 rows=1 width=0)
             Index Cond: (name = 'hans2'::text)
       ->  Bitmap Index Scan on idx_name (cost=0.00..4.44 rows=1 width=0)
             Index Cond: (name = 'paul2'::text)
```

The most important point to learn here is that execution plans depend on input values. They are not static and not independent of the data inside the table. This is a very important observation, which has to be kept in mind all the time. In real-world examples, the fact that plans change can often be the reason for unpredictable runtimes.

Improving speed using clustered tables

In this section, you will learn about the power of correlation and the power of clustered tables. What is the whole idea? Consider you want to read a whole area of data. This might be a certain time range, some block, IDs, or so. The runtime of such queries will vary depending on the amount of data and the physical arrangement of data on disk. So, even if you are running queries that return the same number of rows, two systems might not provide the answer within the same time span as a physical disk layout might make a difference.

Here is an example:

```
test=# EXPLAIN (analyze true, buffers true, timing true)
  SELECT *
  FROM t_test
  WHERE id < 10000;
                          QUERY PLAN
-----------------------------------------------------------------
 Index Scan using idx_id on t_test (cost=0.43..370.87 rows=10768 width=9)
(actual time=0.011..2.897 rows=9999 loops=1)
   Index Cond: (id < 10000)
   Buffers: shared hit=85
 Planning time: 0.078 ms
 Execution time: 4.081 mundefined
(5 rows)
```

As you might remember, the data has been loaded in an organized and sequential way. Data has been added ID after ID and so it can be expected that data will be on disk in sequential order. This holds true if data is loaded into an empty table using some auto increment column.

You have already seen EXPLAIN in action. In this example, EXPLAIN (analyze true, buffers true, timing true) has been utilized. The idea is that analyze will not just show the plan but also execute the query and show us what has happened. EXPLAIN analyze is perfect for comparing planner estimates with what really happened. It is the best way to figure out whether the planner was correct or ways off. The buffers true parameter will tell us how many 8,000 blocks were touched by the query. In this example, a total of 85 blocks were touched. shared hit means that data was coming from the PostgreSQL I/O cache (shared buffers). All together it took PostgreSQL around four milliseconds to retrieve the data.

What happens if the data in your table is somewhat random? Will things change?

To create a table containing the same data but in random order, you can simply use ORDER BY random(). It will make sure that data is indeed shuffled on disk:

```
test=# CREATE TABLE t_random AS SELECT * FROM t_test ORDER BY random();
SELECT 4000000
```

To ensure a fair comparison, the same column is indexed:

```
test=# CREATE INDEX idx_random ON t_random (id);
CREATE INDEX
```

To function properly, PostgreSQL will need optimizer statistics. Those statistics will tell PostgreSQL how much data there is, how values are distributed, and whether the data is correlated on disk. To speed things up even more, I have added a VACUUM call. Please mind that VACUUM will be discussed later in this book in broader detail:

```
test=# VACUUM ANALYZE t_random;
VACUUM
```

Now let's run the same query as before:

```
test=# EXPLAIN (analyze true, buffers true, timing true) SELECT * FROM
t_random WHERE id < 10000;
                           QUERY PLAN
-----------------------------------------------------------------
  Bitmap Heap Scan on t_random
          (cost=203.27..18431.86 rows=10689 width=9)
          (actual time=5.087..13.822 rows=9999 loops=1)
    Recheck Cond: (id < 10000)
    Heap Blocks: exact=8027
    Buffers: shared hit=8057
    ->  Bitmap Index Scan on idx_random
          (cost=0.00..200.60 rows=10689 width=0)
          (actual time=3.558..3.558 rows=9999 loops=1)
        Index Cond: (id < 10000)
        Buffers: shared hit=30
  Planning time: 0.075 ms
  Execution time: 14.411 ms
(9 rows)
```

There are a couple of things to observe here. First of all a staggering total of 8057 blocks were needed and the runtime has skyrocketed to over 14 milliseconds. The only thing here that somewhat rescued performance was the fact that data was again coming from memory and not from disk. Just imagine what it would mean if you had to access the disk 8057 times just to answer this query. It would be a total disaster because disk wait would certainly slow down things dramatically.

However, there is more to see. You can even see that the plan has changed. PostgreSQL is now using a bitmap scan instead of a normal index scan. This is done to reduce the number of blocks needed in the query to prevent even worse behavior.

How does the planner know how data is stored on disk? `pg_stats` is a system view containing all the statistics about the content of columns. The following query reveals the relevant content:

```
test=# SELECT tablename, attname, correlation FROM pg_stats WHERE tablename
IN ('t_test', 't_random') ORDER BY 1, 2;
 tablename | attname | correlation
-----------+---------+-------------
 t_random  | id      |  -0.0114944
 t_random  | name    |    0.493675
 t_test    | id      |           1
 t_test    | name    |           1
(4 rows)
```

You can see that PostgreSQL takes care of every single column. The content of the view is created by a thing called `ANALYZE`, which is vital to performance:

```
test=# \h ANALYZE
Command:     ANALYZE
Description: collect statistics about a database
Syntax:
ANALYZE [ VERBOSE ] [ table_name [ ( column_name [, ...] ) ] ]
```

Usually, `ANALYZE` is automatically executed in the background using the so called autovacuum daemon, which will be covered later in this book.

Back to our query. As you can see, both tables have two columns (`id` and `name`). In the case of `t_test.id`, the correlation is 1, which means that the next value somewhat depends on the previous one. In my example, numbers are simply ascending. The same applies to `t_test.name`. First, we have entries containing `hans` and then we have values containing `paul`. All identical names are therefore stored together.

In `t_random`, the situation is quite different: A negative correlation means that data is shuffled. You can also see that the correlation for the `name` column is around 0.5. In reality, it means that there is usually no straight sequence of identical names in the table, but it rather means that names keep switching all the time when the table is read in physical order.

Why does this lead to so many blocks hit by the query? The answer is relatively simple. If the data we need is not packed together tightly but spread out over the table evenly, more blocks are needed to extract the same amount of information, which in turn leads to worse performance.

Clustering tables

In PostgreSQL, there is a command called CLUSTER that allows us to rewrite a table in a desired order. It is possible to point to an index and store data in the same order as the index:

```
test=# \h CLUSTER
Command:     CLUSTER
Description: cluster a table according to an index
Syntax:
CLUSTER [VERBOSE] table_name [ USING index_name ]
CLUSTER [VERBOSE]
```

The CLUSTER command has been around for many years and serves its purpose well. But, there are some things to consider before blindly running it on a production system:

- The CLUSTER command will lock the table while it is running. You cannot insert or modify data while CLUSTER is running. This might not be acceptable on a production system.
- Data can only be organized according to one index. You cannot order a table by postal code, name, ID, birthday, and so on, at the same time. It means that CLUSTER will make sense if there is a search criteria, which is used most of the time.
- Keep in mind that the example outlined in this book is more of a *worst case* scenario. In reality, the performance difference between a clustered and a non-clustered table will depend on the workload, the amount of data retrieved, cache hit rates, and a lot more.
- The clustered state of a table will not be maintained as changes are made to a table during normal operations. Correlation might deteriorate as time goes by.

Here is an example of how to run the CLUSTER command:

```
test=# CLUSTER t_random USING idx_random;
CLUSTER
```

Depending on the size of the table, the time needed to cluster will vary.

Making use of index only scans

So far, you have seen when an index is used and when it is not. In addition to that, bitmap scans have been discussed.

However, there is more to indexing. The following two examples will only differ slightly although the performance difference might be fairly large. Here is the first query:

```
test=# EXPLAIN SELECT * FROM t_test WHERE id = 34234;
                        QUERY PLAN
-----------------------------------------------------------------
  Index Scan using idx_id on t_test
    (cost=0.43..8.45 rows=1 width=9)
    Index Cond: (id = 34234)
```

There is nothing unusual here. PostgreSQL uses an index to find a single row. What happens if only a single column is selected?

```
test=# EXPLAIN SELECT id FROM  t_test WHERE id = 34234;
                        QUERY PLAN
-----------------------------------------------------------------
  Index Only Scan using idx_id on t_test
    (cost=0.43..8.45 rows=1 width=4)
    Index Cond: (id = 34234)
(2 rows)
```

As you can see, the plan has changed from an *index scan* to a so called *index only scan*. In our example, the id column has been indexed so its content is naturally in the index. There is no need to go to the table in most cases if all the data can already be taken out of the index. Going to the table is (almost) only required if additional fields are queried, which is not the case here. Therefore, the index-only scan will promise significantly better performance than a normal index scan.

Practically, it can even make sense to include an additional column into an index here and there to enjoy the benefit of this feature. In MS SQL, adding additional columns is known as **covering indexes**. Similar behavior can be achieved in PostgreSQL as well.

Understanding additional B-tree features

In PostgreSQL, indexing is a large field and covers many aspects of database work. As I have outlined in this book already, indexing is key to performance. There is no good performance without proper indexing. Therefore, it is worth inspecting those indexing-related features in more detail.

Combined indexes

In my job as a professional PostgreSQL support vendor, I am often asked about the difference between a combined and individual indexes. In this section, I will try to shed some light on this question.

The general rule is this: if a single index can answer your question, it is usually the best choice. However, you cannot index all possible combinations of fields people are filtering on. What you can do is use the properties of combined indexes to achieve as much gain as possible.

Let us suppose we have a table containing three columns: postal_code, last_name, and first_name. A telephone book would make use of a combined index like that. You will see that data is ordered by location. Within the same location, data will be sorted by last name and first name.

The following table will show which operations are possible given the three column index:

Query	Possible	Remarks
postal_code = 2700 AND last_name = 'Schönig' AND first_name = 'Hans'	Yes	This is the ideal use case for this index.
postal_code = 2700 AND last_name = 'Schönig'	Yes	No restrictions.
last_name = 'Schönig AND postal_code = 2700	Yes	PostgreSQL will simply swap conditions.
postal_code = 2700	Yes	This is just like an index on postal_code, the combined index just needs more space on disk.
first_name = 'Hans'	Yes, but a different use case	PostgreSQL cannot use the sorted property of the index anymore. However, in some rare cases (usually very broad tables, including countless columns), PostgreSQL will scan the entire index if it is as cheap as reading the very broad table.

If columns are indexes separately, you will most likely end up seeing bitmap scans. Of course, a single hand-tailored index is better.

Adding functional indexes

So far you have seen how to index the content of a column as it is. However, this might not always be what you really want. Therefore, PostgreSQL allows the creation of *functional indexes*. The basic idea is very simple; instead of indexing a value, the output of a function is stored inside the index.

The following example shows how the cosine of the `id` column can be indexed:

```
test=# CREATE INDEX idx_cos ON t_random (cos(id));
CREATE INDEX
test=# ANALYZE ;
ANALYZE
```

All you have to do is put the function inside the list of columns and you are done. Of course, this won't work for all kinds of functions. Functions can only be used if their output is immutable:

```
test=# SELECT age('2010-01-01 10:00:00'::timestamptz);
            age
--------------------------
 6 years 9 mons 14:00:00
(1 row)
```

Functions such as `age` are not really suitable for indexing because their output is not constant. Time goes on and consequently the output of `age` will change too. PostgreSQL will explicitly prohibit functions that have the potential to change their result given the same input. The `cos` function is fine in this respect because the cosine of a value will still be the same in 1,000 years from now.

To test the index, I have written a simple query to show what will happen:

```
test=# EXPLAIN SELECT * FROM  t_random WHERE cos(id) = 10;
                       QUERY PLAN
------------------------------------------------------------------
 Index Scan using idx_cos on t_random (cost=0.43..8.45 rows=1 width=9)
   Index Cond: (cos((id)::double precision) = '10'::double precision)
(2 rows)
```

As expected, the functional index will be used just like any other index.

Reducing space consumption

Indexing is nice and its main purpose is to speed up things as much as possible. As with all good stuff, indexing comes with a price tag: space consumption. To do its magic, an index has to store values in an organized fashion. If your table contains 10 million integer values, the index belonging to the table will logically contain those 10 million integer values.

A B-tree will contain a pointer to each row in the table, and so it is certainly not free of charge. To figure out how much space an index will need, you can ask psql using the `\di+` command:

```
test=# \di+
                          List of relations
  Schema |    Name     | Type  | Owner |   Table    | Size
 --------+-------------+-------+-------+------------+-------
  public | idx_cos     | index | hs    | t_random   | 86 MB
  public | idx_id      | index | hs    | t_test     | 86 MB
  public | idx_name    | index | hs    | t_test     | 86 MB
  public | idx_random  | index | hs    | t_random   | 86 MB
 (4 rows)
```

In my database, the staggering amount of 344 MB has been burned to store those indexes. Now, compare this to the amount of storage burned by the underlying tables:

```
test=# \d+
                          List of relations
  Schema |     Name      |   Type   | Owner |    Size
 --------+---------------+----------+-------+------------
  public | t_random      | table    | hs    | 169 MB
  public | t_test        | table    | hs    | 169 MB
  public | t_test_id_seq | sequence | hs    | 8192 bytes
 (3 rows)
```

The size of both tables combined is just 338 MB. In other words, our indexing needs more space than the actual data. In the real world, this is common and actually pretty likely. Recently I visited a Cybertec customer in Germany and I saw a database in which 64% of the database size was made up of indexes that were never used (not a single time over the period of months). So, over-indexing can be an issue just like under-indexing. Remember, those indexes don't just consume space. Every INSERT or UPDATE must maintain the values in the indexes as well. In extreme cases like our example, this vastly decreases write throughput.

If there are just a handful of different values in the table, partial indexes are a solution:

```
test=# DROP INDEX idx_name;
DROP INDEX
test=# CREATE INDEX idx_name ON t_test (name) WHERE name NOT IN ('hans',
'paul');
CREATE INDEX
```

In this case, the majority has been excluded from the index and a small, efficient index can be enjoyed:

```
test=# \di+ idx_name
                      List of relations
 Schema |   Name     | Type  | Owner | Table  |    Size
--------+-----------+-------+-------+--------+-----------
 public | idx_name  | index | hs    | t_test | 8192 bytes
(1 row)
```

Note that it only makes sense to exclude very frequent values that make up a large part of the table (at least 25% or so). Ideal candidates for partial indexes are gender (we assume that most people are male or female), nationality (assuming that most people in your country have the same nationality), and so on. Of course, applying this kind of trickery requires some deep knowledge of your data, but it certainly pays off.

Adding data while indexing

Creating an index is easy. However, keep in mind that you cannot modify a table, while an index is being built. The CREATE INDEX command will lock up a table using a SHARE lock to ensure that no changes happen. While this is clearly no problem for small tables, it will cause issues on large ones on production systems. Indexing a terabyte of data or so will take some time and therefore blocking a table for too long can become an issue.

The solution to the problem is CREATE INDEX CONCURRENTLY command. Building the index will take a lot longer (usually at least twice as long) but you can use the table normally during index creation.

Here is how it works:

```
test=# CREATE INDEX CONCURRENTLY idx_name2 ON t_test (name);
CREATE INDEX
```

Note that PostgreSQL does not guarantee success if you are using the CREATE INDEX CONCURRENTLY command. An index can end up being marked as invalid if the operations going on on your system somehow conflict with index creation.

Introducing operator classes

So far, the goal was to figure out what to index and to blindly apply an index on this column or on a group of columns. There is one assumption, however, that we have silently accepted to make this work. Up to now, we have been working on the assumption that the order in which data has to be sorted is a somewhat fixed constant. In reality, this assumption might not hold true. Sure, numbers will always be in the same order, but other kinds of data will most likely not have a predefined, fixed sort order.

To prove my point, I have compiled a real-world example. Take a look at the following two records:

```
1118 09 08 78
2345 01 05 77
```

My question now is: are those two rows ordered properly? They might because one comes before another. However, this is wrong because those two rows do have some hidden semantics. What you see here is two Austrian social security numbers. 09 08 78 actually means August 9, 1978 and 01 05 77 actually means May 1, 1977. The first four numbers consist of a checksum and some sort of auto-incremented three digit number. So in reality, 1977 comes before 1978 and we might consider swapping those two lines to achieve the desired sort order.

The problem is that PostgreSQL has no idea what those two rows actually mean. If a column is marked as text, PostgreSQL will apply the standard rules to sort text. If the column is marked as a number, PostgreSQL will apply the standard rules to sort numbers. Under no circumstances will it ever use something as odd as I've described. If you think that the facts I outlined previously are the only things to consider when processing those numbers, you are wrong. How many months does a year have? 12? Far from true. In the Austrian social security system, these numbers can hold up to 14 months? Why? Remember... three digits are simply an auto-increment value. The trouble is this: if an immigrant or a refugee has no valid paperwork and if his birthday is not known, he will be assigned an artificial birthday in the 13th month. During the Balkan wars in 1990, Austria offered asylum to over 115,000 refugees. Naturally, this three digit number was not enough and a 14th month was added. Now, which standard data type can handle this kind of COBOL-leftover from the early 1970 (that was when the layout of the social security number was introduced)? The answer is: none.

To handle special-purpose fields in a sane way, PostgreSQL offers operator classes:

```
test=# \h CREATE OPERATOR CLASS
Command:     CREATE OPERATOR CLASS
Description: define a new operator class
Syntax:
CREATE OPERATOR CLASS name [ DEFAULT ] FOR TYPE data_type
  USING index_method [ FAMILY family_name ] AS
  {  OPERATOR strategy_number operator_name [ ( op_type, op_type ) ] [ FOR
SEARCH | FOR ORDER BY sort_family_name ]
    | FUNCTION support_number [ ( op_type [ , op_type ] ) ] function_name (
argument_type [, ...] )
    | STORAGE storage_type
  } [, ... ]
```

An operator class will tell an index how to behave. Let's take a look at a standard binary tree. It can perform five operations:

Strategy	Operator	Description
1	<	Less than
2	<=	Less than or equal to
3	=	Equal to
4	>=	Greater than or equal to
5	>	Greater than

The standard operator classes support the standard datatypes and standard operators we have been using throughout this book. If you want to handle social security numbers, it is necessary to come up with your own operators capable of providing you with the logic you need. Those custom operators can then be used to form an operator class, which is nothing more than a strategy passed to the index to configure how it should behave.

Hacking up an operator class for a B-tree

To give you a practical example of what an operator class looks like, I have hacked up some code to handle social security numbers. To keep it simple, I have paid no attention to details such as checksums and so on.

Creating new operators

The first thing, which has to be done, is to come up with the desired operators. Note that five operators are needed. There is one operator for each strategy. A strategy of an index is really like a plugin, which allows you to put in your own code.

Before getting started, I have compiled some test data:

```
CREATE TABLE t_sva (sva text);

INSERT INTO t_sva VALUES ('1118090878');
INSERT INTO t_sva VALUES ('2345010477');
```

Now that the test data is there, it is time to create an operator. For that purpose, PostgreSQL offers the CREATE OPERATOR command:

```
test=# \h CREATE OPERATOR
Command:     CREATE OPERATOR
Description: define a new operator
Syntax:
CREATE OPERATOR name (
    PROCEDURE = function_name
    [, LEFTARG = left_type ] [, RIGHTARG = right_type ]
    [, COMMUTATOR = com_op ] [, NEGATOR = neg_op ]
    [, RESTRICT = res_proc ] [, JOIN = join_proc ]
    [, HASHES ] [, MERGES ]
)
```

Basically, the concept is as follows: an operator calls a function, which gets one or two parameters, one for the left argument and one for the right argument of the operator.

As you can see, an operator is nothing more than a function call. So consequently, it is necessary to implement the logic needed into those functions hidden by the operators. In order to fix the sort order, I have written a function called normalize_si:

```
CREATE OR REPLACE FUNCTION normalize_si(text) RETURNS text AS $$
        BEGIN
        RETURN substring($1, 9, 2) ||
                substring($1, 7, 2) ||
                substring($1, 5, 2) ||
                substring($1, 1, 4);
        END; $$
LANGUAGE 'plpgsql' IMMUTABLE;
```

Calling the function will return the following result:

```
test=# SELECT normalize_si('1118090878');
 normalize_si
---------------
 7808091118
(1 row)
```

As you can see, all we did is swap some digits. It is now possible to just use the normal string sort order. In the next step, this function can already be used to compare social security numbers directly. The first function needed is the lower than function, which is needed by first strategy:

```
CREATE OR REPLACE FUNCTION si_lt(text, text) RETURNS boolean AS $$
        BEGIN
        RETURN normalize_si($1) < normalize_si($2);
        END;
$$ LANGUAGE 'plpgsql' IMMUTABLE;
```

There are two important things to note here:

- The function must not be written in SQL. It only works in a procedural or in a compiled language. The reason for that is that SQL functions can be inline under some circumstances and this would cripple the entire endeavor.
- The second issue is that you should stick to the naming convention used in this chapter—it is widely accepted by the community. Less than functions should be called _lt, less or equal to functions should be called _le, and so on.

Given this knowledge, the next functions needed by our future operators can be defined:

```
-- lower equals
CREATE OR REPLACE FUNCTION si_le(text, text) RETURNS boolean AS $$
        BEGIN
        RETURN normalize_si($1) <= normalize_si($2);
        END;
$$ LANGUAGE 'plpgsql' IMMUTABLE;

-- greater equal
CREATE OR REPLACE FUNCTION si_ge(text, text) RETURNS boolean AS $$
    BEGIN
    RETURN normalize_si($1) >= normalize_si($2);
    END;
$$ LANGUAGE 'plpgsql' IMMUTABLE;

-- greater
CREATE OR REPLACE FUNCTION si_gt(text, text) RETURNS boolean AS $$
    BEGIN
```

```
      RETURN normalize_si($1) > normalize_si($2);
      END;
$$ LANGUAGE 'plpgsql' IMMUTABLE;
```

So far, four functions have been defined. A fifth function for the equals operator is not necessary. We can simply take the existing operator because equals does not depend on sort order anyway.

Now that all functions are in place, it is time to define those operators:

```
-- define operators
CREATE OPERATOR <# ( PROCEDURE=si_lt,
                     LEFTARG=text,
                     RIGHTARG=text);
```

The design of the operator is actually very simple. The operator needs a name (in my case <#), a procedure, which is supposed to be called, as well as the datatype of the left and the right argument. When the operator is called, the left argument will be the first parameter of si_lt and the right argument will be the second argument.

The remaining three operators follow the same principle:

```
CREATE OPERATOR <=# ( PROCEDURE=si_le,
                      LEFTARG=text,
                      RIGHTARG=text);

CREATE OPERATOR >=# ( PROCEDURE=si_ge,
                      LEFTARG=text,
                      RIGHTARG=text);

CREATE OPERATOR ># ( PROCEDURE=si_gt,
                     LEFTARG=text,
                     RIGHTARG=text);
```

Depending on the type of index you are using, a couple of *support functions* are needed. In the case of standard B-trees, there is only one support function needed, which is used to speed things up internally:

```
CREATE OR REPLACE FUNCTION si_same(text, text) RETURNS int AS $$
        BEGIN
                IF      normalize_si($1) < normalize_si($2)
                THEN
                        RETURN -1;
                ELSIF   normalize_si($1) > normalize_si($2)
                THEN
                        RETURN +1;
                ELSE
```

```
                      RETURN 0;
             END IF;
       END;
  $$ LANGUAGE 'plpgsql' IMMUTABLE;
```

The `si_same` function will either return `-1` if the first parameter is smaller, `0` if both parameters are equal, and `1` if the first parameter is greater. Internally, the `_same` function is the workhorse, so you should make sure that your code is optimized.

Creating operator classes

Finally, all components are in place and it is finally possible to create the operator class needed by the index:

```
CREATE OPERATOR CLASS sva_special_ops
FOR TYPE text USING btree
AS
    OPERATOR        1        <#  ,
    OPERATOR        2        <=# ,
    OPERATOR        3        =  ,
    OPERATOR        4        >=# ,
    OPERATOR        5        >#  ,

    FUNCTION        1        si_same(text, text);
```

The `CREATE OPERATOR CLASS` command connects strategies and operators. `OPERATOR 1 <#` means that strategy 1 will use the `<#` operator. Finally the `_same` function is connected with the operator class.

Note that the operator class has a name and that it has been explicitly defined to work with B-trees.

The operator class can already be used during index creation:

```
CREATE INDEX idx_special ON t_sva (sva sva_special_ops);
```

Creating the index works in a slightly different way than previously: `sva sva_special_ops` means that the `sva` column is indexed using the `sva_special_ops` operator class. If `sva_special_ops` is not explicitly used, then PostgreSQL will not go for our special sort order but decide on the default operator class.

Testing custom operator classes

In our example, the test data consists of just two rows. Therefore, PostgreSQL will never use an index because the table is just too small to justify the overhead of even opening the index. To be able to still test without having to load too much data, you can advise the optimizer to make sequential scans more expensive. Making operations more expensive can be done inside your session using the following instruction:

```
SET enable_seqscan TO off;
```

The index works as expected:

```
test=# explain SELECT * FROM t_sva WHERE sva = '0000112273';
                                QUERY PLAN
-------------------------------------------------------------------
 Index Only Scan using idx_special on t_sva (cost=0.13..8.14 rows=1
width=32)
   Index Cond: (sva = '0000112273'::text)
(2 rows)

test=# SELECT * FROM t_sva;
sva
-------------
 2345010477
 1118090878
(2 rows)
```

Understanding PostgreSQL index types

So far only binary trees have been discussed. However, in many cases B-trees are just not enough. Why is that the case? As discussed in this chapter, B-trees are basically based on sorting. Operators <, <=, =, >= and > can be handled using B-trees. The trouble is: not all data types can be sorted in a useful way. Just imagine a polygon. How would you sort those objects in a useful way? Sure, you can sort by the area covered, its length or so, but doing that won't allow you to actually find them using a geometric search.

The solution to the problem is to provide more than just one index type. Each index will serve a special purpose and do exactly what is needed. The following index types are available (as of PostgreSQL 9.6):

```
test=# SELECT * FROM pg_am;
 amname |  amhandler  | amtype
--------+-------------+--------
 btree  | bthandler   | i
```

```
hash    | hashhandler | i
GiST    | GiSThandler | i
gin     | ginhandler  | i
spGiST  | spghandler  | i
brin    | brinhandler | i
(6 rows)
```

There are six types of indexes. B-trees have already been discussed in great detail but what are those other index types good for? The following sections will outline the purpose of each index type available in PostgreSQL.

Note that there are some extensions out there that can be used on top of what you can see here. Additional index types available on the web are rum, vodka, and in future, cognac.

Hash indexes

Hash indexes have been around for many years. The idea is to hash the input value and store it for later lookups. Having hash indexes actually makes sense. However, it is not advised to use them in PostgreSQL. The reason for that is that hashes are not very good at concurrency and have no support for the PostgreSQL transaction log. In short, you should not use them in real-world systems in the foreseeable future.

GiST indexes

Generalized search tree (**GiST**) indexes are highly important index types because they are used for a variety of different things. GiST indexes can be used to implement R-tree behavior and it is even possible to act as B-tree. However, abusing GiST for B-tree indexes is not recommended.

Typical use cases for GiST are:

- Range types
- Geometric indexes (for example, used by the highly popular PostGIS extension)
- Fuzzy searching

Understanding how GiST works

To many people, GiST is still a black box. Therefore, I have decided to add a section to this section outlining how GiST works internally.

Consider the following diagram:

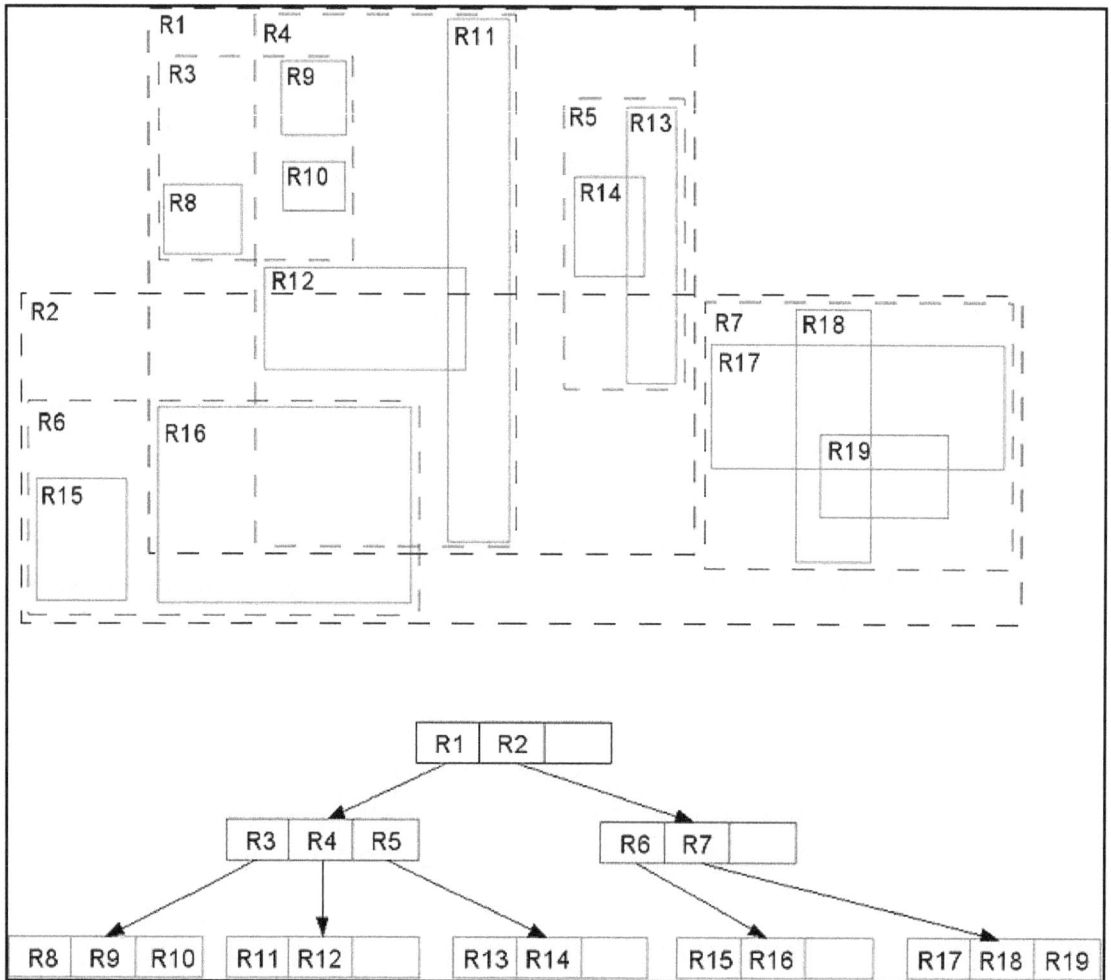

Figure 3.1: Source:
http://leopard.in.ua/assets/images/postgresql/pg_indexes/pg_indexes2.jpg

Take a look at the tree. You will see that **R1** and **R2** are on top. **R1** and **R2** are the bounding boxes containing everything else. **R3**, **R4**, and **R5** are contained by **R1**. **R8**, **R9**, and **R10** are contained by **R3** and so on. A GiST index is therefore hierarchically organized. What you can see in the diagram is that some operations, which are not available in B-trees are supported. Some of those operations are overlaps, left of, right of, and so on. The layout of a GiST tree is ideal for geometric indexing.

Extending GiST

Of course, it is also possible to come up with your own operator classes. The following strategies are supported:

Operation	Strategy number
Strictly left of	1
Does not extend to right of	2
Overlaps	3
Does not extend to left of	4
Strictly right of	5
Same	6
Contains	7
Contained by	8
Does not extend above	9
Strictly below	10
Strictly above	11
Does not extend below	12

If you want to write operator classes for GiST, a couple of support functions have to be provided. In the case of a B-tree, there is only the `same` function - GiST indexes provide a lot more:

Function	Description	Support function number
`consistent`	The functions determine whether a key satisfies the query qualifier. Internally, strategies are looked up and checked.	1
`union`	Calculate the union of a set of keys. In case of numeric values simply the upper and lower values or a range are computed. It is especially important to geometries.	2
`compress`	Compute a compressed representation of a key or value.	3

Function	Description	Support function number
decompress	This is the counterpart of the compress function.	4
penalty	During insertion, the cost of inserting into the tree will be calculated. The cost determines where the new entry will go inside the tree. Therefore, a good penalty function is key to good overall performance of the index.	5
picksplit	Determines where to move entries in case of a page split. Some entries have to stay in the old page while others will go to the new page being created. Having a good picksplit function is essential to good index performance.	6
equal	The equal function is similar to the same function you have already seen in B-trees.	7
distance	Calculates the distance (a number) between a key and the query value. The distance function is optional and is needed in case KNN search is supported.	8
fetch	Determine the original representation of a compressed key. This function is needed to handle index only scans as supported by recent version of PostgreSQL.	9

Implementing operator classes for GiST indexes is usually done in C. If you are interested in a good example, I advise you to check out the btree_GiST module in the contrib directory. It shows how to index standard data types using GiST and is a good source of information as well as inspiration.

GIN indexes

Generalized inverted (**GIN**) indexes are a good way to index text. Suppose you want to index a million text documents. A certain word may occur millions of times. In a normal B-tree this would mean that the key is stored millions of times. Not so in a GIN. Each key (or *word*) is stored once and assigned to a document list. Keys are organized in a standard B-tree. Each entry will have a document list pointing to all entries in the table having the same key. A GIN index is very small and compact. However, it lacks an important feature found in B-trees—Sorted data. In a GIN, the list of item pointers associated with a certain key is sorted by the position of the row in the table and not by some arbitrary criteria.

Extending GIN

Just like any other index, GIN can be extended. The following strategies are available:

Operation	Strategy number
Overlap	1
Contains	2
Is contained by	3
Equal	4

On top of that, the following support functions are available:

Function	Description	Support function number
compare	The compare function is similar to the same function you have seen in B-trees. If two keys are compared, it returns -1 (lower), 0 (equal), or 1 (higher).	1
extractValue	Extract keys from a value to be indexed. A value can have many keys. For example, a text value might consist of more than one word.	2
extractQuery	Extract keys from a query condition.	3
consistent	Check whether a value matches a query condition.	4

Function	Description	Support function number
comparePartial	Compare a partial key from query and a key from the index. Returns −1, 0, or 1 (similar to the same function supported by B-trees).	5
triConsistent	Determine whether a value matches a query condition (ternary variant). It is optional if the consistent function is present.	6

If you are looking for a good example of how to extend GIN, consider looking at the btree_gin module in the PostgreSQL contrib directory. It is a valuable source of information and a good way to start your own implementation.

If you are interested in full text search, more information will be provided later on in this chapter.

SP-GiST indexes

Space partitioned GiST (SP-GiST) has mainly been designed for in-memory use. The reason for that is that an SP-GiST stored on disk needs a fairly high number of disk hits to function. Disk hits are way more expensive than just following a couple of pointers in RAM.

The beauty is that SP-GiST can be used to implement various types of trees such as quad-trees, k-d trees, and radix trees (tries).

The following strategies are provided:

Operation	Strategy number
Strictly left of	1
Strictly right of	5
Same	6
Contained by	8
Strictly below	10
Strictly above	11

To write your own operator classes for SP-GiST, a couple of functions have to be provided:

Function	Description	Support function number
config	Provides information about the operator class in use	1
choose	Figures out how to insert a new value into an inner tuple	2
picksplit	Figures out how to partition/split a set of values	3
inner_consistent	Determine which subpartitions need to be searched for a query	4
leaf_consistent	Determine whether key satisfies the query qualifier	5

BRIN indexes

Block range indexes (**BRIN**) are of great practical use. All indexes discussed until now need quite a lot of disk space. Although a lot of work has gone into shrinking GIN indexes and the like, they still need quite a lot because an index pointer is needed for each entry. So if there are 10 million entries, there will be 10 million index pointers. Space is the main concern addressed by BRIN indexes. A BRIN index does not keep an index entry for each tuple but will store the minimum and the maximum value of 128 (default) blocks of data (1 MB). The index is therefore very small but *lossy*. Scanning the index will return more data than we asked for. PostgreSQL has to filter out those additional rows in a later step.

The following example demonstrates how small a BRIN index really is:

```
test=# CREATE INDEX idx_brin ON t_test USING brin(id);
CREATE INDEX
test=# \di+ idx_brin
                          List of relations
 Schema |   Name    | Type  | Owner | Table  | Size
--------+-----------+-------+-------+--------+-------------
 public | idx_brin  | index | hs    | t_test | 48 KB
(1 row)
```

In my example, the BRIN index is 2,000 times smaller than a standard B-tree. The question naturally arising now is: why don't we always use BRIN indexes? To answer this kind of question, it is important to reflect on the layout of BRIN; the minimum and maximum value for 1 MB are stored. If the data is sorted (high correlation), BRIN is pretty efficient because we can fetch 1 MB of data, scan it, and we are done. However, what if data is shuffled? In this case, BRIN won't be able to exclude chunks of data anymore because it is very likely that something close to the overall high and the overall low is within 1 MB of data. Therefore, BRIN is mostly made for highly correlated data. In reality, correlated data is quite likely in data warehousing applications. Often data is loaded every day and therefore dates can be highly correlated.

Extending BRIN indexes

BRIN supports the same strategies as a B-tree and therefore needs the same set of operators. Code can be reused nicely:

Operation	Strategy number
Less than	1
Less than or equal	2
Equal	3
Greater than or equal	4
Greater than	5

The support functions needed by BRIN are as follows:

Function	Description	Support function number
opcInfo	Provide internal information about the indexed columns	1
add_value	Add an entry to an existing summary tuple	2
consistent	Check whether a value matches a condition	3
union	Calculate the union of two summary entries (minimum/maximum values)	4

Adding additional indexes

Since PostgreSQL 9.6, there has been an easy way to deploy entirely new index types as extensions. This is pretty cool because if those index types provided by PostgreSQL are not enough, it is possible to add additional ones serving precisely your purpose. The instruction to do that is CREATE ACCESS METHOD:

```
test=# \h CREATE ACCESS METHOD
Command:     CREATE ACCESS METHOD
Description: define a new access method
Syntax:
CREATE ACCESS METHOD name
    TYPE access_method_type
    HANDLER handler_function
```

Don't worry too much about this command—just in case you ever deploy your own index type, it will come as a ready to use extension.

One of those extensions implement *bloom filters*. Bloom filters are probabilistic data structures. They sometimes return too many rows but never too few. Therefore, a bloom filter is a good method to pre-filter data.

How does it work? A bloom filter is defined on a couple of columns. A bitmask is calculated based on the input values, which is then compared to your query. The upside of a bloom filter is that you can index as many columns as you want. The downside is that the entire bloom filter has to be read. Of course, the bloom filter is smaller than the underlying data and so it is, in many cases, very beneficial.

To use bloom filters, just activate the extension, which is part of the PostgreSQL contrib package:

```
test=# CREATE EXTENSION bloom;
CREATE EXTENSION
```

As stated previously, the idea behind a bloom filter is that it allows you to index as many columns as you want. In many real-world applications, the challenge is to index many columns without knowing which combinations the user will actually need at runtime. In the case of a large table, it is totally impossible to create standard B-tree indexes on, say, 80 fields or more. A bloom filter might be an alternative in this case:

```
test=# CREATE TABLE t_bloom (x1 int, x2 int, x3 int, x4 int, x5 int, x6
int, x7 int);
CREATE TABLE
```

Creating the index is easy:

```
test=# CREATE INDEX idx_bloom ON t_bloom (x1, x2, x3, x4, x5, x6, x7);
CREATE INDEX
```

If sequential scans are turned off, the index can be seen in action:

```
test=# explain SELECT * FROM t_bloom WHERE x5 = 9 AND x3 = 7;
                              QUERY PLAN
-------------------------------------------------------------------------
 Bitmap Heap Scan on t_bloom   (cost=18.50..22.52 rows=1 width=28)
   Recheck Cond: ((x3 = 7) AND (x5 = 9))
   ->  Bitmap Index Scan on idx_bloom   (cost=0.00..18.50 rows=1 width=0)
         Index Cond: ((x3 = 7) AND (x5 = 9))
```

Note that I have queried a combination of random columns; they are not related to the actual order in the index. The bloom filter will still be beneficial.

If you are interested in bloom filters, consider checking out the following website: `https://en.wikipedia.org/wiki/Bloom_filter`.

Achieving better answers with fuzzy searching

Performing precise searching is not the only thing expected by users these days. Modern websites have educated users in a way that they always expect a result regardless of the user input. If you search on Google, there will always be an answer even if the user input is wrong, full of typos, or simply pointless. People expect good results regardless of the input data.

Taking advantage of pg_trgm

To do fuzzy searching with PostgreSQL, you can add the `pg_trgm` extension. To activate the extension, just run the following instruction:

```
test=# CREATE EXTENSION pg_trgm;
CREATE EXTENSION
```

The `pg_trgm` extension is pretty powerful, and to show what it is capable of, I have compiled some sample data consisting of 2,354 names of villages and cities here in Austria, Europe.

Our sample data can be stored in a simple table:

```
test=# CREATE TABLE t_location (name text);
CREATE TABLE
```

My company website has all the data and PostgreSQL enables you to load the data directly:

```
test=# COPY t_location FROM PROGRAM 'curl www.cybertec.at/secret/orte.txt';
COPY 2354
```

> **TIP**
>
> Note that `curl` (a command-line tool to fetch data) has to be installed. If you don't have this tool, download the file normally and import it from your local filesystem.

Once the data has been loaded, it is possible to check out the content of the table:

```
test=# SELECT * FROM t_location LIMIT 4;
              name
---------------------------------
 Eisenstadt
 Rust
 Breitenbrunn am Neusiedler See
 Donnerskirchen
(4 rows)
```

If German is not your mother tongue, it will be impossible to spell the names of those locations without severe mistakes. Fortunately, `pg_trgm` will come to the rescue:

```
test=# CREATE EXTENSION pg_trgm;
CREATE EXTENSION
```

The `pg_trgm` provides us with a distance operator, which computes the distance between two strings:

```
test=# SELECT 'abcde' <-> 'abdeacb';
 ?column?
----------
 0.833333
(1 row)
```

The distance is a number between zero and one. The lower the number, the more similar two strings are.

How does that work? Trigrams take a string and dissect it into sequences of three characters each:

```
test=# SELECT show_trgm('abcdef');
              show_trgm
--------------------------------------
 {"  a","  ab",abc,bcd,cde,def,"ef "}
(1 row)
```

Those sequences will then be used to come up with the distance you have just seen. Of course, the distance operator can be used inside a query to find the closest match:

```
test=# SELECT * FROM  t_location ORDER BY name <-> 'Kramertneusiedel' LIMIT
3;
       name
------------------
 Gramatneusiedl
 Klein-Neusiedl
 Potzneusiedl
(3 rows)
```

Gramatneusiedl is pretty close to Kramertneusiedel. It sounds similar and using a K instead of a G is a pretty common mistake. On Google, you will sometimes see **Did you mean...**. It is quite likely that Google is using n-grams here to do that.

In PostgreSQL, it is possible to use GiST to index on text using trigrams:

```
test=# CREATE INDEX idx_trgm ON t_location USING GiST(name GiST_trgm_ops);
CREATE INDEX
```

pg_trgm provides us with the GiST_trgm_ops operator class designed to do similarity searches. The following listing shows that the index is used as expected:

```
test=# explain SELECT * FROM t_location ORDER BY name <->
'Kramertneusiedel' LIMIT 5;
                            QUERY PLAN
-------------------------------------------------------------------
 Limit   (cost=0.14..0.58 rows=5 width=17)
    ->  Index Scan using idx_trgm on t_location
           (cost=0.14..207.22 rows=2354 width=17)
           Order By: (name <-> 'Kramertneusiedel'::text)
(3 rows)
```

Speed up LIKE queries

LIKE queries definitely cause some of the worst performance problems faced by people around the globe these days. In most database systems, LIKE is pretty slow and requires a sequential scan. In addition to that, end users quickly figure out that a fuzzy search will in many cases return better results than precise queries. A single type of LIKE query on a large table can, therefore, often cripple the performance of an entire database server if it is called often enough.

Fortunately, PostgreSQL offers a solution to the problem and the solution happens to be installed already:

```
test=# explain SELECT * FROM t_location WHERE name LIKE '%neusi%';
                            QUERY PLAN
---------------------------------------------------------------
 Bitmap Heap Scan on t_location
   (cost=4.33..19.05 rows=24 width=13)
   Recheck Cond: (name ~~ '%neusi%'::text)
   ->  Bitmap Index Scan on idx_trgm  (cost=0.00..4.32 rows=24 width=0)
         Index Cond: (name ~~ '%neusi%'::text)
(4 rows)
```

The trigram index deployed in the previous section is also suitable to speed up LIKE. Note that the % symbols can be used at any point in the search string. This is a major advantage over standard B-trees, which just happen to speed up wild cards at the end of the query.

Handling regular expressions

However, this is still not everything. Trigram indexes are even capable of speeding up simple regular expressions. The following example shows how this can be done:

```
test=# SELECT * FROM t_location WHERE name ~ '[A-C].*neu.*';
     name
---------------
 Bruckneudorf
(1 row)

test=# explain SELECT * FROM t_location WHERE name ~ '[A-C].*neu.*';
                            QUERY PLAN
---------------------------------------------------------------
 Index Scan using idx_trgm on t_location  (cost=0.14..8.16
   rows=1 width=13)
   Index Cond: (name ~ '[A-C].*neu.*'::text)
(2 rows)
```

PostgreSQL will inspect the regular expression and use the index to answer the question.

> Internally, PostgreSQL can transform the regular expression into a graph and traverse the index accordingly.

Understanding full-text search - FTS

If you are looking up names or for simple strings, you are usually querying the entire content of a field. In FTS, this is different. The purpose of full-text search is to look for words or groups of words, which can be found inside a text. Therefore, FTS is more of a *contains* operation as you are basically never looking for an exact string.

In PostgreSQL, FTS can be done using GIN indexes. The idea is to dissect a text, extract valuable lexemes, and index those elements rather than the underlying text. To make your search even more successful, those words are preprocessed.

Here is an example:

```
test=# SELECT to_tsvector('english', 'A car, I want a car. I would not even
mind having many cars');
                            to_tsvector
-----------------------------------------------------------------
 'car':2,6,14 'even':10 'mani':13 'mind':11 'want':4 'would':8
(1 row)
```

The example shows a simple sentence. The to_tsvector function will take the string, apply English rules and perform a stemming process. Based on the configuration (english), PostgreSQL will parse the string, throw away stop words and stem individual words. For example, car and cars will be transformed to car. Note that this is not about finding the word stem. In the case of many, PostgreSQL will simply transform the string to mani by applying standard rules working nicely with the English language.

Note that the output of the `to_tsvector` function is highly language dependent. If you tell PostgreSQL to treat the string as Dutch, the result will be totally different:

```
test=# SELECT to_tsvector('dutch', 'A car, I want a car. I would not even
mind having many cars');
                          to_tsvector
----------------------------------------------------------------
 'a':1,5 'car':2,6,14 'even':10 'having':12 'i':3,7 'many':13
   'mind':11 'not':9 'would':8
(1 row)
```

To figure out which configurations are supported, consider running the following query:

```
SELECT cfgname FROM pg_ts_config;
```

Comparing strings

After taking a brief look at the stemming process, it is time to figure out how a stemmed text can be compared to a user query. The following code snippet checks for `wanted`:

```
test=# SELECT to_tsvector('english', 'A car, I want a car. I would not even
mind having many cars') @@ to_tsquery('english', 'wanted');
 ?column?
----------
 t
(1 row)
```

Note that `wanted` does not actually show up in the original text. Still, PostgreSQL will return true. The reason is that `want` and `wanted` are both transformed to the same lexeme so the result is true. Practically, this makes a lot of sense. Imagine you are looking for *car* on Google. If you find pages selling *cars*, this is totally fine. Finding common lexemes is therefore an intelligent idea.

Sometimes, people are not only looking for a single word but want to find a set of words. With `to_tsquery`, this is possible as shown in the next example:

```
test=# SELECT to_tsvector('english', 'A car, I want a car. I would not even
mind having many cars') @@ to_tsquery('english', 'wanted & bmw');
 ?column?
----------
 f
(1 row)
```

In this case, false is returned because bmw cannot be found in our input string. In the to_tsquery function, & means and and | means or. It is therefore easily possible to build complex search strings.

Defining GIN indexes

If you want to apply text search to a column or a group of columns, there are basically two choices:

- Create a functional index using GIN
- Add a column containing ready to use tsvectors and a trigger to keep them in sync

In this section, both options will be outlines. To show how things work, I have created some sample data:

```
test=# CREATE TABLE t_fts AS SELECT comment FROM pg_available_extensions;
SELECT 43
```

Indexing the column directly with a functional index is definitely a slower but more space-efficient way to get things done:

```
test=# CREATE INDEX idx_fts_func ON t_fts USING gin(to_tsvector('english',
comment));
CREATE INDEX
```

Deploying an index on the function is easy but it can lead to some overhead. Adding a materialized column needs more space but will lead to better runtime behavior:

```
test=# ALTER TABLE t_fts ADD COLUMN ts tsvector;
ALTER TABLE
```

The only trouble is: how do you keep this column in sync? The answer is by using a trigger:

```
test=# CREATE TRIGGER tsvectorupdate
BEFORE INSERT OR UPDATE ON t_fts
FOR EACH ROW
EXECUTE PROCEDURE
tsvector_update_trigger(somename, 'pg_catalog.english', "comment");
```

Fortunately, PostgreSQL already provides a C function that can be used by a trigger to sync the `tsvector` column. Just pass a name, the desired language, as well as a couple of columns to the function, and you are already done. The trigger function will take care of all that is needed. Note that a trigger will always operate within the same transaction as the statement making the modification. Therefore there is no risk of being inconsistent.

Debugging your search

Sometimes it is not quite clear why a query matches a given search string. To debug your query, PostgreSQL offers the `ts_debug` function. From a user's point of view it can be used just like `to_tsvector`. It reveals a lot about the inner workings of the FTS infrastructure:

```
test=# \x
Expanded display is on.
test=# SELECT * FROM ts_debug('english', 'go to
www.postgresql-support.de');
-[ RECORD 1 ]+---------------------------
alias        | asciiword
description  | Word, all ASCII
token        | go
dictionaries | {english_stem}
dictionary   | english_stem
lexemes      | {go}
-[ RECORD 2 ]+---------------------------
alias        | blank
description  | Space symbols
token        |
dictionaries | {}
dictionary   |
lexemes      |
-[ RECORD 3 ]+---------------------------
alias        | asciiword
description  | Word, all ASCII
token        | to
dictionaries | {english_stem}
dictionary   | english_stem
lexemes      | {}
-[ RECORD 4 ]+---------------------------
alias        | blank
description  | Space symbols
token        |
dictionaries | {}
dictionary   |
lexemes      |
-[ RECORD 5 ]+---------------------------
```

```
alias        | host
description  | Host
token        | www.postgresql-support.de
dictionaries | {simple}
dictionary   | simple
lexemes      | {www.postgresql-support.de}
```

`ts_debug` will list every token found and display information about the token. You will see which token was found by the parser, the dictionary used, as well as the type of object. In my example, blanks, words, and hosts have been found. You might also see numbers, e-mail addresses, and a lot more. Depending on the type of string, PostgreSQL will handle things differently. For example, it makes absolutely no sense to stem hostnames and e-mail addresses.

Gathering word statistics

Full-text search can handle a lot of data. To give end users more insights into their texts, PostgreSQL offers the `pg_stat` function, which returns a list of words:

```
SELECT * FROM ts_stat('SELECT to_tsvector(''english'', comment) FROM
pg_available_extensions') ORDER BY 2 DESC LIMIT 3;
   word     | ndoc | nentry
-----------+------+--------
 function  |  10  |   10
 data      |  10  |   10
 type      |   7  |    7
(3 rows)
```

The `word` column contains the stemmed word, `ndoc` tells us about the number of documents a certain word occurs. `nentry` indicates how often a word was found all together

Taking advantage of exclusion operators

So far, indexes have been used to speed up things and to ensure uniqueness. However, a couple of years ago somebody come up with the idea of using indexes for even more. As you have seen in this chapter, GiST supports operations such as *intersects*, *overlaps*, *contains*, and a lot more. So why not use those operations to manage data integrity?

Here is an example:

```
test=# CREATE EXTENSION btree_gist;
test=# CREATE TABLE t_reservation (
        room            int,
        from_to         tsrange,
        EXCLUDE USING GiST (room with =,
                            from_to with &&)
);
CREATE TABLE
```

The EXCLUDE USING GiST clause defines additional constraints. If you are selling rooms, you might want to allow different rooms to be booked at the same time. However, you don't want to sell the same room twice during the same period. What the EXCLUDE clause says in my example is this: if the room is equal, the data in from_to with must not overlap (&&).

The following two rows will not violate constraints:

```
test=# INSERT INTO t_reservation VALUES (10, '["2017-01-01",
"2017-03-03"]');
INSERT 0 1
test=# INSERT INTO t_reservation VALUES (13, '["2017-01-01",
"2017-03-03"]');
INSERT 0 1
```

However, the next INSERT will cause a violation because the data overlaps:

```
test=# INSERT INTO t_reservation VALUES (13, '["2017-02-02",
"2017-08-14"]');
ERROR:  conflicting key value violates exclusion constraint
"t_reservation_room_from_to_excl"
DETAIL:  Key (room, from_to)=(13, ["2017-02-02 00:00:00","2017-08-14
00:00:00"]) conflicts with existing key (room, from_to)=(13, ["2017-01-01
00:00:00","2017-03-03 00:00:00"]).
```

The use of exclusion operators is very useful and can provide you with highly advanced means to handle integrity.

Summary

This chapter was all about indexes. You learned when PostgreSQL will decide on an index and which types of indexes exist. On top of just using indexes, it is also possible to implement your own strategies to speed up your applications with custom operators and indexing strategies.

For those of you who really want to take things to the limit, PostgreSQL offers custom access methods.

The next chapter is all about advanced SQL. Many people are not aware of what SQL is really capable of, and therefore I am going to show people some efficient, more advanced SQL stuff.

4
Handling Advanced SQL

In the previous chapter, you learned about indexing as well as about PostgreSQL's ability to run custom indexing code to speedup queries. In this chapter you will learn about advanced SQL. Most readers of this book will have some experience of using SQL. However, experience has shown that those advanced features outlined in this book are not widely known and therefore it makes sense to cover them in this context to help people to achieve their goals faster and more efficiently.

The topics of this chapter are:

- Grouping sets
- Ordered sets
- Hypothetical aggregates
- Windowing functions and analytics

At the end of the chapter, you will be able to understand and use advanced SQL.

Introducing grouping sets

Every advanced user of SQL should be familiar with GROUP BY and HAVING clauses. But are you also aware of CUBE, ROLLUP, and GROUPING SETS? If not, this chapter might be worth reading for you.

Loading some sample data

To make this chapter a pleasant experience for you, I have compiled some sample data, which has been taken from the BP energy report: `http://www.bp.com/en/global/corporate/energy-economics/statistical-review-of-world-energy.html`.

Here is the data structure that will be used:

```
test=# CREATE TABLE t_oil (
   region          text,
   country         text,
   year            int,
   production      int,
   consumption     int
);
CREATE TABLE
```

The test data can be downloaded from our website using `curl` directly:

```
test=# COPY t_oil FROM PROGRAM ' curl www.cybertec.at/secret/oil_ext.txt ';
COPY 644
```

As in the previous chapter, you can download the file before importing it. On some operating systems, `curl` is not there by default or has not been installed, so downloading the file before might be an easier option for many people.

There is data for 14 nations between 1965 and 2010, which are in two regions of the world:

```
test=# SELECT region, avg(production) FROM    t_oil GROUP BY region;
    region     |          avg
---------------+----------------------
 Middle East   | 1992.6036866359447005
 North America | 4541.3623188405797101
(2 rows)
```

Applying grouping sets

The GROUP BY clause will turn many rows into one row per group. However, if you do reporting in real life, you might also be interested in the overall average. One additional line might be needed.

Here is how this can be achieved:

```
test=# SELECT region, avg(production) FROM t_oil GROUP BY ROLLUP (region);
    region     |          avg
---------------+-----------------------
 Middle East   | 1992.6036866359447005
 North America | 4541.3623188405797101
               | 2607.5139860139860140
(3 rows)
```

`ROLLUP` will inject an additional line, which will contain the overall average. If you do reporting, it is highly likely that a summary line will be needed. Instead of running two queries, PostgreSQL can provide the data running just a single query.

Of course, this kind of operation can also be used if you are grouping by more than just one column:

```
test=# SELECT   region, country, avg(production) FROM t_oil WHERE country
IN ('USA', 'Canada', 'Iran', 'Oman') GROUP BY ROLLUP (region, country);
    region     | country |          avg
---------------+---------+-----------------------
 Middle East   | Iran    | 3631.6956521739130435
 Middle East   | Oman    |  586.4545454545454545
 Middle East   |         | 2142.9111111111111111
 North America | Canada  | 2123.2173913043478261
 North America | USA     | 9141.3478260869565217
 North America |         | 5632.2826086956521739
               |         | 3906.7692307692307692
(7 rows)
```

In this example, PostgreSQL will inject three lines into the result set. One line will be injected for `Middle East`, one for `North America`. On top of that we will get a line for the overall averages. If you are building a web application the current result is ideal because you can easily build a GUI to drill into the result set by filtering out the null values.

`ROLLUP` is nice in case you instantly want to display a result. I always used it to display final results to end users. However, if you are doing reporting, you might want to pre-calculate more data to ensure more flexibility. The `CUBE` keyword is what you might have been looking for:

```
test=# SELECT   region, country, avg(production) FROM    t_oil WHERE
country IN ('USA', 'Canada', 'Iran', 'Oman') GROUP BY CUBE (region,
country);
    region     | country |          avg
---------------+---------+-----------------------
 Middle East   | Iran    | 3631.6956521739130435
 Middle East   | Oman    |  586.4545454545454545
```

```
Middle East    |          | 2142.9111111111111111
North America  | Canada   | 2123.2173913043478261
North America  | USA      | 9141.3478260869565217
North America  |          | 5632.2826086956521739
               |          | 3906.7692307692307692
               | Canada   | 2123.2173913043478261
               | Iran     | 3631.6956521739130435
               | Oman     |  586.4545454545454545
               | USA      | 9141.3478260869565217
(11 rows)
```

Note that even more rows have been added to the result. CUBE will create the same data as: GROUP BY region, country + GROUP BY region + GROUP BY country + the overall average. So, the whole idea is to extract many results and various levels of aggregation at once. The resulting cube contains all possible combinations of groups.

ROLLUP and CUBE are really just convenience features on top of GROUPING SETS clause. With the GROUPING SETS clause, you can explicitly list the aggregates you want:

```
test=# SELECT    region, country, avg(production)
FROM    t_oil
WHERE   country IN ('USA', 'Canada', 'Iran', 'Oman')
GROUP BY GROUPING SETS ( (), region, country);
    region      | country |          avg
----------------+---------+------------------------
 Middle East    |         | 2142.9111111111111111
 North America  |         | 5632.2826086956521739
                |         | 3906.7692307692307692
                | Canada  | 2123.2173913043478261
                | Iran    | 3631.6956521739130435
                | Oman    |  586.4545454545454545
                | USA     | 9141.3478260869565217
(7 rows)
```

In this, I went for three grouping sets: the overall average, GROUP BY region and GROUP BY country. If you want regions and countries combined, use (region, country).

Investigating performance

Grouping sets are a powerful feature; they help to reduce the number of expensive queries. Internally, PostgreSQL will basically turn to traditional GroupAggregates to make things work. A GroupAggregate node requires sorted data, so be prepared that PostgreSQL might do a lot of temporary sorting:

```
test=# explain SELECT    region, country, avg(production)
```

```
FROM    t_oil
WHERE   country IN ('USA', 'Canada', 'Iran', 'Oman')
GROUP BY GROUPING SETS ( (), region, country);
                           QUERY PLAN
-----------------------------------------------------------
 GroupAggregate  (cost=22.58..32.69 rows=34 width=52)
   Group Key: region
   Group Key: ()
   Sort Key: country
     Group Key: country
   -> Sort  (cost=22.58..23.04 rows=184 width=24)
         Sort Key: region
         -> Seq Scan on t_oil
               (cost=0.00..15.66 rows=184 width=24)
               Filter: (country = ANY
                   ('{USA,Canada,Iran,Oman}'::text[]))
(9 rows)
```

Hash aggregates are only supported for normal GROUP BY clauses involving no grouping sets. According to the developer of grouping sets (Atri Shama), whom I talked to shortly before writing this chapter, adding support for hashes is not worth the effort; so it seems PostgreSQL already has an efficient implementation even if the optimizer has fewer choices than it has with normal GROUP BY statements.

Combining grouping sets with the FILTER clause

In real-world applications, grouping sets can often be combined with FILTER clauses. The idea behind the FILTER clause is to be able to run partial aggregates.

Here is an example:

```
test=# SELECT    region,
avg(production) AS all,
avg(production) FILTER (WHERE year < 1990) AS old,
avg(production) FILTER (WHERE year >= 1990) AS new
FROM    t_oil
GROUP BY ROLLUP (region);
```

region	all	old	new
Middle East	1992.603686635	1747.325892857	2254.233333333
North America	4541.362318840	4471.653333333	4624.349206349
	2607.513986013	2430.685618729	2801.183150183

```
(3 rows)
```

The idea here is that not all columns will use the same data for aggregation. The FILTER clauses allow you to selectively pass data to those aggregates. In my example, the second aggregate will only consider data before 1990, while the second aggregate will take care of more recent data.

> **TIP**
>
> Note that if it is possible to move conditions to a WHERE clause it is always more desirable as less data has to be fetched from the table. FILTER is only useful if the data left by the WHERE clause is not needed by each aggregate.

FILTER works for all kinds of aggregates and offers a simple way to pivot your data.

Making use of ordered sets

Ordered sets are a powerful feature, which is not widely regarded and not widely known in the developer community. The idea is actually quite simple: data is grouped normally and then the data inside each group is ordered given a certain condition. The calculation is then performed on this sorted data.

A classical example would be the calculation of the median.

> **TIP**
>
> The median is the middle value. If you are for example earning the median income the number of people earning less and more than you is identical. 50% of people do better and 50% of people do worse.

One way to get the median is to take sorted data and move 50% into the dataset. This is an example of what the WITHIN GROUP clause will ask PostgreSQL to do:

```
test=# SELECT region, percentile_disc(0.5) WITHIN GROUP (ORDER BY
production) FROM     t_oil GROUP BY 1;
    region      | percentile_disc
----------------+------------------
 Middle East    |            1082
 North America  |            3054
(2 rows)
```

`percentile_disc` will skip 50% of the group and return the desired value. Note that the median can significantly deviate from the average. In economics, the deviation between median and average income can even be used as an indicator for social equality or inequality. The higher the median compared to the average, the more the income inequality. To provide more flexibility, the ANSI standard does not just propose a median function. Instead, `percentile_disc` allows you to use any value between 0 and 1.

The beauty is that you can even use ordered sets along with grouping sets:

```
test=# SELECT region,
          percentile_disc(0.5) WITHIN GROUP (ORDER BY production)
FROM      t_oil
GROUP BY ROLLUP (1);
    region      | percentile_disc
----------------+------------------
 Middle East    |            1082
 North America  |            3054
                |            1696
(3 rows)
```

In this case PostgreSQL will again inject additional lines into the result set.

As proposed by the ANSI SQL standard, PostgreSQL provides you with two `percentile_` functions. `percentile_disc` will return a value, which is really contained by the dataset. `percentile_cont` will interpolate a value if no exact match is found. The following example shows, how this works:

```
test=# SELECT
          percentile_disc(0.62) WITHIN GROUP (ORDER BY id),
          percentile_cont(0.62) WITHIN GROUP (ORDER BY id)
FROM      generate_series(1, 5) AS id;
 percentile_disc | percentile_cont
-----------------+------------------
              4 |            3.48
(1 row)
```

4 is a value, which really exists—3.48 has been interpolated.

The `percentile_` functions are not the only ones provided by PostgreSQL. To find the most frequent value within a group the `mode` function is available. Before showing an example of how to use `mode` function, I have compiled a query telling us a bit more about the content of the table:

```
test=# SELECT production, count(*)
   FROM    t_oil
   WHERE   country = 'Other Middle East'
   GROUP BY production
   ORDER BY 2 DESC
   LIMIT 4;
 production | count
------------+-------
         50 |     5
         48 |     5
         52 |     5
         53 |     4
(4 rows)
```

Three different values occur exactly five times. Of course, the `mode` function can only give us one of them:

```
test=# SELECT country, mode() WITHIN GROUP (ORDER BY production)
   FROM    t_oil
   WHERE   country = 'Other Middle East'
   GROUP BY 1;
      country      | mode
-------------------+------
 Other Middle East |   48
(1 row)
```

The most frequent value is returned but SQL won't tell us how often the number actually shows up. It can even happen that the number only shows up once.

Understanding hypothetical aggregates

Hypothetical aggregates are pretty similar to standard ordered sets. However, they help to answer a different kind of question: what would be the result if a value was there? As you can see, this is not about values inside the database but about the result, if a certain value was actually there.

The only hypothetical function provided by PostgreSQL is `rank`. It tells us:

```
test=# SELECT       region,
                    rank(9000) WITHIN GROUP
```

```
                (ORDER BY production DESC NULLS LAST)
FROM        t_oil
GROUP BY ROLLUP (1);
    region      | rank
----------------+------
 Middle East    |   21
 North America  |   27
                |   47
(3 rows)
```

If somebody produced 9000 barrels per day, it would be the 27 best year in North America and 21 in the Middle East.

> **TIP**
>
> Note that in my example, I used NULLS LAST. When data is sorted, nulls are usually at the end. However, if sort order is reversed, nulls should still be at the end of the list. NULLS LAST ensures exactly that.

Utilizing windowing functions and analytics

After discussing ordered sets, it is time to take a look at windowing functions. Aggregates follow a fairly simple principle: take many rows and turn them into fewer, aggregated rows. A windowing function is different. It compares the current row with all rows in the group. The number of rows returned does not change.

Here is an example:

```
test=# SELECT avg(production) FROM t_oil;
    avg
-----------
 2607.5139
(1 row)

test=# SELECT country, year, production, consumption, avg(production) OVER
()
FROM        t_oil
LIMIT 4;
 country | year | production | consumption |    avg
---------+------+------------+-------------+-----------
 USA     | 1965 |       9014 |       11522 | 2607.5139
 USA     | 1966 |       9579 |       12100 | 2607.5139
 USA     | 1967 |      10219 |       12567 | 2607.5139
 USA     | 1968 |      10600 |       13405 | 2607.5139
(4 rows)
```

The average production in our dataset is around 2.6 million barrels per day. The goal of this query is to add this value as a column. It is now easy to compare the current row to the overall average.

Keep in mind that the OVER clause is essential. PostgreSQL is not able to process the query without it:

```
test=# SELECT country, year, production, consumption, avg(production)
FROM t_oil;
ERROR:  column "t_oil.country" must appear in the GROUP BY clause or be
used in an aggregate function
LINE 1: SELECT country, year, production, consumption, avg(productio...
```

This actually makes sense because the average has to be defined precisely. The database engine cannot just take any value, which *might be right* by doing guesswork.

> **TIP**
>
> Other database engines can accept aggregate functions without an OVER or even a GROUP BY clause. However, from a logical point of view this is wrong and on top of that a violation of SQL.

Partitioning data

So far the same result can also easily be achieved using a subselect. However, if you want more than just the overall average, subselects will turn your queries into nightmares. Suppose, you just don't want the overall average but the average of the country you are dealing with. A PARTITION BY clause is what you need:

```
test=# SELECT country, year, production, consumption, avg(production) OVER
(PARTITION BY country) FROM     t_oil;
    country      | year | production | consumption |    avg
-----------------+------+------------+-------------+-----------
   Canada        | 1965 |        920 |        1108 | 2123.2173
   Canada        | 2010 |       3332 |        2316 | 2123.2173
   Canada        | 2009 |       3202 |        2190 | 2123.2173
...
   Iran          | 1966 |       2132 |         148 | 3631.6956
   Iran          | 2010 |       4352 |        1874 | 3631.6956
   Iran          | 2009 |       4249 |        2012 | 3631.6956
...
```

The point here is that each country will be assigned to the average of the country. The OVER clause defines the window we are looking at. In this case the window is the country the row belongs to. In other words the query returns the rows compared to all rows in this country.

Note that the `year` column is not sorted. The query does not contain an explicit sort order so it might happen that data is returned in random order. Remember, SQL does not promise sorted output unless you explicitly state what you want.

Basically, a `PARTITION BY` clause takes any expression. Usually most people will use a column to partition the data. Here is an example:

```
test=# SELECT year, production,
    avg(production) OVER (PARTITION BY year < 1990)
FROM       t_oil
WHERE      country = 'Canada'
ORDER BY year;
 year | production |          avg
------+------------+-----------------------
 1965 |        920 | 1631.6000000000000000
 1966 |       1012 | 1631.6000000000000000
 ...
 1990 |       1967 | 2708.4761904761904762
 1991 |       1983 | 2708.4761904761904762
 1992 |       2065 | 2708.4761904761904762
 ...
```

The point is that data is split using the expression. `year < 1990` can return two values: true and false. Depending on the group a year is in, it will be assigned to the pre-1990 average or to the post-1990 average. PostgreSQL is really flexible here. Using functions to determine group membership is not uncommon in real-world applications.

Ordering data inside a window

A `PARTITION BY` clause is not the only possible thing you can put into an `OVER` clause. Sometimes it is necessary to sort data inside a window. `ORDER BY` will provide data to your aggregate functions in a certain way. Here is an example:

```
test=# SELECT country, year, production,
    min(production) OVER (PARTITION BY country ORDER BY year)
FROM       t_oil
WHERE      year BETWEEN 1978 AND 1983
           AND country IN ('Iran', 'Oman');
 country | year | production | min
---------+------+------------+------
 Iran    | 1978 |       5302 | 5302
 Iran    | 1979 |       3218 | 3218
 Iran    | 1980 |       1479 | 1479
 Iran    | 1981 |       1321 | 1321
```

```
Iran      | 1982 |        2397 | 1321
Iran      | 1983 |        2454 | 1321
Oman      | 1978 |         314 |  314
Oman      | 1979 |         295 |  295
Oman      | 1980 |         285 |  285
Oman      | 1981 |         330 |  285
. . .
```

Two countries (Iran and Oman) are chosen from our dataset for the period 1978 to 1983. Keep in mind, there was a revolution going on in Iran in 1979 so this had some impact on the production of oil. The data reflects that.

What the query does is to calculate the minimum production up to a certain point in our time series. Up to this point is a good way for SQL students to remember what an ORDER BY clause does inside an OVER clause. In this example the PARTITION BY clause will create one group for each country and order data inside the group. min function will loop over the sorted data and provide the required minimums.

In case you are new to windowing functions there is something you should be aware of: it really makes a difference whether you use an ORDER BY clause or not:

```
test=# SELECT country, year, production,
           min(production) OVER (),
           min(production) OVER (ORDER BY year)
    FROM   t_oil
    WHERE  year BETWEEN 1978 AND 1983
           AND country = 'Iran';
 country | year | production | min  | min
---------+------+------------+------+------
 Iran    | 1978 |       5302 | 1321 | 5302
 Iran    | 1979 |       3218 | 1321 | 3218
 Iran    | 1980 |       1479 | 1321 | 1479
 Iran    | 1981 |       1321 | 1321 | 1321
 Iran    | 1982 |       2397 | 1321 | 1321
 Iran    | 1983 |       2454 | 1321 | 1321
(6 rows)
```

If the aggregate is used without ORDER BY it will automatically take the minimum of the entire dataset inside your windows. Not so if there is an ORDER BY: in this case it will always be the minimum up to this point given the order you have defined.

Using sliding windows

So far the window we have used inside our query has been static. However, for calculations such as a moving average, this is not enough. A moving average needs a sliding window, which moves along as data is processed.

Here is an example of how a moving average can be achieved:

```
test=# SELECT country, year, production,
   min(production) OVER (PARTITION BY country
                        ORDER BY year ROWS
                        BETWEEN 1 PRECEDING
                        AND 1 FOLLOWING)
   FROM    t_oil
   WHERE   year BETWEEN 1978 AND 1983
           AND country IN ('Iran', 'Oman');
 country | year | production | min
---------+------+------------+------
 Iran    | 1978 |       5302 | 3218
 Iran    | 1979 |       3218 | 1479
 Iran    | 1980 |       1479 | 1321
 Iran    | 1981 |       1321 | 1321
 Iran    | 1982 |       2397 | 1321
 Iran    | 1983 |       2454 | 2397
 Oman    | 1978 |        314 |  295
 Oman    | 1979 |        295 |  285
 Oman    | 1980 |        285 |  285
 Oman    | 1981 |        330 |  285
 Oman    | 1982 |        338 |  330
 Oman    | 1983 |        391 |  338
(12 rows)
```

The most important thing is that a moving window should be used with an ORDER BY clause. Otherwise there will be major problems. PostgreSQL would actually accept the query but the result would be total crap. Remember, feeding data to a sliding window without ordering it first, will simply lead to random data.

ROWS BETWEEN 1 PRECEDING and 1 FOLLOWING 1 defines the window. In my example up to three rows will be in use: the current row, the one before, and the one after the current row. To illustrate how the sliding window works, consider checking out the following example:

```
test=# SELECT *,
          array_agg(id) OVER
              (ORDER BY id ROWS BETWEEN 1 PRECEDING AND 1 FOLLOWING)
   FROM    generate_series(1, 5) AS id;
```

```
 id | array_agg
----+-----------
  1 | {1,2}
  2 | {1,2,3}
  3 | {2,3,4}
  4 | {3,4,5}
  5 | {4,5}
(5 rows)
```

`array_agg` function will turn a list of values into a PostgreSQL array. It will help to explain how the sliding window operates.

Actually this trivial query has some very important aspects. What you see is that the first array contains only two values. There is no entry before `1` and therefore the array is not full. PostgreSQL does not add null entries because they would be ignored by aggregates anyway. The same happens at the end of the data.

However, sliding windows offer more. There are a couple of keywords, which can be used to specify the sliding window:

```
test=# SELECT *,
          array_agg(id) OVER
                 (ORDER BY id ROWS BETWEEN UNBOUNDED PRECEDING
                  AND 0 FOLLOWING)
   FROM   generate_series(1, 5) AS id;
 id | array_agg
----+-------------
  1 | {1}
  2 | {1,2}
  3 | {1,2,3}
  4 | {1,2,3,4}
  5 | {1,2,3,4,5}
(5 rows)
```

`UNBOUNDED PRECEDING` that everything before the current line will be in the window. The counterpart to `UNBOUNDED PRECEDING` is `UNBOUNDED FOLLOWING`:

```
test=# SELECT *,
          array_agg(id) OVER
                 (ORDER BY id ROWS BETWEEN 2 FOLLOWING
                  AND UNBOUNDED FOLLOWING)
   FROM   generate_series(1, 5) AS id;
 id | array_agg
----+-----------
  1 | {3,4,5}
  2 | {4,5}
  3 | {5}
```

```
    4 |
    5 |
(5 rows)
```

As you can see it is also possible to use a window, which is in the future. PostreSQL is very flexible here.

Abstracting window clauses

A windowing function allows us to add columns to the result set, which have been calculated on the fly. However, it happens quite frequently that many columns are based on the same window. Putting the same clauses into your queries over and over again is definitely not a good idea because your queries will be hard to read and therefore hard to maintain.

The WINDOW clause allows developers to predefine a window and use it at various places in the query. Here is how it works:

```
SELECT country, year, production, min(production) OVER (w), max(production)
OVER (w)
FROM       t_oil
WHERE      country = 'Canada'
           AND year BETWEEN 1980 AND 1985
WINDOW w AS (ORDER BY year);
 country | year | production |  min  |  max
---------+------+------------+-------+------
 Canada  | 1980 |       1764 | 1764  | 1764
 Canada  | 1981 |       1610 | 1610  | 1764
 Canada  | 1982 |       1590 | 1590  | 1764
 Canada  | 1983 |       1661 | 1590  | 1764
 Canada  | 1984 |       1775 | 1590  | 1775
 Canada  | 1985 |       1812 | 1590  | 1812
(6 rows)
```

The example shows that min and max will use the same clause.

Of course, it is possible to have more than just one WINDOW clause—PostgreSQL does not impose serious restrictions on users here.

Making use of onboard windowing functions

After introducing you to basic concepts it is time to take a look at which windowing functions PostgreSQL will support out of the box. You have already seen that windowing works with all standard aggregate functions. On top of those functions PostgreSQL offers some additional functions, which are exclusively for windowing and analytics.

In this section, some highly important functions will be explained and discussed.

rank and dense_rank functions

rank() and dense_rank() functions are in my judgment the most prominent functions around. The rank() function returns the number of the current row within its window. Counting starts at one.

Here is an example:

```
test=# SELECT year, production,
          rank() OVER (ORDER BY production)
   FROM   t_oil
   WHERE  country = 'Other Middle East'
   ORDER BY rank
   LIMIT 7;
 year | production | rank
------+------------+------
 2001 |         47 |    1
 2004 |         48 |    2
 2002 |         48 |    2
 1999 |         48 |    2
 2000 |         48 |    2
 2003 |         48 |    2
 1998 |         49 |    7
(7 rows)
```

The rank column will number those rows. Note that many rows in my sample are equal. Therefore rank will jump from 2 to 7 directly. If you want to avoid that, dense_rank() function is the way to go:

```
test=# SELECT year, production,
          dense_rank() OVER (ORDER BY production)
   FROM   t_oil
   WHERE  country = 'Other Middle East'
   ORDER BY dense_rank
   LIMIT 7;
 year | production | dense_rank
```

```
------+------------+------------
2001 |         47 |          1
2004 |         48 |          2
...
2003 |         48 |          2
1998 |         49 |          3
(7 rows)
```

PostgreSQL will pack the numbers more tightly. There will be no more gaps.

ntile() function

Some applications require data to be split into ideally equal groups. ntile() function will do exactly that for you.

The following example shows how data can be split into groups:

```
test=# SELECT year, production,
           ntile(4) OVER (ORDER BY production)
    FROM   t_oil
    WHERE  country = 'Iraq'
           AND year BETWEEN 2000 AND 2006;
 year | production | ntile
------+------------+-------
 2003 |       1344 |     1
 2005 |       1833 |     1
 2006 |       1999 |     2
 2004 |       2030 |     2
 2002 |       2116 |     3
 2001 |       2522 |     3
 2000 |       2613 |     4
(7 rows)
```

The query splits data into four groups. The trouble is that only seven rows are selected, which makes it impossible to create four even groups. As you can see, PostgreSQL will fill up the first three groups and make the last one a bit smaller. You can rely on the fact that the groups at the end will always tend to be a bit smaller than the rest.

> Note that in this example only a handful of rows are used. In real-world applications millions of rows will be involved and therefore it is no problem, if groups are not perfectly equal.

ntile() function is usually not used alone. Sure, it helps to assign a group ID to a row. However, in real-world applications, people want to perform calculations on top of those groups. Suppose you want to create a quantile distribution for your data. Here is how it works:

```
test=# SELECT grp, min(production), max(production), count(*)
FROM (
SELECT   year, production,
            ntile(4) OVER (ORDER BY production) AS grp
FROM     t_oil
WHERE    country = 'Iraq'
) AS x
GROUP BY ROLLUP (1);
 grp | min  | max  | count
-----+------+------+--------
   1 |  285 | 1228 |    12
   2 | 1313 | 1977 |    12
   3 | 1999 | 2422 |    11
   4 | 2428 | 3489 |    11
     |  285 | 3489 |    46
(5 rows)
```

The most important thing is that the calculation cannot be done in one step. When doing SQL training courses here at Cybertec (www.cybertec.at), I try to explain to students that whenever you don't know how to do it all at once, consider using a subselect. In analytics this is usually a good idea. In this example, the first thing done (in the subselect) is to attach a group label to each group. Then those groups are taken and processed in the main query.

The result is already something which could be used in a real-world application (maybe as a legend located next to a graph or so).

lead() and lag() functions

While ntile() function is essential to split a dataset into groups, lead() and lag() functions are here to move lines within the result set. A typical use case is to calculate the difference in production from one year to the next:

```
test=# SELECT year, production,
            lag(production, 1) OVER (ORDER BY year)
    FROM    t_oil
    WHERE   country = 'Mexico'
    LIMIT 5;
 year | production | lag
------+------------+-----
 1965 |        362 |
```

```
1966 |          370 | 362
1967 |          411 | 370
1968 |          439 | 411
1969 |          461 | 439
(5 rows)
```

Before actually calculating the change in production it makes sense to sit back and see what `lag()` functions actually does. You can see that the column is moved by one row. The data moved as defined in the `ORDER BY` clause. In my example, it means down. An `ORDER BY DESC` clause would of course have moved data up.

From this point on the query is easy:

```
test=# SELECT year, production,
            production - lag(production, 1) OVER (ORDER BY year)
    FROM    t_oil
    WHERE   country = 'Mexico'
    LIMIT 3;
 year | production | ?column?
------+------------+----------
 1965 |        362 |
 1966 |        370 |        8
 1967 |        411 |       41
(3 rows)
```

All you have to do is to calculate the difference as you would with any other column. Note that `lag()` function has two parameters. The first one indicates which column is to be displayed. The second column tells PostgreSQL how many rows you want to move. Putting in 7 therefore means that everything is off by seven rows.

> Note that the first value is null (and all other lagged rows without a preceding value).

`lead()` function is the counterpart of `lag()` function; it will move rows up instead of down:

```
test=# SELECT year, production,
            production - lead(production, 1) OVER (ORDER BY year)
FROM        t_oil
WHERE       country = 'Mexico'
LIMIT 3;
 year | production | ?column?
------+------------+----------
 1965 |        362 |       -8
```

```
1966 |        370 |      -41
1967 |        411 |      -28
(3 rows)
```

Basically, PostgreSQL will also accept negative values for lead and
lag columns. lag(production, -1) is therefore a replacement for lead(production,
1). However, it is definitely cleaner to use the right function to move data into the direction
you want.

So far you have seen, how to lag a single column. In most applications lagging a single
value will be the standard case used by most developers. The point is, PostgreSQL can do a
lot more than that. It is possible to lag entire lines:

```
test=# \x
Expanded display is on.
test=# SELECT year, production,
           lag(t_oil, 1) OVER (ORDER BY year)
    FROM   t_oil
    WHERE  country = 'USA'
    LIMIT 3;
-[ RECORD 1 ]-------------------------------------
year       | 1965
production | 9014
lag        |
-[ RECORD 2 ]-------------------------------------
year       | 1966
production | 9579
lag        | ("North America",USA,1965,9014,11522)
-[ RECORD 3 ]-------------------------------------
year       | 1967
production | 10219
lag        | ("North America",USA,1966,9579,12100)
```

The beauty here is that more than just a single value can be compared to the previous row.
The trouble here is just that PostgreSQL will return the entire row as a composite type and
therefore it is hard to work with. To dissect a composite type, you can use parentheses and
a star:

```
test=# SELECT year, production,
           (lag(t_oil, 1) OVER (ORDER BY year)).*
    FROM   t_oil
    WHERE  country = 'USA'
    LIMIT 3;
 year | prod |    region    | country | year | prod | consumption
------+------+--------------+---------+------+------+-------------
 1965 | 9014 |              |         |      |      |
 1966 | 9579 | N. America   | USA     | 1965 | 9014 |       11522
```

```
    1967 | 10219 | N. America | USA      | 1966 | 9579 |        12100
    (3 rows)
```

Why is that useful? Lagging an entire row will make it possible to see, if data has been inserted more than once. It is pretty simple to detect duplicate rows (or close to duplicate rows) in your time series.

Check out the following example:

```
test=# SELECT   *   FROM (
SELECT t_oil, lag(t_oil)
OVER (ORDER BY year)
FROM    t_oil
WHERE country = 'USA'
) AS x
WHERE   t_oil = lag;
  t_oil | lag
-------+-----
(0 rows)
```

Of course, the sample data does not contain duplicates. However, in real-world examples, duplicates can easily happen, and it is easy to detect them even if there is no primary key.

> Note that `t_oil` is really the entire row. The `lag` returned by the subselect is also a complete row. In PostgreSQL, composite types can be compared directly in case the fields are identical. PostgreSQL will simply compare one field after the other.

first_value(), nth_value(), and last_value() functions

Sometimes, it is necessary to calculate data based on the first value of a data window. Unsurprisingly the function to do that is `first_value()`:

```
test=# SELECT year, production,
                first_value(production) OVER (ORDER BY year)
    FROM    t_oil
    WHERE   country = 'Canada'
    LIMIT 4;
 year | production | first_value
------+------------+-------------
 1965 |        920 |         920
 1966 |       1012 |         920
 1967 |       1106 |         920
 1968 |       1194 |         920
(4 rows)
```

Again a sort order is needed to tell the system where the first value actually is. PostgreSQL will then put the same value into the last column. If you want to find the last value in the window, simply use `last_value()` function instead of `first_value()` function.

If you are not interested in the first or the last value but are looking for something in the middle, PostgreSQL provides `nth_value()` function:

```
test=# SELECT year, production,
          nth_value(production, 3) OVER (ORDER BY year)
    FROM   t_oil
    WHERE  country = 'Canada';
 year | production | nth_value
------+------------+-----------
 1965 |        920 |
 1966 |       1012 |
 1967 |       1106 |       1106
 1968 |       1194 |       1106
 . . .
```

In this, the third value will be put into the last column. However, note that the first two rows are empty. The trouble is that when PostgreSQL starts going through the data, the third value is not known yet. Therefore, null is added. The question now is: how can we make the time series more complete and replace those two null values with the data to come?

Here is one way to do it:

```
test=# SELECT  *,
          min(nth_value) OVER ()
FROM (
SELECT year, production,
nth_value(production, 3) OVER (ORDER BY year)
FROM t_oil
WHERE country = 'Canada'
) AS x
LIMIT 4;
 year | production | nth_value | min
------+------------+-----------+------
 1965 |        920 |           | 1106
 1966 |       1012 |           | 1106
 1967 |       1106 |      1106 | 1106
 1968 |       1194 |      1106 | 1106
(4 rows)
```

The subselect will create the incomplete time series. The SELECT clause on top of that will complete the data. The clue here is: just completing the data might be more complex and therefore a subselect might open a couple of opportunities to add some more complex logic than doing it just in one step.

row_number() function

The last function discussed in this section is row_number() function, which can simply be used to return a virtual ID. Sounds simple? Here it is:

```
test=# SELECT country, production,
            row_number() OVER (ORDER BY production)
   FROM   t_oil
   LIMIT 3;
 country | production | row_number
---------+------------+------------
 Yemen   |         10 |          1
 Syria   |         21 |          2
 Yemen   |         26 |          3
(3 rows)
```

row_number() function simply assigns a number to the row. There are definitely no duplicates.

The interesting point here is that this can even be done without an order (in case it is not relevant to you):

```
test=# SELECT country, production,
            row_number() OVER ()
   FROM   t_oil
   LIMIT 3;
 country | production | row_number
---------+------------+------------
 USA     |       9014 |          1
 USA     |       9579 |          2
 USA     |      10219 |          3
(3 rows)
```

Writing your own aggregates

In this book you have most of the onboard functions provided by PostgreSQL. However, what SQL provides might not be enough for you. The good news is that it is possible to add your own aggregates to the database engine. In this section you will learn how that can be done.

Creating simple aggregates

For the purpose of this example the goal is to solve a very simple problem: if you take a taxi, you usually have to pay for getting in the taxi (for example, 2.50 EUR). Then let us assume that for each kilometer the customer has to pay 2.20 EUR. The question now is: what is the total price of a trip?

Of course, this example is simple enough to solve the problem without a custom aggregate, however, let's see how it works. First some test data is created:

```
test=# CREATE TABLE t_taxi (trip_id int, km numeric);
CREATE TABLE
test=# INSERT INTO t_taxi VALUES
    (1, 4.0), (1, 3.2), (1, 4.5),
    (2, 1.9), (2, 4.5);
INSERT 0 5
```

To create aggregates PostgreSQL offers the CREATE AGGREGATE command. The syntax of this command has become so powerful and long over time that it does not make sense anymore to include the output of \h here in this book. Instead I recommend going to the PostgreSQL documentation, which can be found at: https://www.postgresql.org/docs/devel/static/sql-createaggregate.html.

The first thing needed when writing an aggregate is a function, which is called for every line. It will take an intermediate value and data taken from the line processed. Here is an example:

```
test=# CREATE FUNCTION taxi_per_line (numeric, numeric)
RETURNS numeric AS
$$
BEGIN
RAISE NOTICE 'intermediate: %, per row: %', $1, $2;
RETURN $1 + $2*2.2;
END;
$$ LANGUAGE 'plpgsql';
CREATE FUNCTION
```

Now it is already possible to create a simple aggregate:

```
test=# CREATE AGGREGATE taxi_price (numeric)
(
            INITCOND = 2.5,
            SFUNC = taxi_per_line,
            STYPE = numeric
);
CREATE AGGREGATE
```

As stated every trip starts at 2.50 EUR for getting in the taxi, which is defined by the INITCOND (init condition). It represents the starting value for each group. Then a function is called for each line in the group. In my example this function is taxi_per_line and has already been defined. As you can see, it needs two parameters. The first parameter is an intermediate value. Those additional parameters (can be many) are the parameters passed to the function by the user.

The following statement shows which data is passed when and how:

```
test=# SELECT trip_id, taxi_price(km)
            FROM    t_taxi
            GROUP BY 1;
NOTICE:    intermediate: 2.5, per row: 4.0
NOTICE:    intermediate: 11.30, per row: 3.2
NOTICE:    intermediate: 18.34, per row: 4.5
NOTICE:    intermediate: 2.5, per row: 1.9
NOTICE:    intermediate: 6.68, per row: 4.5
 trip_id | taxi_price
---------+------------
       1 |      28.24
       2 |      16.58
(2 rows)
```

The system starts with trip one and 2.50 EUR (the init condition). Then 4 kilometers are added. Overall the price is now 2.50 + 4 x 2.2. Then the next line is added, which will add 3.2 x 2.2, and so on. The first trip therefore costs 28.24.

Then the next trip starts. Again there is a fresh init condition and PostgreSQL will call one function per line.

In PostgreSQL an aggregate can automatically be used as windowing function too. No additional steps are needed—you can use the aggregate directly:

```
test=# SELECT *, taxi_price(km) OVER (PARTITION BY trip_id ORDER BY km)
FROM    t_taxi;
NOTICE:  intermediate: 2.5, per row: 3.2
NOTICE:  intermediate: 9.54, per row: 4.0
NOTICE:  intermediate: 18.34, per row: 4.5
NOTICE:  intermediate: 2.5, per row: 1.9
NOTICE:  intermediate: 6.68, per row: 4.5
 trip_id | km  | taxi_price
---------+-----+------------
       1 | 3.2 |       9.54
       1 | 4.0 |      18.34
       1 | 4.5 |      28.24
       2 | 1.9 |       6.68
       2 | 4.5 |      16.58
(5 rows)
```

What the query does is to give us the price up to a given point of the trip.

The aggregate we have defined will call one function per line. However, how would users be able to calculate an average or so? Without adding a FINALFUNC calculations like that are not possible. To demonstrate how the FINALFUNC works it is possible to extend our example. Suppose you want to give the taxi driver a 10% tip as soon as you leave the taxi. That 10% has to be added at the end as soon as the total price is known. That is the point when the FINALFUNC kicks in. Here is how it works:

```
test=# DROP AGGREGATE taxi_price(numeric);
DROP AGGREGATE
```

First of all, the old aggregate is dropped. The FINALFUNC is defined. It will get the intermediate result as parameter and do its magic:

```
test=# CREATE FUNCTION taxi_final (numeric)
    RETURNS numeric AS
$$
    SELECT $1 * 1.1;
$$
LANGUAGE sql IMMUTABLE;
CREATE FUNCTION
```

The calculation is pretty simple in this case—as stated previously 10% is added to the final sum.

Once the function has been deployed, it is already possible to recreate the aggregate:

```
test=# CREATE AGGREGATE taxi_price (numeric)
    (
            INITCOND = 2.5,
            SFUNC = taxi_per_line,
            STYPE = numeric,
            FINALFUNC = taxi_final
    );
CREATE AGGREGATE
```

At the end of the day the price will simply be a bit higher than before:

```
test=# SELECT trip_id, taxi_price(km)
    FROM    t_taxi
    GROUP BY 1;
NOTICE:  intermediate: 2.5, per row: 4.0
...
 trip_id | taxi_price
---------+------------
       1 |     31.064
       2 |     18.238
(2 rows)
```

PostgreSQL takes care of all the grouping and so on automatically.

For simple calculations, simple datatypes can be used for the intermediate result. However, not all operations can be done by just passing simple numbers and texts around. Fortunately, PostgeSQL allows the use of composite data types, which can be used as intermediate results.

Imagine you want to calculate an average of some data (maybe a time series or so). An intermediate result might look as follows:

```
test=# CREATE TYPE my_intermediate AS (c int4, s numeric);
CREATE TYPE
```

Feel free to compose any arbitrary type serving your purpose. Just pass it as the first parameter and add data as additional parameters as needed.

Adding support for parallel queries

What you have just seen is a simple aggregate, which has no support for parallel queries and all that. To solve those challenges the next couple of examples are all about improvements and speedups.

When creating an aggregate you can optionally define the following things:

```
[ , PARALLEL = { SAFE | RESTRICTED | UNSAFE } ]
```

By default, an aggregate does not support parallel queries. For performance reasons it does make sense, however, to explicitly state, what the aggregate is capable of:

- UNSAFE: In this mode no parallel queries are allowed
- RESTRICTED: In this mode the aggregate can be executed in parallel mode, but the execution is restricted to parallel group leader
- SAFE: It provides full support for parallel queries

If you mark a function as SAFE you have to keep in mind that the function must not have side effects. An execution order must not have an impact on the result of the query. Only then PostgreSQL should be allowed to execute operations in parallel. Examples of functions without side effects would be sin(x), length(s), and so on. An IMMUTABLE functions are a good candidate for this, since they're guaranteed to return the same result given the same inputs. STABLE can work if certain restrictions apply.

Improving efficiency

The aggregates defined so far can already achieve quite a lot. However, if you are using sliding windows the number of function calls will simply explode. Here is what happens:

```
test=# SELECT taxi_price(x::numeric)
          OVER ( ROWS BETWEEN 0 FOLLOWING AND 3 FOLLOWING)
    FROM generate_series(1, 5) AS x;
NOTICE:   intermediate: 2.5, per row: 1
NOTICE:   intermediate: 4.7, per row: 2
NOTICE:   intermediate: 9.1, per row: 3
NOTICE:   intermediate: 15.7, per row: 4
NOTICE:   intermediate: 2.5, per row: 2
NOTICE:   intermediate: 6.9, per row: 3
NOTICE:   intermediate: 13.5, per row: 4
NOTICE:   intermediate: 22.3, per row: 5
...
```

For every line PostgreSQL will process the full window. If the sliding window is large, efficiency will go down the drain. To fix that, our aggregates can be extended. Before that the old aggregate can be dropped:

```
DROP AGGREGATE taxi_price(numeric);
```

Basically two functions are needed: The `msfunc` function will add the next row in the window to the intermediate result:

```
CREATE FUNCTION taxi_msfunc(numeric, numeric)
RETURNS numeric AS
$$
        BEGIN
          RAISE NOTICE 'taxi_msfunc called with % and %', $1, $2;
          RETURN $1 + $2;
        END;
$$ LANGUAGE 'plpgsql' STRICT;
```

The `minvfunc` function will remove the value falling out of the window from the intermediate result:

```
CREATE FUNCTION taxi_minvfunc(numeric, numeric)
RETURNS numeric AS
$$
        BEGIN
          RAISE NOTICE 'taxi_minvfunc called with % and %', $1, $2;
          RETURN $1 - $2;
        END;
$$ LANGUAGE 'plpgsql' STRICT;
```

In my example, all we do is add and subtract. In a more sophisticated example the calculation can be arbitrarily complex.

The next statement shows how the aggregate can be recreated:

```
CREATE AGGREGATE taxi_price (numeric)
(
        INITCOND = 0,
        STYPE = numeric,
        SFUNC = taxi_per_line,
        MSFUNC = taxi_msfunc,
        MINVFUNC = taxi_minvfunc,
        MSTYPE = numeric
);
```

Let us run the same query again now:

```
test# SELECT taxi_price(x::numeric)
          OVER (ROWS BETWEEN 0 FOLLOWING AND 3 FOLLOWING)
FROM    generate_series(1, 5) AS x;
NOTICE:  taxi_msfunc called with 1 and 2
NOTICE:  taxi_msfunc called with 3 and 3
NOTICE:  taxi_msfunc called with 6 and 4
NOTICE:  taxi_minfunc called with 10 and 1
NOTICE:  taxi_msfunc called with 9 and 5
NOTICE:  taxi_minfunc called with 14 and 2
NOTICE:  taxi_minfunc called with 12 and 3
NOTICE:  taxi_minfunc called with 9 and 4
```

The number of function calls has decreased dramatically. Only a fixed handful of calls per row have to be performed. There is no need anymore to calculate the same frame all over and over again.

Writing hypothetical aggregates

Writing aggregates is not hard and it can be highly beneficial to perform more complex operations. In this section the plan is to write a hypothetical aggregate, which has already been discussed in this chapter.

Implementing hypothetical aggregates is not too different from writing normal aggregates. The really hard part is to figure out, when to actually use one. To make this section as easy to understand as possible I have decided to include a trivial example: given a specific order, what would the result be if we added abc to the end of the string?

Here is how it works:

```
CREATE AGGREGATE name ( [ [ argmode ] [ argname ] arg_data_type [ , ... ] ]
                        ORDER BY [ argmode ] [ argname ] arg_data_type [ ,
... ] ) (
    SFUNC = sfunc,
    STYPE = state_data_type
    [ , SSPACE = state_data_size ]
    [ , FINALFUNC = ffunc ]
    [ , FINALFUNC_EXTRA ]
    [ , INITCOND = initial_condition ]
    [ , PARALLEL = { SAFE | RESTRICTED | UNSAFE } ]
    [ , HYPOTHETICAL ]
)
```

Two functions will be needed. The `sfunc` function will be called for every line.:

```
CREATE FUNCTION hypo_sfunc(text, text)
RETURNS text AS
$$
BEGIN
    RAISE NOTICE 'hypo_sfunc called with % and %',
        $1, $2;
    RETURN $1 || $2;
  END;
$$ LANGUAGE 'plpgsql';
```

Two parameters will be passed to the procedure. The logic is the same as before. Just like earlier, a `final` function call can be defined:

```
CREATE FUNCTION hypo_final(text, text, text)
    RETURNS text AS
$$
BEGIN
    RAISE NOTICE 'hypo_final called with %, %, and %',
        $1, $2, $3;
    RETURN $1 || $2;
  END;
$$ LANGUAGE 'plpgsql';
```

Once those functions are in place the hypothetical aggregate can already be created:

```
CREATE AGGREGATE whatif(text ORDER BY text) (
  INITCOND = 'START',
  STYPE = text,
  SFUNC = hypo_sfunc,
  FINALFUNC = hypo_final,
  FINALFUNC_EXTRA = true,
  HYPOTHETICAL
);
```

Note that the aggregate has been marked as hypothetical, so that PostgreSQL will know, what kind of aggregate it actually is.

After the aggregate has been created, it is already possible to run it:

```
test=# SELECT whatif('abc'::text) WITHIN GROUP (ORDER BY id::text)
    FROM    generate_series(1, 3) AS id;
NOTICE:   hypo_sfunc called with START and 1
NOTICE:   hypo_sfunc called with START1 and 2
NOTICE:   hypo_sfunc called with START12 and 3
NOTICE:   hypo_final called with START123, abc, and <NULL>
    whatif
--------------
  START123abc
(1 row)
```

The key to understanding all those aggregates is really to fully see when which kind of function is called and how the overall machinery works.

Summary

In this chapter, you learned about the advanced features provided by SQL. On top of simple aggregates PostgreSQL provides ordered sets, grouping sets, windowing functions, recursions, as well as an interface to create custom aggregates. The advantage of running aggregations in the database is that code is easy to write and a database engine will usually have an edge when it comes to efficiency.

In the next chapter, we will turn our attention to more administrative tasks such as handling log files, understanding system statistics, and implementing monitoring.

5
Log Files and System Statistics

In the previous chapter, you learned a lot about advanced SQL and ways to see SQL in a different light. However, database work does not only consist of hacking up fancy SQL. Sometimes, it is also about keeping things running in a professional manner. To do that, it is highly important to keep an eye on system statistics, log files, and so on. Monitoring is the key to running databases professionally.

In this chapter, you will learn these topics:

- Collecting runtime statistics
- Creating log files
- Gathering important information
- Making sense of a database statistics

Gathering runtime statistics

The first thing you really have to learn is to use and understand what PostgreSQL's onboard statistics have got to offer. As I keep saying, there is no way to improve performance and reliability without first collecting the data to make prudent decisions.

This section will guide you through PostgreSQL's runtime statistics and explain in detail how you can extract more data from your database setups.

Working with PostgreSQL system views

PostgreSQL offers a large set of system views that allow administrators and developers alike to take a deep look into what is really going on in their system. The trouble is that many people actually collect all this data but cannot make real sense out of it. The general rule is this: there is no point in drawing a graph for something you don't understand anyway. The goal in this section, therefore, is to shed some light on what PostgreSQL has to offer to hopefully make it easier for people to fully take advantage of what is there to serve them.

Checking live traffic

Whenever I inspect a system, there is a system view I like to inspect first before digging deeper. I am, of course, talking about `pg_stat_activity`. The idea behind the view is to give you a chance to figure out what is going on right now.

Here is how it works:

```
test=# \d pg_stat_activity
            View "pg_catalog.pg_stat_activity"
      Column       |            Type             | Modifiers
-------------------+-----------------------------+-----------
 datid             | oid                         |
 datname           | name                        |
 pid               | integer                     |
 usesysid          | oid                         |
 usename           | name                        |
 application_name  | text                        |
 client_addr       | inet                        |
 client_hostname   | text                        |
 client_port       | integer                     |
 backend_start     | timestamp with time zone    |
 xact_start        | timestamp with time zone    |
 query_start       | timestamp with time zone    |
 state_change      | timestamp with time zone    |
 wait_event_type   | text                        |
 wait_event        | text                        |
 state             | text                        |
 backend_xid       | xid                         |
 backend_xmin      | xid                         |
 query             | text                        |
```

`pg_stat_activity` will provide you with one line per active connection. You will see the internal object ID of the database (`datid`), the name of the database somebody is connected to, as well as the process ID serving this connection (`pid`). On top of that, PostgreSQL will tell you who is connected (`usename`; note the missing r) and that user's internal object ID (`usesysid`).

Then there is a field called `application_name`, which is worth commenting on a bit more extensively. In general, `application_name` can be set freely by the end user:

```
test=# SET application_name TO 'postgresql-support.de';
SET
test=# SHOW application_name ;
    application_name
-----------------------
 postgresql-support.de
(1 row)
```

The point is this: assume thousands of connections are coming from a single IP. Can you, as the administrator, tell what a specific connection is really doing right now? You might not know all the SQL by heart. If the client is kind enough to set an `application_name` parameter, it is a lot easier to see what the purpose of a connection really is. In my example, I have set the name to the domain the connection belongs to. This makes it easy to find similar connections, which might cause similar problems.

The next three columns (`client_`) will tell you where a connection comes from. PostgreSQL will show IP addresses and (if it has been configured) even hostnames.

`backend_start` will tell you when a certain connection has started. `xact_start` indicates when a transaction has started. Then there are `query_start` and `state_change`. Back in the dark old days, PostgreSQL would only show active queries. During a time when queries took a lot longer than today, this made sense of course. On modern hardware, OLTP queries might only consume a fraction of a millisecond, and therefore it is hard to catch such queries doing potential harm. The solution was to either show the active query or the previous query executed by the connection you are looking at.

Here is what you might see:

```
test=# SELECT pid, query_start, state_change, state, query FROM
pg_stat_activity;
. . .
-[ RECORD 2 ]+---------------------------------------------------------------
----
pid            | 28001
query_start    | 2016-11-05 10:03:57.575593+01
state_change   | 2016-11-05 10:03:57.575595+01
state          | active
query          | SELECT pg_sleep(10000000);
```

In this case, you can see that pg_sleep is being executed in a second connection.

As soon as this query is terminated, the output will change:

```
-[ RECORD 2 ]+---------------------------------------------------------------
---
pid            | 28001
query_start    | 2016-11-05 10:03:57.575593+01
state_change   | 2016-11-05 10:05:10.388522+01
state          | idle
query          | SELECT pg_sleep(10000000);
```

The query is now marked as idle. The difference between state_change and query_start is the time the query needed to execute.

pg_stat_activity will therefore give you a great overview of what is going on in your system right now. The new state_change field makes it a lot more likely to spot expensive queries.

The question now is this: once you have found bad queries, how can you actually get rid of them? PostgreSQL provides two functions to take care of these things: pg_cancel_backend and pg_terminate_backend. The pg_cancel_backend function will terminate the query but will leave the connection in place.
The pg_terminate_backend function is a bit more radical and will kill the entire database connection along with the query.

if you want to disconnect all other users but yourself, here is how you can do that:

```
test=# SELECT pg_terminate_backend(pid) FROM  pg_stat_activity WHERE pid <>
pg_backend_pid();
 pg_terminate_backend
----------------------
 t
 t
(2 row)
```

If you happen to be kicked out, the following message will be displayed:

```
test=# SELECT pg_sleep(10000000);
FATAL:  terminating connection due to administrator command
server closed the connection unexpectedly
    This probably means the server terminated abnormally
    before or while processing the request.
The connection to the server was lost. Attempting reset: Succeeded.
```

> Only psql will try to reconnect. This is not true for most other clients,
> especially not for client libraries.

Inspecting databases

Once you have inspected active database connections, you can dig deeper and inspect database-level statistics. pg_stat_database will return one line per database inside your PostgreSQL instance.

This is what you can find there:

```
test=# \d pg_stat_database
          View "pg_catalog.pg_stat_database"
      Column       |           Type           | Modifiers
-------------------+--------------------------+-----------
 datid             | oid                      |
 datname           | name                     |
 numbackends       | integer                  |
 xact_commit       | bigint                   |
 xact_rollback     | bigint                   |
 blks_read         | bigint                   |
 blks_hit          | bigint                   |
 tup_returned      | bigint                   |
 tup_fetched       | bigint                   |
 tup_inserted      | bigint                   |
```

```
tup_updated    | bigint                    |
tup_deleted    | bigint                    |
conflicts      | bigint                    |
temp_files     | bigint                    |
temp_bytes     | bigint                    |
deadlocks      | bigint                    |
blk_read_time  | double precision          |
blk_write_time | double precision          |
stats_reset    | timestamp with time zone  |
```

Next to the database ID and the database name, there is a column called `numbackends` that shows the number of database connections that are currently open.

Then there are `xact_commit` and `xact_rollback`. These two columns indicate whether your application tends to commit or roll back. `blks_hit` and `blks_read` will tell you about cache hits and cache misses. When inspecting these two columns, keep in mind that we are mostly talking about shared buffer hits and shared buffer misses. There is no reasonable way on the database level to distinguish filesystem cache hits and real disk hits. At Cybertec (`www.postgresql-support.de`), we like to correlate disk wait with cache misses in `pg_stat_database` to get an idea of what really goes on in the system.

The `tup_` columns will tell you whether there is a lot of reading or a lot of writing going on in your system.

Then we have `temp_files` and `temp_bytes`. These two columns are of incredible importance because they will tell you whether your database has to write temporary files to disk, which will inevitably slow down operations. What can be the reasons for high temporary file usage? The major reasons are as follows:

- **Poor settings**: If your `work_mem` settings are too low, there is no way to do anything in RAM, and therefore PostgreSQL will go to disk.
- **Stupid operations**: It happens quite frequently that people torture their system with fairly expensive, pointless queries. If you see many temporary files on an OLTP system, consider checking for expensive queries.
- **Indexing and other administrative tasks**: Once in a while, indexes might be created or people might run DDLs. These operations can lead to temporary file I/O but are not necessarily considered a problem (in many cases).

In short, temporary files can happen even if your system is perfectly fine. However, it definitely makes sense to keep an eye on them and ensure that temp files are not needed frequently.

Finally there are two more important fields: blk_read_time and blk_write_time. By default, these two fields are empty and no data is collected. The idea behind these fields is to give you a way to see how much time was spent on I/O. The reason these fields are empty is that track_io_timing is off by default. This is for good reasons. Imagine you want to check how long it takes to read 1 million blocks. To do that, you have to call the time function in your C library twice, which leads to 2 million additional function calls just to read 8 GB of data. It really depends on the speed of your system whether this will lead to a lot of overhead or not.

Fortunately there is a tool that helps you to determine how expensive the timing is:

```
[hs@zenbook ~]$ pg_test_timing
Testing timing overhead for 3 seconds.
Per loop time including overhead: 23.16 nsec
Histogram of timing durations:
< usec    % of total        count
      1    97.70300    126549189
      2     2.29506      2972668
      4     0.00024          317
      8     0.00008          101
     16     0.00160         2072
     32     0.00000            5
     64     0.00000            6
    128     0.00000            4
    256     0.00000            0
    512     0.00000            0
   1024     0.00000            4
   2048     0.00000            2
```

In my case, the overhead of turning track_io_timing on for a session or in the postgresql.conf file is around 23 nanoseconds, which is fine. Professional high-end servers can provide you with numbers as low as 14 nanoseconds, while really bad virtualization can return values up to 1,400 nanoseconds or even 1,900 nanoseconds. In case you are confronted with four digit values, measuring the I/O timing might surely lead to real measurable overhead, which will slow down your system. The general rule is this: on real hardware, timing is not an issue; on virtual systems, check it out before you turn it on.

> It is also possible to turn things on selectively by using ALTER DATABASE, ALTER USER, or the like.

Inspecting tables

Once you have gained an overview of what is going on in your databases, it might be a good idea to dig deeper and see what is going on in individual tables. Two system views are here to help you: `pg_stat_user_tables` and `pg_statio_user_tables`. Here is the first one:

```
test=# \d pg_stat_user_tables
              View "pg_catalog.pg_stat_user_tables"
         Column          |            Type             | Modifiers
-------------------------+-----------------------------+-----------
 relid                   | oid                         |
 schemaname              | name                        |
 relname                 | name                        |
 seq_scan                | bigint                      |
 seq_tup_read            | bigint                      |
 idx_scan                | bigint                      |
 idx_tup_fetch           | bigint                      |
 n_tup_ins               | bigint                      |
 n_tup_upd               | bigint                      |
 n_tup_del               | bigint                      |
 n_tup_hot_upd           | bigint                      |
 n_live_tup              | bigint                      |
 n_dead_tup              | bigint                      |
 n_mod_since_analyze     | bigint                      |
 last_vacuum             | timestamp with time zone    |
 last_autovacuum         | timestamp with time zone    |
 last_analyze            | timestamp with time zone    |
 last_autoanalyze        | timestamp with time zone    |
 vacuum_count            | bigint                      |
 autovacuum_count        | bigint                      |
 analyze_count           | bigint                      |
 autoanalyze_count       | bigint                      |
```

By my judgment, `pg_stat_user_tables` is one of the most important but also one of the most misunderstood or even ignored system views. I have a feeling that many people read it but fail to extract the full potential of what can really be seen here. When used properly, `pg_stat_user_tables` can, in some cases, be nothing short of a revelation.

Before we dig into the interpretation of data, it is important to understand which fields are actually there. First of all, there is one entry for each table, which will show us the number of sequential scans that happened on the table (`seq_scan`). Then we have `seq_tup_read`, which tells us how many tuples the system has to read during those sequential scans.

Remember the `seq_tup_read` column, it contains vital information, which can help to find performance problems.

`idx_scan` is next on the list. It will show us how often an index was used for this table. PostgreSQL will also show how many rows those scans returned. Then there are a couple of columns starting with `n_tup_`. Those will tell us how much we inserted, updated, and deleted. The most important thing here is related to HOT `UPDATE`. When running an `UPDATE`, PostgreSQL has to copy a row to ensure that `ROLLBACK` will work correctly. HOT `UPDATE` is pretty good because it allows PostgreSQL to ensure that a row does not have to leave a block. The copy of the row stays inside the same block, which is beneficial for performance in general. A fair amount of HOT `UPDATE` indicates that you are on the right track in case of `UPDATE` intense workload. The perfect ratio between normal and HOT `UPDATE` cannot be stated here for all use cases. People have really got to think for themselves to figure, which workload benefits from many in-place operations. The general rule is this: the more `UPDATE` intense your workload is, the better it is to have many HOT `UPDATE` clauses.

Finally there are some `VACUUM` statistics, which mostly speak for themselves.

Making sense of pg_stat_user_tables

Reading all this data might be interesting; however, unless you are able to make sense out of it, it is pretty pointless. One way to use `pg_stat_user_tables` is to detect which tables might need an index. One way to get a clue of the right direction is to use the following query, which has served me well over the years:

```
SELECT schemaname, relname,
       seq_scan,
       seq_tup_read,
       seq_tup_read / seq_scan AS avg,
       idx_scan
FROM   pg_stat_user_tables
WHERE  seq_scan > 0
ORDER BY seq_tup_read
DESC LIMIT 25;
```

The idea is to find large tables, which have been used frequently in a sequential scan. Those tables will naturally come out on top of the list to bless us with enormously high `seq_tup_read` values, which can be mind-blowing.

> Work your way from top to bottom and look for expensive scans. Keep in mind that sequential scans are not necessarily bad. They appear naturally in backups, analytical statements, and so on without causing any harm. However, if you are running large sequential scans all the time, your performance will go down the drain.

Note that this query is really golden--it will help you to spot tables with missing indexes. Practical experience of close to two decades has shown again and again that missing indexes are the single most important reason for bad performance. Therefore the query you are looking at is literally gold.

Once you are done looking for potentially missing indexes, consider taking a brief look on the caching behavior of your tables. `pg_statio_user_tables` will contain information about all kinds of things such as caching behavior of the table (`heap_blks_`), of your indexes (`idx_blks_`), as well as **the oversized attribute storage technique (TOAST)** tables. Finally you can find out more about TID scans, which is usually not relevant to the overall performance of the system:

```
test=# \d pg_statio_user_tables
View "pg_catalog.pg_statio_user_tables"
     Column       |  Type  | Modifiers
-----------------+--------+-----------
 relid           | oid    |
 schemaname      | name   |
 relname         | name   |
 heap_blks_read  | bigint |
 heap_blks_hit   | bigint |
 idx_blks_read   | bigint |
 idx_blks_hit    | bigint |
 toast_blks_read | bigint |
 toast_blks_hit  | bigint |
 tidx_blks_read  | bigint |
 tidx_blks_hit   | bigint |
```

Although `pg_statio_user_tables` contains important information, it is usually the case that `pg_stat_user_tables` is more likely to provide you with a really relevant insight (such as a missing index or so).

Digging into indexes

While `pg_stat_user_tables` is important to spotting missing indexes, it is sometimes necessary to find indexes which should really not exist. Recently, I was on a business trip to Germany and discovered a system that contained mostly pointless indexes (74% of the total storage consumption). While this might not be a problem if your database is really small, it does make a difference in case of large systems--having hundreds of gigabytes of pointless indexes can seriously harm your overall performance.

`pg_stat_user_indexes` can be inspected to find those pointless indexes:

```
test=# \d pg_stat_user_indexes
View "pg_catalog.pg_stat_user_indexes"
    Column      |  Type   | Modifiers
----------------+---------+-----------
 relid          | oid     |
 indexrelid     | oid     |
 schemaname     | name    |
 relname        | name    |
 indexrelname   | name    |
 idx_scan       | bigint  |
 idx_tup_read   | bigint  |
 idx_tup_fetch  | bigint  |
```

The view tells us, for every index on every table in every schema, how often it has been used (`idx_scan`). To enrich this view a bit, I suggest the following SQL:

```
SELECT  schemaname,
        relname,
        indexrelname,
        idx_scan,
        pg_size_pretty(pg_relation_size(indexrelid)),
        pg_size_pretty(sum(pg_relation_size(indexrelid))
                    OVER (ORDER BY idx_scan, indexrelid)) AS total
FROM    pg_stat_user_indexes
ORDER BY 6 ;
```

The output of this statement is highly useful. It doesn't only contain information about how often an index was used--it also tells us how much space has been wasted for each index. Finally, it adds up all the space consumption in column 6. You can now go through the table and rethink all those indexes that have rarely been used. It is hard to come up with a general rule when to drop an index so some manual checking makes a lot of sense.

> **TIP**
>
> Do not just blindly drop indexes. In some cases, indexes are simply not used because end users use the application differently than expected. In case end users change (a new secretary is hired or so on), an index might very well turn into a useful object again.

There is also a view called `pg_statio_user_indexes`, which contains caching information about an index. Although it is interesting, it usually does not contain information leading to big leaps forward.

Tracking the background worker

In this section, it is time to take a look at the background writer statistics. As you might know, database connections will in many cases not write blocks to disks directly. Instead, data is written by the background writer process or by the checkpointer.

To see how data is written, the `pg_stat_bgwriter` view can be inspected:

```
test=# \d pg_stat_bgwriter
            View "pg_catalog.pg_stat_bgwriter"
        Column          |          Type           | Modifiers
------------------------+-------------------------+-----------
 checkpoints_timed      | bigint                  |
 checkpoints_req        | bigint                  |
 checkpoint_write_time  | double precision        |
 checkpoint_sync_time   | double precision        |
 buffers_checkpoint     | bigint                  |
 buffers_clean          | bigint                  |
 maxwritten_clean       | bigint                  |
 buffers_backend        | bigint                  |
 buffers_backend_fsync  | bigint                  |
 buffers_alloc          | bigint                  |
 stats_reset            | timestamp with time zone |
```

The first thing that should catch your attention here is the first two columns. You will learn later in this book that PostgreSQL will perform regular checkpoints, which are necessary to ensure that data has really made it to disk. If your checkpoints are too close to each other, `checkpoint_req` might point you in the right direction. If requested checkpoints are high, it can mean that a lot of data is written and that checkpoints are always triggered because of high throughput. In addition to that, PostgreSQL will tell you about the time needed to write data during a checkpoint and the time needed to sync. In addition to that, `buffers_checkpoint` indicates how many buffers were written during the checkpoint, and how many were written by the background writer (`buffers_clean`).

But there is more: `maxwritten_clean` tells us about the number of times the background writer stopped a cleaning scan because it had written too many buffers.

Finally, there are `buffers_backend` (number of buffers directly written by a backend database connection), `buffers_backend_fsync` (number of buffers flushed by a database connection), and `buffers_alloc`, which contains the number of buffers allocated.

Tracking, archiving, and streaming

In this section, we will take a look at some replication and transaction log archiving related features. The first thing to inspect is `pg_stat_archiver`, which tells us about the archiver process moving the transaction log (WAL) from the main server to some backup device:

```
test=# \d pg_stat_archiver
            View "pg_catalog.pg_stat_archiver"
       Column        |            Type            | Modifiers
---------------------+----------------------------+-----------
 archived_count      | bigint                     |
 last_archived_wal   | text                       |
 last_archived_time  | timestamp with time zone   |
 failed_count        | bigint                     |
 last_failed_wal     | text                       |
 last_failed_time    | timestamp with time zone   |
 stats_reset         | timestamp with time zone   |
```

`pg_stat_archiver` contains important information about your archiving process. First of all, it will inform you about the number of transaction log files, which have been archived (`archived_count`). It will also know the last file, that was archived and when that happened (`last_archived_wal` and `last_achived_time`).

While knowing the number of WAL files is certainly interesting, it is not really that important. Therefore consider taking a look at `failed_count` and `last_failed_wal`. If your transaction log archiving failed, it will tell you the latest file that failed and when that happened. It is recommended to keep an eye on those fields because otherwise it might happen that archiving does not work without you even noticing.

If you are running streaming replication, the following two views will be really important for you. The first one is called `pg_stat_replication` and will provide information about the streaming process from the master to the slave. One entry per WAL sender process will be visible. If there is no single entry, there is no transaction log streaming going on, which might not be what you want.

Let us take a look at `pg_stat_replication`:

```
test=# \d pg_stat_replication
          View "pg_catalog.pg_stat_replication"
        Column        |             Type             | Modifiers
----------------------+------------------------------+-----------
 pid                  | integer                      |
 usesysid             | oid                          |
 usename              | name                         |
 application_name     | text                         |
 client_addr          | inet                         |
 client_hostname      | text                         |
 client_port          | integer                      |
 backend_start        | timestamp with time zone     |
 backend_xmin         | xid                          |
 state                | text                         |
 sent_location        | pg_lsn                       |
 write_location       | pg_lsn                       |
 flush_location       | pg_lsn                       |
 replay_location      | pg_lsn                       |
 sync_priority        | integer                      |
 sync_state           | text                         |
```

You will find columns to indicate the username connected via streaming replication. Then there is the application name along with connection data (`client_`). Then, PostgreSQL will tell us when the streaming connection has started. In production, a young connection can point to a network problem or to something even worse (reliability issues and so on). The `state` column shows in which state the other side of the stream is. Note that there will be more information on this in `Chapter 10`, *Making Sense of Backups and Replication*.

There are fields telling us how much transaction log has been sent over the network connection (`sent_location`), how much has been sent to the kernel (`write_location`), how much has been flushed to disk (`flush_location`), and how much has already been replayed (`replay_location`). Finally the sync status is listed.

While `pg_stat_replication` can be queried on the sending server of a replication setup, `pg_stat_wal_receiver` can be consulted on the receiving end. It provides similar information and allows this information to be extracted on the replica (or alike).

Here is the definition of the view:

```
test=# \d pg_stat_wal_receiver
            View "pg_catalog.pg_stat_wal_receiver"
        Column          |             Type             | Modifiers
------------------------+------------------------------+-----------
 pid                    | integer                      |
 status                 | text                         |
 receive_start_lsn      | pg_lsn                       |
 receive_start_tli      | integer                      |
 received_lsn           | pg_lsn                       |
 received_tli           | integer                      |
 last_msg_send_time     | timestamp with time zone     |
 last_msg_receipt_time  | timestamp with time zone     |
 latest_end_lsn         | pg_lsn                       |
 latest_end_time        | timestamp with time zone     |
 slot_name              | text                         |
 conninfo               | text                         |
```

First of all, PostgreSQL will tell us the process ID of the WAL receiver process. Then the view shows us the status of the connection in use. `receive_start_lsn` will tell us the transaction log position used when the WAL receiver was started. `receive_start_tli` contains the timeline in use, when the WAL receiver was started. At some point, you might want to know the latest WAL position and timeline. To get those two numbers, use `received_lsn` and `received_tli`.

In the next two columns, there are two timestamps: `last_msg_send_time` and `last_msg_receipt_time`. The first one says when a message was last sent and when it was received.

`latest_end_lsn` contains the last transaction log position reported to the WAL sender process at `latest_end_time`. Finally, there are the `slot_name` and an obfuscated version of the connection information.

Checking SSL connections

Many people running PostgreSQL use SSL to encrypt connections from the server to the client. More recent versions of PostgreSQL provide a view to gain an overview of those encrypted connections, which is `pg_stat_ssl`:

```
test=# \d pg_stat_ssl
   View "pg_catalog.pg_stat_ssl"
  Column     |  Type   | Modifiers
-------------+---------+-----------
 pid         | integer |
```

```
ssl         | boolean |
version     | text    |
cipher      | text    |
bits        | integer |
compression | boolean |
clientdn    | text    |
```

Every process is represented by the process ID. If a connection uses SSL, the second column is set to true. The third and fourth column will define the version as well as the cipher. Finally, there are the number of bits used by the encryption algorithm, an indicator of whether compression is used or not, as well as the **distinguished name** (**DN**) field from the client certificate.

Inspecting transactions in real time

Up to now, a couple of statistics tables have already been discussed. The idea behind all of them is to see what is going on in the entire system. But what if you are a developer who wants to inspect an individual transaction? pg_stat_xact_user_tables is here to help. It does not contain system-wide transactions but only data about your current transaction:

```
test=# \d pg_stat_xact_user_tables
View "pg_catalog.pg_stat_xact_user_tables"
     Column      |  Type   | Modifiers
-----------------+---------+-----------
 relid           | oid     |
 schemaname      | name    |
 relname         | name    |
 seq_scan        | bigint  |
 seq_tup_read    | bigint  |
 idx_scan        | bigint  |
 idx_tup_fetch   | bigint  |
 n_tup_ins       | bigint  |
 n_tup_upd       | bigint  |
 n_tup_del       | bigint  |
 n_tup_hot_upd   | bigint  |
```

Developers can therefore look into a transaction just before it commits to see whether it has caused any performance issues. It helps to distinguish overall data from what has just been caused by your application.

The ideal way for application developers to use this view is to add a function call in the application before commit to track, what the transaction has done. This data can then be inspected so that the output of the current transaction can be distinguished from the overall workload.

Tracking vacuum progress

In PostgreSQL 9.6, the community introduced a system view many people have been waiting for. For many years, people wanted to track the progress of a vacuum process to see how long things might still take.

`pg_stat_progress_vacuum` has been invented to answer those questions:

```
test=# \d pg_stat_progress_vacuum
View "pg_catalog.pg_stat_progress_vacuum"
        Column          |   Type   | Modifiers
------------------------+----------+-----------
 pid                    | integer  |
 datid                  | oid      |
 datname                | name     |
 relid                  | oid      |
 phase                  | text     |
 heap_blks_total        | bigint   |
 heap_blks_scanned      | bigint   |
 heap_blks_vacuumed     | bigint   |
 index_vacuum_count     | bigint   |
 max_dead_tuples        | bigint   |
 num_dead_tuples        | bigint   |
```

Most of the columns speak for themselves, and therefore I won't go into too much detail. There are just a couple of things that should be kept in mind. First of all, the process is not linear--it can jump quite a bit. In addition to that, vacuum is usually pretty fast so progress can be rapid and hard to track.

Using pg_stat_statements

After discussing the first couple of views, it is time to turn our attention to one of the most important views, which can be used to spot performance problems. I am of course speaking about `pg_stat_statements`. The idea is to have information about queries on your system. It helps figure out which types of queries are slow and how often queries are called.

To use the module, three steps are necessary:

1. Add `pg_stat_statements` to `shared_preload_libraries` in the `postgresql.conf` file.
2. Restart the database server.
3. Run `CREATE EXTENSION pg_stat_statements` in the database(s) of your choice.

Let's inspect the definition of the view:

```
test=# \d pg_stat_statements
            View "public.pg_stat_statements"
         Column         |       Type       | Modifiers
------------------------+------------------+-----------
 userid                 | oid              |
 dbid                   | oid              |
 queryid                | bigint           |
 query                  | text             |
 calls                  | bigint           |
 total_time             | double precision |
 min_time               | double precision |
 max_time               | double precision |
 mean_time              | double precision |
 stddev_time            | double precision |
 rows                   | bigint           |
 shared_blks_hit        | bigint           |
 shared_blks_read       | bigint           |
 shared_blks_dirtied    | bigint           |
 shared_blks_written    | bigint           |
 local_blks_hit         | bigint           |
 local_blks_read        | bigint           |
 local_blks_dirtied     | bigint           |
 local_blks_written     | bigint           |
 temp_blks_read         | bigint           |
 temp_blks_written      | bigint           |
 blk_read_time          | double precision |
 blk_write_time         | double precision |
```

`pg_stat_statements` provides simply fabulous information. For every user in every database, it provides one line per query. By default it tracks 5,000 (can be changed by setting `pg_stat_statements.max`).

> **TIP**
>
> Queries and parameters are separated. PostgreSQL will put placeholders into the query. This allows identical queries, which just use different parameters, to be aggregated. `SELECT ... FROM x WHERE y = 10` will be turned into `SELECT ... FROM x WHERE y = ?`.

For each query, PostgreSQL will tell us the total time it has consumed along with the number of calls. In more recent versions, `min_time`, `max_time`, `mean_time`, and `stddev` have been added. The standard deviation is especially noteworthy because it will tell us whether a query has stable or fluctuating runtimes. Unstable runtimes can happen for various reasons:

- If the data is not fully cached in RAM queries, which have to go to disk, they will take a lot longer than their cached counterparts
- Different parameters can lead to different plans and totally different result sets
- Concurrency and locking can have an impact

PostgreSQL will also tell us about the caching behavior of a query. The `shared_` columns show how many blocks came from the cache (`_hit`) or from the operating system (`_read`). If many blocks come from the operating system, the runtime of a query might fluctuate.

The next block of columns is all about local buffers. Local buffers are memory blocks allocated by the database connection directly.

On top of all this information, PostgreSQL provides information about temporary file I/O. Note that temporary file I/O will naturally happen in case a large index is built or in case some other large DDL is executed. However, temporary files are usually a very bad thing to have in OLTP as it will slow down the entire system by potentially blocking the disk. A high amount of temporary file I/O can point to a couple of undesirable things. The following list contains my top three:

- Undesirable `work_mem` settings (OLTP)
- Suboptimal `maintenance_work_mem` settings (DDLs)
- Queries, which should not be run in the first place

Finally there are two fields containing information about I/O timing. By default, those two fields are empty. The reason for this is that measuring timing can be quite a lot of overhead on some systems. Therefore, the default value for `track_io_timing` is false--remember to turn it on if you need this data.

Once the module has been enabled, PostgreSQL is already collecting data and you can use the view.

> **TIP**
>
> Never run `SELECT * FROM pg_stat_statements` in front of a customer. More than once, people have started pointing at queries. They happened to know and started to explain why, who, what, when, and so on. When you use this view, always create a sorted output so that the most relevant information can be seen instantly.

Here at Cybertec, we have found the following query very helpful to gain an overview of what is happening on the database server:

```
test=# SELECT  round((100 * total_time / sum(total_time) OVER ()))::numeric,
2) percent,
        round(total_time::numeric, 2) AS total,
        calls,
        round(mean_time::numeric, 2) AS mean,
        substring(query, 1, 40)
FROM    pg_stat_statements
ORDER BY total_time DESC
LIMIT 10;
 percent |    total    |  calls  |  mean  | substring
---------+-------------+---------+--------+-------------------------------------
   54.47 | 111289.11 | 122161 |  0.91 | UPDATE pgbench_branches SET
                                        bbalance = b
   43.01 |  87879.25 | 122161 |  0.72 | UPDATE pgbench_tellers SET
                                        tbalance = tb
    1.46 |   2981.06 | 122161 |  0.02 | UPDATE pgbench_accounts SET
                                        abalance = a
    0.50 |   1019.83 | 122161 |  0.01 | SELECT abalance FROM
                                        pgbench_accounts WH
    0.42 |    856.22 | 122161 |  0.01 | INSERT INTO pgbench_history
                                        (tid, bid, a
    0.04 |     85.63 |      1 | 85.63 | copy pgbench_accounts from
                                        stdin
    0.02 |     44.11 |      1 | 44.11 | vacuum analyze pgbench_accounts
    0.02 |     42.86 | 122161 |  0.00 | END;
    0.02 |     34.08 | 122171 |  0.00 | BEGIN;
    0.01 |     22.46 |      1 | 22.46 | alter table pgbench_accounts
                                        add primary
(10 rows)
```

It shows the top 10 queries and their runtime including a percentage. It also makes sense to display the average execution time of the query so that you can decide whether the runtime of those queries is too high or not.

Work your way down the list and inspect all queries, which seem to run too long on average.

Keep in mind that working through the top 1,000 queries is usually not worth it. In most cases, the first queries are already responsible for most of the load on the system.

> In my example, I have used a substring to shorten the query to fit on a page. This makes no sense if you really want to see what is going on.

Remember that `pg_stat_statements` will by default cut off queries at 1024 bytes:

```
test=# SHOW track_activity_query_size;
 track_activity_query_size
---------------------------
 1024
(1 row)
```

Consider increasing this value to, say, 16,384. If your clients are running Java applications based on Hibernate, a larger value of `track_activity_query_size` will ensure that queries are not cut off before the interesting part is shown.

At this point, I want to use the situation to point out how important `pg_stat_statements` really is. It is by far the easiest way to track down performance problems. A slow query log can never be as useful as `pg_stat_statements`, because a slow query log will only point to individual slow queries--it won't show us problems caused by tons of medium queries. Therefore, it is recommended to always turn this module on. The overhead is really small and in no way harms the overall performance of the system.

By default, 5,000 types of queries are tracked (as of PostgreSQL 9.6). In most reasonably sane applications, this will be enough.

To reset the data, consider using the following instruction:

```
test=# SELECT pg_stat_statements_reset();
 pg_stat_statements_reset
---------------------------

(1 row)
```

Creating log files

After taking a deep look at the system views provided by PostgreSQL, it is time to configure logging. Fortunately, PostgreSQL provides easy means to work with log files and helps people to set up a good configuration easily. Collecting log is important because it can point to errors and potential database problems.

The `postgresql.conf` file has all the parameters you need to provide you with all the parameters.

Configuring postgresql.conf file

In this section, we will go through some of the most important entries in the `postgresql.conf` file to configure logging and see how logging can be used in the most beneficial way.

Before we get started, I want to say a few words about logging in PostgreSQL in general. On Unix systems, PostgreSQL will send log information to `stderr` by default. However, `stderr` is not a good place for logs to go because you will surely want to inspect the log stream at some point. Therefore, it really makes sense to work through this chapter to adjust things to your needs.

Defining log destination and rotation

Let us go through the `postgresql.conf` file and see what can be done:

```
#------------------------------------------------------------------
# ERROR REPORTING AND LOGGING
#------------------------------------------------------------------

# - Where to Log -

#log_destination = 'stderr'
                    # Valid values are combinations of
                    # stderr, csvlog, syslog, and eventlog,
                          # depending on platform.  csvlog
                          # requires logging_collector to be on.

# This is used when logging to stderr:
#logging_collector = off
                    # Enable capturing of stderr and csvlog
                    # into log files. Required to be on for
                    # csvlogs.
```

```
# (change requires restart)
```

The first configuration option defines how the log is processed. By default, it will go to stderr (on Unix). On Windows, the default is eventlog, which is the Windows onboard tool to handle logging. Alternatively, you can choose to go with csvlog or syslog.

In case you want to make PostgreSQL log files, you should go for stderr and turn the logging collector on. PostgreSQL will then create log files.

The logical question now is: what will the names of those log files be and where will those files be stored? postgresql.conf has the answer:

```
# These are only used if logging_collector is on:
#log_directory = 'pg_log'
                # directory where log files are written,
                # can be absolute or relative to PGDATA
#log_filename = 'postgresql-%Y-%m-%d_%H%M%S.log'
                # log file name pattern,
                # can include strftime() escapes
```

log_directory will tell the system where to store the log. If you are using an absolute path, you can explicitly configure where logs will go. If you prefer the logs to be in the PostgreSQL data directly, simply go for a relative path. The advantage is that the data directory will be self-contained and you can move it without having to worry.

In the next step, you can define the filename PostgreSQL is supposed to use. PostgreSQL is very flexible and allows you to use all the shortcuts provided by strftime. To give you an impression of how powerful this feature is, a quick count on my platform reveals that strftime provides 43 (!) placeholders to create the filename. Everything people usually need is certainly possible.

Once the filename has been defined, it makes sense to briefly think about cleanup. The following settings will be available:

```
#log_truncate_on_rotation = off
#log_rotation_age = 1d
#log_rotation_size = 10MB
```

By default, PostgreSQL will keep producing log files in case files are older than one day or larger than 10 MB. log_truncate_on_rotation specifies if you want to append to a log file or not. Sometimes a log_filenames is defined in a way that it becomes cyclic. The log_truncate_on_rotation parameter defines whether to overwrite or to append to the file, which already exists. Given the default log file, this will of course not happen.

One way to handle auto-rotation is to use something like `postgresql_%a.log` or so along with `log_truncate_on_rotation = on`. `%a` means that the day of the week will be used inside the log file. The advantage here is that the day of the week tends to repeat itself every seven days. Therefore the log will be kept for a week and recycled. If you are aiming for weekly rotation, a 10 MB file size might not be enough. Consider turning the maximum file size off.

Configuring syslog

Some people prefer to use `syslog` to collect log files. PostgreSQL offers the following configuration parameters:

```
# These are relevant when logging to syslog:
#syslog_facility = 'LOCAL0'
#syslog_ident = 'postgres'
#syslog_sequence_numbers = on
#syslog_split_messages = on
```

`syslog` is pretty popular among `sysadmins`. Fortunately it is easy to configure. Basically you set a facility and an identifier. If `log_destination` is set to `syslog`, this is already everything there is to do.

Logging slow queries

The log can also be used to track down individual slow queries. Back in the old days, this was pretty much the only way to spot performance problems.

How does it work? `postgresql.conf` has a variable called `log_min_duration_statement`. If this is set to a value greater than zero, every query exceeding our chosen setting will make it to the log:

```
# log_min_duration_statement = -1
```

Most people see the slow query log as the ultimate source of wisdom. However, I would like to add a word of caution. There are many slow queries, and they just happen to eat up a lot of CPU: index creation, data exports, analytics, and so on.

Those long-running queries are totally expected and are in many cases not the root cause of all evil. It happens frequently that many shorter queries are to blame. Here is an example: 1,000 queries x 500 milliseconds is worse than 2 queries x 5 seconds. The slow query log can be misleading in some cases.

Still, it does not mean that it is pointless--it just means that it is *a* source of information and not *the* source of information.

Defining what and how to log

After taking a look at some basic settings, it is time to decide what to log. By default, only errors will be logged. However, this might not be enough. In this section, you will learn what can be logged and what a logline will look like.

By default, PostgreSQL does not log information about checkpoints. The following setting is here to change exactly that:

```
#log_checkpoints = off
```

The same applies to connections; whenever a connection is established or properly destroyed, PostgreSQL can create log entries:

```
#log_connections = off
#log_disconnections = off
```

In most cases, it does not make sense to log connections as extensive logging significantly slows down the systems. Analytical systems won't suffer much. However, OLTP might be seriously impacted.

If you want to see how long statements take, consider switching the following setting to on:

```
#log_duration = off
```

Let us move on to one of the most important settings. So far, we have not defined the layout of the messages yet. And so far, the log files contain errors in the following form:

```
test=# SELECT 1 / 0;
ERROR:  division by zero
```

The log will state ERROR along with the error message. There is no timestamp, no username, and so on. To change that, take a look at `log_line_prefix`:

```
#log_line_prefix = ''          # special values:
                               #   %a = application name
                               #   %u = user name
                               #   %d = database name
                               #   %r = remote host and port
                               #   %h = remote host
                               #   %p = process ID
                               #   %t = timestamp without milliseconds
                               #   %m = timestamp with milliseconds
                               #   %n = timestamp with milliseconds (as a
                               Unix epoch)
                               #   %i = command tag
                               #   %e = SQL state
                               #   %c = session ID
                               #   %l = session line number
                               #   %s = session start timestamp
                               #   %v = virtual transaction ID
                               #   %x = transaction ID (0 if none)
                               #   %q = stop here in non-session processes
                               #   %% = '%'
```

`log_line_prefix` is pretty flexible and allows you to configure the log line to exactly match your needs. In general, it is a good idea to log a timestamp. Otherwise, it is close to impossible to see when something bad has happened. Personally I also like to know the username, the transaction ID, and the database. However, it is up to you to decide on what you really need.

Sometimes slowness is caused by bad locking behavior. In general locking related issues can be hard to track down. `log_lock_waits` can help to detect such issues. If a lock is held longer than `deadlock_timeout` then a line will be sent to the log, provided the following configuration variable is turned on:

```
#log_lock_waits = off
```

Finally, it is time to tell PostgreSQL what to actually log. So far, only errors, slow queries, and the like have been sent to the log. `log_statement` has three possible settings:

```
#log_statement = 'none'
# none, ddl, mod, all
```

`none` means that only errors will be logged. `ddl` means that errors as well as DDLs (`CREATE TABLE`, `ALTER TABLE`, and so on) will be logged. `mod` will already include data changes and `all` will send every statement to the log.

> Note that `all` can lead to a lot of logging information, which can slow down your system. To give you an impression of how much impact there can be, I have compiled a blog post. It can be found here: `http://www.cyb ertec.at/2014/03/logging-the-hidden-speedbrakes/`.

If you want to inspect replication in more detail, consider turning the following setting to on:

```
#log_replication_commands = off
```

It will send replication related commands to the log (for more information visit the following website: `https://www.postgresql.org/docs/9.6/static/protocol-replicati on.html`).

It can happen quite frequently that performance problems are caused by temporary file I/O. To see which queries cause the problem, the following setting can be used:

```
#log_temp_files = -1      # log temporary files equal or larger
                          # than the specified size in kilobytes;
                          # -1 disables, 0 logs all temp files
```

While `pg_stat_statements` contains aggregated information, `log_temp_files` will point to specific queries causing issues. It usually makes sense to set this one to a reasonably low value. The correct value depends on your workload but maybe 4 MB is already a good start.

By default, PostgreSQL will write log files in the time zone where the server is located. However, if you are running a system that is spread all over the world, it can make sense to adjust the time zone in a way that you can go and compare log entries:

```
log_timezone = 'Europe/Vienna'
```

Keep in mind that on the SQL side, you will still see the time in your local time zone. However, if this variable is set, log entries will be in a different time zone.

Summary

This chapter was all about system statistics. You learned how to extract information from PostgreSQL and how to use system statistics in a beneficial way. The most important views were discussed in detail.

The next chapter is all about query optimization. You will learn to inspect queries and how they are optimized.

6
Optimizing Queries for Good Performance

In previous chapters, you have learned how to read system statistics and how to make use of what PostgreSQL provides. Armed with this knowledge, this chapter is all about good query performance. You will learn more about the following topics:

- Optimizer internals
- Execution plans
- Partitioning data
- Enabling and disabling optimizer settings
- Parameters for good query performance

At the end of the chapter, I hope that you will be able to write better and faster queries. And if your queries still happen to be bad, you should be able to understand why this is the case.

Learning what the optimizer does

Before even attempting to think about query performance, it makes sense to familiarize yourself with what the query optimizer does. Having a deeper understanding of what is going on under the hood makes a lot of sense because it helps you to see what the database is really up to and what it is doing.

Optimizations by example

To demonstrate how the optimizer works, I have compiled an example, one which I have used over the years in PostgreSQL training. Suppose there are three tables:

```
CREATE TABLE a (aid int, ...);        -- 100 million rows
CREATE TABLE b (bid int, ...);        -- 200 million rows
CREATE TABLE c (cid int, ...);        -- 300 million rows
```

Let us assume further that those tables contain millions or maybe hundreds of millions of rows. In addition to that there are indexes:

```
CREATE INDEX idx_a ON a (aid);
CREATE INDEX idx_b ON a (bid);
CREATE INDEX idx_c ON a (cid);

CREATE VIEW v AS
        SELECT  *
        FROM    a, b
        WHERE   aid = bid;
```

Finally, there is a view joining the first two tables together.

Let us suppose now the end user wants to run the following query. What will the optimizer do with this query? Which choices are there?

```
SELECT  *
FROM    v, c
WHERE   v.aid = c.cid
        AND cid = 4;
```

Before looking at the real optimization process, I want to focus on some options the planner has.

Evaluating join options

The planner has a couple of options here and I want to use the chance to show what can go wrong if trivial approaches are used.

Suppose, the planner would just steam ahead and calculate the output of the view. What is the best way to join 100 million with 200 million rows?

In this section, a couple of (not all) join options will be discussed to show what PostgreSQL is able to do.

Nested loops

One way to join two tables is to use a nested loop. The principle is simple. Here is some pseudo code:

```
for x in table1:
    for y in table2:
        if x.field == y.field
            issue row
        else
            keep doing
```

Nested loops are often used if one of the sides is very small and contains only a limited set of data. In our example, a nested loop would lead to 100 million x 200 million iterations through the code. This is clearly not an option because runtime would simply explode.

A nested loop is generally $O(n^2)$ so it is only efficient if one side of the join is very small. In my example, this is not the case so a nested loop can be ruled out to calculate the view.

Hash joins

The second option is a hash join. The following strategy could be applied to solve our little problem:

```
← Hash join
      ← Sequential scan table 1
      ← Sequential scan table 2
```

Both sides can be hashed and the hash keys could be compared leaving us with the result of the join. The trouble here is that all the values have to be hashed and put somewhere.

Merge joins

Finally, there is a merge join. The idea here is to use sorted lists to join the results. If both sides of the join are sorted, the system can just take rows from the top and see if they match and return them. The main requirement here is that the lists are sorted. Here is a sample plan:

```
← Merge join
    ← Sort table 1
          ← Sequential scan table 1
    ← Sort table 2
          ← Sequential scan table 2
```

To join, data has to be provided in sorted order. In many cases, PostgreSQL will just sort the data. However, there are other options to provide the join with sorted data. One way is to consult an index, as shown in the next example:

```
← Merge join
    ← Index scan table 1
    ← Sort table 2
        ← Sequential scan table 2
```

One side of the join or both sides can use sorted data coming from lower levels of the plan. If the table is accessed directly, an index is the obvious choice to do that.

The beauty of a merge join is that it can handle a lot of data. The downside is that data has to be sorted or taken from an index at some point.

Sorting is $O(n * log(n))$. Therefore, sorting 300 million rows to perform the join is not attractive either.

Applying transformations

Obviously, doing the obvious thing (joining the view first) makes no sense at all. A nested loop would send execution times through the roof. A hash join has to hash millions of rows and a nested loop has to sort 300 million rows. All three options are clearly not suitable here. The way out is to apply logical transformations to make the query fast. In this section, you will learn what the planner does to speedup the query. A couple of steps will be performed.

Inlining the view

The first transformation done by the optimizer is to inline views. Here is what happens:

```
SELECT   *
FROM     (SELECT   *
         FROM     a, b
         WHERE    aid = bid ) AS v, c
WHERE    v.aid = c.cid
         AND cid = 4;
```

The view is inlined and transformed to a subselect. What does this one buy us? Actually, nothing. All it does is to open the door for further optimization, which will really be a game changer to this query.

Flattening subselects

The next thing is to flatten subselects. By getting rid of subselects, a couple more options to optimize the query will appear.

Here is what the query will look like after flattening the subselects:

```
SELECT  *
FROM    a, b, c
WHERE   a.aid = c.cid
        AND aid = bid
        AND cid = 4;
```

It is now a normal join. Note, we would have done that on our own but the planner will take care of those transformations for us anyway. The door is open for a key optimization.

Applying equality constraints

The following process creates equality constraints. The idea is to detect additional constraints, join options, and filters. Let us take a deep breath and take a look at the query: If `aid = cid` and `aid = bid`, we know that `bid = cid`. If `cid = 4` and all the others are equal too, we know that `aid` and `bid` have to be 4 as well, which leads us to the following query:

```
SELECT  *
FROM    a, b, c
WHERE   a.aid = c.cid
        AND aid = bid
        AND cid = 4
        AND bid = cid
        AND aid = 4
        AND bid = 4
```

The importance of this optimization cannot be stressed enough. What the planner did here was to open the door for two additional indexes, which were not clearly visible in the original query.

By being able to use indexes on all three columns, there is no need to calculate this expensive horror view anymore. PostgreSQL has the option to just retrieve a couple of rows from the index and use whatever join option makes sense.

Exhaustive searching

Now that those formal transformations have been done, PostgreSQL will perform an exhaustive search. It will try out all possible plans and come up with the cheapest solution to your query. PostgreSQL knows which indexes are possible and just uses the cost model to determine how to do things in the best way possible.

During an exhaustive search, PostgreSQL will also try to determine the best join order. In the original query, the join order was fixed to $A \circledcirc B$ and $A \circledcirc C$. However, using those equality constraints we could join $B \circledcirc C$ and join A later. All options are open to the planner.

When it comes to joining, the general rule is to join large tables first to get rid of as much data as possible early on in the process. If the data is gone, it won't be there to haunt you later and to reduce speed.

Trying it all out

Now that all those optimizations have been discussed, it is time to see which plan PostgreSQL might create for us:

```
test=# explain SELECT  *
FROM     v, c
WHERE    v.aid = c.cid
AND cid = 4;
                          QUERY PLAN
---------------------------------------------------------------
 Nested Loop  (cost=1.71..17.78 rows=1 width=12)
    ->  Nested Loop  (cost=1.14..9.18 rows=1 width=8)
          ->  Index Only Scan using idx_a on a
                (cost=0.57..4.58 rows=1 width=4)
                Index Cond: (aid = 4)
          ->  Index Only Scan using idx_b on b
                (cost=0.57..4.59 rows=1 width=4)
                Index Cond: (bid = 4)
    ->  Index Only Scan using idx_c on c
                (cost=0.57..8.59 rows=1 width=4)
          Index Cond: (cid = 4)
(8 rows)
```

As you can see, PostgreSQL will use three indexes. It is also interesting to see that PostgreSQL decides to go for a nested loop to join the data. This makes perfect sense because there is virtually no data coming back from the index scans. Therefore, using a loop to join things is perfectly feasible and highly efficient.

Making the process fail

So far you have seen what PostgreSQL can do for you and how the optimizer helps to speedup queries. PostgreSQL is pretty smart but it needs smart users. There are some cases in which the end user cripples the entire optimization process by doing stupid things. Let us drop the view:

```
test=# DROP VIEW v;
DROP VIEW
```

Now the view is recreated. Note that OFFSET 0 has been added to the end of the view:

```
test=# CREATE VIEW v AS
SELECT   *
FROM     a, b
WHERE    aid = bid
OFFSET 0;
CREATE VIEW
```

While this view is logically equivalent to the example shown previously, the optimizer has to treat things differently. Every OFFSET other than 0 will change the result and therefore the view has to be calculated. The entire optimization process is crippled by adding things such as OFFSET.

> The PostgreSQL community did not dare to optimize the stupid case of having an OFFSET 0 in a view. People are simply not supposed to do that. I am using this just as an example to show that some operations can cripple performance and that developers should be aware of the underlying optimization process.

Here is the new plan:

```
test=# EXPLAIN SELECT   *
FROM     v, c
WHERE    v.aid = c.cid
AND cid = 4;
                         QUERY PLAN
-----------------------------------------------------------------
 Nested Loop  (cost=120.71..7949879.40 rows=1 width=12)
    ->  Subquery Scan on v
                 (cost=120.13..7949874.80 rows=1 width=8)
          Filter: (v.aid = 4)
          ->  Merge Join  (cost=120.13..6699874.80
                              rows=100000000 width=8)
                Merge Cond: (a.aid = b.bid)
                ->  Index Only Scan using idx_a on a
```

```
                        (cost=0.57..2596776.57 rows=100000000
                        width=4)
                ->    Index Only Scan using idx_b on b
                        (cost=0.57..5193532.33 rows=199999984
                        width=4)
        ->    Index Only Scan using idx_c on c
                (cost=0.57..4.59 rows=1 width=4)
                Index Cond: (cid = 4)
    (9 rows)
```

Just take a look at the costs predicted by the planner. Costs have skyrocketed from a two digit number to a staggering one. Cleary, this query is going to provide you with bad performance.

There are more ways to cripple performance and it makes sense to keep the optimization process in mind.

Constant folding

However, there are many more optimizations in PostgreSQL, which happen behind the scenes and which contribute to overall good performance. One of those features is called **constant folding**. The idea is to turn expressions into constants, as shown in the following example:

```
test=# explain SELECT * FROM a WHERE aid = 3 + 1;
                        QUERY PLAN
-----------------------------------------------------------------
  Index Only Scan using idx_a on a
            (cost=0.57..4.58 rows=1 width=4)
        Index Cond: (aid = 4)
  (2 rows)
```

As you can see, PostgreSQL will try to look for 4. As `aid` is indexed, PostgreSQL will go for an index scan. Note that our table has just one column so PostgreSQL even figured that all the data it needs can be found in the index.

What happens if the expression is on the left-hand side?

```
test=# explain SELECT * FROM a WHERE aid - 1 = 3;
                        QUERY PLAN
-----------------------------------------------------------
 Seq Scan on a   (cost=0.00..1942478.48 rows=500000 width=4)
   Filter: ((aid - 1) = 3)
(2 rows)
```

In this case, the index lookup code will fail and PostgreSQL has to go for a sequential scan.

Understanding function inlining

As outlined in this section already, there are many optimizations which help to speedup queries. One of them is called **function inlining**. PostgreSQL is able to inline immutable SQL functions. The main idea is to reduce the number of function calls which have to be made to speed things up.

Here is an example of a function:

```
test=# CREATE OR REPLACE FUNCTION ld(int)
RETURNS numeric AS
$$
    SELECT log(2, $1);
$$
LANGUAGE 'sql' IMMUTABLE;
CREATE FUNCTION
```

The function will calculate the *logarithmus dualis* of the input value:

```
test=# SELECT ld(1024);
         ld
--------------------
 10.0000000000000000
(1 row)
```

To demonstrate how things work, I will recreate the table with less content to speedup the index creation:

```
test=# TRUNCATE a;
TRUNCATE TABLE
```

Then data can be added again and the index can be applied:

```
test=# INSERT INTO a SELECT * FROM generate_series(1, 10000);
INSERT 0 10000
test=# CREATE INDEX idx_ld ON a (ld(aid));
CREATE INDEX
```

As expected, the index created on the function will be used just like any other index. However, take a closer look at the indexing condition:

```
test=# EXPLAIN SELECT * FROM  a WHERE ld(aid) = 10;
                        QUERY PLAN
-----------------------------------------------------------------
 Index Scan using idx_ld on a  (cost=0.29..8.30 rows=1 width=4)
   Index Cond: (log('2'::numeric, (aid)::numeric) = '10'::numeric)
(2 rows)
```

The important observation here is that the indexing condition actually looks for log function instead of ld function. The optimizer has completely gotten rid of the function call.

Logically, this opens the door for the following query:

```
test=# EXPLAIN SELECT * FROM  a WHERE log(2, aid) = 10;
                        QUERY PLAN
-----------------------------------------------------------------
 Index Scan using idx_ld on a  (cost=0.29..8.30 rows=1 width=4)
   Index Cond: (log('2'::numeric, (aid)::numeric) = '10'::numeric)
(2 rows)
```

Join pruning

PostgreSQL provides an optimization called **join pruning**. The idea is to remove joins if they are not needed by the query. This can come in handy in case queries are generated by some middleware or some ORM. If a join can be removed, it naturally speeds things up dramatically and leads to less overhead.

The question now is: how does join pruning work? Here is an example:

```
CREATE TABLE x (id int, PRIMARY KEY (id));
CREATE TABLE y (id int, PRIMARY KEY (id));
```

First of all, two tables are created. Make sure that both sides of the join conditions are actually unique. Those constraints will be important in a minute.

Now we can write a simple query:

```
test=# EXPLAIN SELECT *
FROM    x LEFT JOIN y
ON (x.id = y.id)
WHERE x.id = 3;
                              QUERY PLAN
---------------------------------------------------------------
 Nested Loop Left Join   (cost=0.31..16.36 rows=1 width=8)
   Join Filter: (x.id = y.id)
   ->  Index Only Scan using x_pkey on x
         (cost=0.15..8.17 rows=1 width=4)
         Index Cond: (id = 3)
   ->  Index Only Scan using y_pkey on y
         (cost=0.15..8.17 rows=1 width=4)
         Index Cond: (id = 3)
(6 rows)
```

As you can see, PostgreSQL will join those tables directly. So far there are no surprises. However, the following query is slightly modified. Instead of selecting all columns, it only selects those columns on the left-hand side of the join:

```
test=# explain SELECT x.*
FROM    x LEFT JOIN y
ON (x.id = y.id)
WHERE x.id = 3;
                              QUERY PLAN
---------------------------------------------------------------
 Index Only Scan using x_pkey on x
   (cost=0.15..8.17 rows=1 width=4)
   Index Cond: (id = 3)
(2 rows)
```

PostgreSQL will go for a direct inside scan and skip the join completely. There are two reasons why this is actually possible and logically correct:

- No columns are selected from the right side of the join; thus looking those columns up does not buy us anything
- The right side is unique, which means that joining cannot increase the number of rows due to duplicates on the right side

If joins can be pruned automatically, it might happen that queries are a magnitude faster. The beauty here is that the speedup can be achieved by just removing columns which might not be needed by the application anyway.

Speedup set operations

Set operations allow the results of multiple queries to be combined into a single result set. Set operators include UNION, INTERSECT, and EXCEPT. PostgreSQL implements all of them and offers many important optimizations to speed them up.

The planner is able to push restrictions down into the set operation, opening the door for fancy indexing and speedups in general. Let us take a look at the following query, which shows how this works:

```
test=# EXPLAIN SELECT     *
FROM (
SELECT   aid AS xid
FROM     a
UNION ALL
SELECT   bid
FROM     b
) AS y
WHERE xid = 3;
                              QUERY PLAN
-----------------------------------------------------------------------
 Append   (cost=0.29..12.89 rows=2 width=4)
    ->  Index Only Scan using idx_a on a
           (cost=0.29..8.30 rows=1 width=4)
           Index Cond: (aid = 3)
    ->  Index Only Scan using idx_b on b
           (cost=0.57..4.59 rows=1 width=4)
           Index Cond: (bid = 3)
 (5 rows)
```

What you see here is that two relations are added to each other. The trouble is that the only restriction is outside the subselect. However, PostgreSQL figures that the filter can be pushed further down the plan. xid = 3 is therefore attached to aid and bid, opening the option to use indexes on both tables. By avoiding the sequential scan on both tables, the query will run a lot faster.

Note that there is a distinction between UNION clause and UNION ALL clause. UNION ALL clause will just blindly append the data and deliver the result of both tables. UNION clause is different: it will filter out duplicates. The following plan shows how that works:

```
test=# EXPLAIN SELECT    *
FROM (
SELECT   aid AS xid
FROM     a
UNION
SELECT   bid
FROM     b
) AS y
WHERE xid = 3;
                           QUERY PLAN
------------------------------------------------------------------
 Unique  (cost=12.92..12.93 rows=2 width=4)
   ->  Sort  (cost=12.92..12.93 rows=2 width=4)
         Sort Key: a.aid
         ->  Append  (cost=0.29..12.91 rows=2 width=4)
               ->  Index Only Scan using idx_a on a
                     (cost=0.29..8.30 rows=1 width=4)
                     Index Cond: (aid = 3)
               ->  Index Only Scan using idx_b on b
                     (cost=0.57..4.59 rows=1 width=4)
                     Index Cond: (bid = 3)
 (8 rows)
```

PostgreSQL has to add a Sort node on top of the Append node to ensure that duplicates can be filtered later on.

> Many people who are not fully aware of the difference between UNION clause and UNION ALL clause complain about bad performance because they are unaware that PostgreSQL has to filter out duplicates, which is especially painful in the case of large datasets.

Understanding execution plans

After digging into some important optimizations implemented into PostgreSQL, I want to shift your attention a bit more to execution plans. You have already seen some plans in this book. However, in order to make full use of plans, it is important to develop a systematic approach to reading this information. Reading plans systematically is exactly within the scope of this section.

Approaching plans systematically

The first thing you have to know is that an EXPLAIN clause can do quite a lot for you and I would highly recommend to make full use of those features.

As many readers might already know, an EXPLAIN ANALYZE clause will execute the query and return the plan including real runtime information. Here is an example:

```
test=# EXPLAIN ANALYZE SELECT *
    FROM (SELECT *
        FROM  b
        LIMIT 1000000
        ) AS b
    ORDER BY cos (bid);
                            QUERY PLAN
------------------------------------------------------------------
  Sort   (cost=146173.12..148673.12 rows=1000000)
            (actual time=837.049..1031.587 rows=1000000)
          Sort Key: (cos((b.bid)::double precision))
          Sort Method: external merge  Disk: 25408kB
      ->  Subquery Scan on b
            (cost=0.00..29424.78 rows=1000000 width=12)
            (actual time=0.011..352.717 rows=1000000)
            ->  Limit   (cost=0.00..14424.78 rows=1000000)
                  (actual time=0.008..169.784 rows=1000000)
                ->  Seq Scan on b b_1  (cost=0.00..2884955.84
                      rows=199999984 width=4)
                      (actual time=0.008..85.710 rows=1000000)
  Planning time: 0.064 ms
  Execution time: 1159.919 ms
(8 rows)
```

The plan looks a bit scary but don't panic, we will go through it step by step. When reading a plan, make sure that you read it from the inside to the outside. In our example, execution starts with a sequential scan on b. There are actually two blocks of information here: the cost block and the actual time block. While the cost block contains estimations, the actual time block is hard evidence. It shows real execution time. In this example, the sequential scan has taken 85.7 milliseconds.

Data is then passed on to Limit node, which ensures that there is not too much data. Note that each stage of execution will also show us the number of rows involved. As you can see, PostgreSQL will only fetch 1 million rows from the table in the first place; the Limit node ensures that this will actually happen. However, there is a price tag: at this stage, the runtime has jumped to 169 milliseconds already.

Finally, data is sorted, which takes a lot of time. The most important thing when looking at the plan is to figure out where time is actually lost. The best way to do that is to take a look at the `actual time` block and try to figure out where time jumps. In this example, the sequential scan takes some time but it cannot be speedup significantly. Instead we see that time skyrockets as sorting starts.

Of course, sorting can be speedup but more on that later in this chapter.

Making EXPLAIN more verbose

In PostgreSQL, the output of an `EXPLAIN` clause can be beefed up a little to provide you with more information. To extract as much as possible out of a plan, consider turning the following options on:

```
test=# EXPLAIN (
          analyze true,
          verbose true,
          costs true,
          timing true,
          buffers true)
     SELECT * FROM a ORDER BY random();
                              QUERY PLAN
-----------------------------------------------------------------
 Sort   (cost=834.39..859.39 rows=10000 width=12)
          (actual time=6.089..7.199 rows=10000 loops=1)
    Output: aid, (random())
    Sort Key: (random())
    Sort Method: quicksort   Memory: 853kB
    Buffers: shared hit=45
    ->  Seq Scan on public.a
          (cost=0.00..170.00 rows=10000 width=12)
          (actual time=0.012..2.625 rows=10000 loops=1)
          Output: aid, random()
          Buffers: shared hit=45
 Planning time: 0.054 ms
 Execution time: 7.992 ms
(10 rows)
```

`analyze true` will actually execute the query as shown previously. `verbose true` will add some more information to the plan (such as column information, and so on). `costs true` will show information about costs. `timing true` is equally important, as it will provide us with good runtime data so that we can see where in the plan time gets lost. Finally, there is `buffers true`, which can be very enlightening. In my example, it reveals that we have needed 45 buffers to execute the query.

Spotting problems

Given all the information shown in the previous chapter, it is already possible to spot a couple of potential performance problems, which are highly important in real life.

Spotting changes in runtime

When looking at a plan, there are always two questions which you have got to ask yourself:

- Is the runtime shown by the EXPLAIN ANALYZE clause justified for the given query?
- If the query is slow, where does the runtime jump?

In my case, the sequential scan is rated at 2.625 milliseconds. The sort is done after 7.199 milliseconds so the sort takes roughly 4.5 milliseconds to complete and is therefore responsible for most of the runtime needed by the query.

Looking for jumps in the execution time of the query will reveal what is really going on. Depending on which type of operation will burn too much time, you have to act accordingly. General advice is not possible here because there are simply too many things which can cause issues.

Inspecting estimates

However, there is something which should always be done: make sure that estimates and real numbers are reasonably close together. In some cases, the optimizer will make poor decisions because the estimates are way off for some reason. It can happen that estimates are off because the system statistics are not up to date. Running an ANALYZE clause is therefore definitely a good thing to start with. However, optimizer stats are mostly taken care of by the autovacuum daemon so it is definitely worth considering other options causing bad estimates. Take a look at the following example:

```
test=# CREATE TABLE t_estimate AS
    SELECT * FROM generate_series(1, 10000) AS id;
SELECT 10000
```

After loading 10,000 rows, optimizer statistics are created:

```
test=# ANALYZE t_estimate;
ANALYZE
```

Let us take a look at the estimates now:

```
test=# EXPLAIN ANALYZE SELECT *
       FROM   t_estimate
       WHERE        cos(id) < 4;
                               QUERY PLAN
--------------------------------------------------------------------
 Seq Scan on t_estimate   (cost=0.00..220.00 rows=3333 width=4)
         (actual time=0.010..4.006 rows=10000 loops=1)
   Filter: (cos((id)::double precision) < '4'::double precision)
 Planning time: 0.064 ms
 Execution time: 4.701 ms
(4 rows)
```

In many cases, PostgreSQL might not be able to process the WHERE clause properly because it only has statistics on columns, not on expressions. What we see here is a nasty underestimation of the data returned from the WHERE clause.

Of course, it can also happen that the amount of data is overestimated:

```
test=# EXPLAIN ANALYZE SELECT *
 FROM t_estimate
 WHERE cos(id) > 4;
 QUERY PLAN
--------------------------------------------------------------------
 Seq Scan on t_estimate (cost=0.00..220.00 rows=3333 width=4)
 (actual time=3.802..3.802 rows=0 loops=1)
 Filter: (cos((id)::double precision) > '4'::double precision)
 Rows Removed by Filter: 10000
 Planning time: 0.037 ms
 Execution time: 3.813 ms
(5 rows)
```

If something like that happens deep inside the plan, the process might very well create a bad plan. Therefore, making sure that estimates are within a certain range makes perfect sense.

Fortunately, there is a way to get around this problem:

```
test=# CREATE INDEX idx_cosine ON t_estimate (cos(id));
CREATE INDEX
```

Creating an index will make PostgreSQL track statistics of the expression:

```
test=# ANALYZE ;
ANALYZE
```

Apart from the fact that this plan will ensure significantly better performance, it will also fix statistics—even if the index is not used:

```
test=# EXPLAIN ANALYZE SELECT *
 FROM t_estimate
 WHERE cos(id) > 4;
 QUERY PLAN
-------------------------------------------------------------------
 Index Scan using idx_cosine on t_estimate
 (cost=0.29..8.30 rows=1 width=4)
 (actual time=0.002..0.002 rows=0 loops=1)
 Index Cond: (cos((id)::double precision)
 > '4'::double precision)
 Planning time: 0.095 ms
 Execution time: 0.011 ms
(4 rows)
```

However, there is more to wrong estimates than meets the eye. One problem which is often underestimated is called **cross-column correlation**. Consider a simple example involving two columns:

- 20% of people like to ski
- 20% of people are from Africa

If we want to count the number of skiers in Africa, mathematics says that the result will be 0.2 x 0.2 = 4% of the overall population. However, there is no snow in Africa and the income is low. Therefore the real result will surely be lower. The observation *Africa* and the observation *skiing* are not statistically independent. In many cases, the fact that PostgreSQL keeps column statistics which do not span more than one column, can lead to bad results. Of course, the planner does a lot to prevent these things from happening as often as possible. Still, it can be an issue.

Starting with PostgreSQL 10.0, we will most likely have multivariate statistics in PostgreSQL, which will put an end to cross-column correlation once and for all.

Inspecting buffer usage

However, the plan itself is not the only thing which can cause issues. In many cases, dangerous things are hidden on some other level. Memory and caching can lead to undesired behavior, which is often hard to understand for end users who are not trained to see the problem described in this section.

Here is an example:

```
test=# CREATE TABLE t_random AS
        SELECT *
        FROM  generate_series(1, 10000000) AS id
        ORDER BY random();
SELECT 10000000
test=# ANALYZE t_random ;
ANALYZE
```

I have generated a simple table containing 10 million rows and created optimizer statistics. In the next step, a simple query retrieving only a handful of rows is executed:

```
test=# EXPLAIN (analyze true, buffers true, costs true, timing true)
    SELECT   *
    FROM     t_random
    WHERE    id < 1000;
                              QUERY PLAN
------------------------------------------------------------------
 Seq Scan on t_random  (cost=0.00..169248.60 rows=1000 width=4)
    (actual time=1.068..685.410 rows=999 loops=1)
    Filter: (id < 1000)
    Rows Removed by Filter: 9999001
    Buffers: shared hit=2112 read=42136
 Planning time: 0.035 ms
 Execution time: 685.551 ms
(6 rows)
```

Before inspecting the data, make sure that you have executed the query twice. Of course, it makes sense to use an index here. However, I want to point to something else. In my query, PostgreSQL has found 2,112 buffers inside the cache and 421136 buffers had to be taken from the operating system. Now there are two things which can happen. If you are lucky, the operating system lands a couple of cache hits and the query is fast. If the filesystem cache is not lucky, those blocks have to be taken from disk. This might look obvious; however, it can lead to wild swings in execution time. A query which runs entirely in cache can be 100 times faster than a query which has to slowly collect random blocks from disk.

Let me try to outline the problem using a simple example. Suppose we have a phone system storing 10 billion rows (which is not uncommon at large phone carriers). Data flows in at a rapid rate and users want to query this data. If you have 10 billion rows, data will only partially fit into memory and therefore a lot of stuff will naturally end up coming from disk.

We can run a simple query now:

```
SELECT * FROM data WHERE phone_number = '+12345678';
```

Even if you are on the phone, your data will be spread all over the place. If you end a phone call just to start the next call, thousands of people will do the same so the odds that two of your calls will end up in the very same 8,000 block is naturally close to zero. Just imagine for the time being that there are 100,000 calls going on at the same time. On disk, data will be randomly distributed. In case your phone number shows up often, it means that for each row at least one block has to be fetched from disk (assuming a very low cache hit rate). Suppose 5,000 rows will be returned. Assuming you have to go to disk 5,000 times, it leads to something like 5,000 x 5 milliseconds = 25 seconds of execution time. Note that the execution time of this query might vary between milliseconds and, say, 30 seconds, depending on how much has been cached by the operating system or by PostgreSQL.

Keep in mind that every server restart will naturally clean out the PostgreSQL and filesystem caches, which can lead to real trouble after a node failure.

Fixing high buffer usage

The question is now: how can the situation be improved? One way to do that is to run a CLUSTER clause:

```
test=# \h CLUSTER
Command:      CLUSTER
Description: cluster a table according to an index
Syntax:
CLUSTER [VERBOSE] table_name [ USING index_name ]
CLUSTER [VERBOSE]
```

The CLUSTER clause will rewrite the table in the same order as a (B-tree) index. If you are running an analytical workload, this can make sense. However, in an OLTP system, the CLUSTER clause might not be feasible because a table lock is required while the table is rewritten.

Understanding and fixing joins

Joins are an important thing; everybody needs them on a regular basis. Consequently, joins are also relevant to maintaining or achieving good performance. To ensure that you can write good joins, I have decided to include a section about joining into this book.

Getting joins right

Before we dive into optimizing joins, it is important to take a look at some of the most common problems arising with joins and which should ring alarm bells to you.

Here is an example:

```
test=# CREATE TABLE a (aid int);
CREATE TABLE
test=# CREATE TABLE b (bid int);
CREATE TABLE
test=# INSERT INTO a VALUES (1), (2), (3);
INSERT 0 3
test=# INSERT INTO b VALUES (2), (3), (4);
INSERT 0 3
```

In the next example, you will see a simple outer join:

```
test=# SELECT * FROM a LEFT JOIN b ON (aid = bid);
 aid | bid
-----+-----
   1 |
   2 |   2
   3 |   3
(3 rows)
```

You can see that PostgreSQL will take all rows from the left-hand side and only list the ones fitting the condition.

The next example might come as a surprise to many people:

```
test=# SELECT * FROM a LEFT JOIN b ON (aid = bid AND bid = 2);
 aid | bid
-----+-----
   1 |
   2 |   2
   3 |
(3 rows)
```

No, the number of rows does not decrease—it will stay constant. Most people assume that there will only be one row in the join but this is not true and will lead to some hidden issues.

Consider the following query:

```
test=# SELECT avg(aid), avg(bid)
    FROM a LEFT JOIN b
         ON (aid = bid AND bid = 2);
        avg         |        avg
--------------------+--------------------
 2.0000000000000000 | 2.0000000000000000
(1 row)
```

Most people assume that the average is calculated based on a single row. However, as stated earlier, this is not the case and therefore queries like that are often considered to be a performance problem because, for some reason, PostgreSQL does not index the table on the left-hand side of the join. Of course, we are not looking at a performance problem here—we are definitely looking at a semantic issue here. It happens on a regular basis that people writing outer joins don't mean what they order PostgreSQL to do. So my personal advice is to always question the semantical correctness of an outer join before attacking the performance problem reported by the client.

I cannot stress enough how important this kind of work is to ensure that your queries are correct and do exactly what is needed.

Processing outer joins

After verifying that your queries are actually correct from a business point of view, it makes sense to check, what the optimizer can do to speedup your outer joins. The most important thing is that PostgreSQL can in many cases reorder inner joins to speedup things dramatically. However, in the case of outer joins, this is not always possible. Only a handful *Pac* of reordering operations are actually allowed:

(A leftjoin B on (Pab)) innerjoin C on (Pac) = (A innerjoin C on (Pac)) leftjoin B on (Pab)

Pac is a predicate referencing *A* and *C*, and so on (in this case, clearly *Pac* cannot reference *B*, or the transformation is nonsensical):

(A leftjoin B on (Pab)) leftjoin C on (Pac) = (A leftjoin C on (Pac)) leftjoin B on (Pab)

(A leftjoin B on (Pab)) leftjoin C on (Pbc) = (A leftjoin (B leftjoin C on (Pbc)) on (Pab)

The last rule only holds if predicate *Pbc* must fail for all null *B* rows (that is, *Pbc* is strict for at least one column of *B*). If *Pbc* is not strict, the first form might produce some rows with non-null *C* columns where the second form would make those entries null.

While some joins can be reordered, a typical type of query cannot benefit from join reordering:

```
SELECT ...
FROM     a LEFT JOIN b ON (aid = bid)
   LEFT JOIN c ON (bid = cid)
   LEFT JOIN d ON (cid = did)
   ...
```

The way to approach this is to check if all outer joins are really necessary. In many cases, it happens that people write outer joins without actually needing them. Often the business case does not even contain the necessity to use outer joins.

Understanding the join_collapse_limit variable

During the planning process, PostgreSQL tries to check all possible join orders. In many cases, this can be pretty expensive because there can be many permutations, which naturally slows down the planning process. The `join_collapse_limit` variable is here to give the developer a tool to actually work around these problems and define, in a more straightforward way, how a query should be processed.

To show what this setting is all about, I have compiled a little example:

```
SELECT    *
FROM      tab1, tab2, tab3
WHERE     tab1.id = tab2.id
          AND tab2.ref = tab3.id;


SELECT    *
FROM      tab1 CROSS JOIN tab2
          CROSS JOIN tab3
WHERE     tab1.id = tab2.id
          AND tab2.ref = tab3.id;


SELECT    *
FROM      tab1 JOIN (tab2 JOIN tab3
              ON (tab2.ref = tab3.id))
          ON (tab1.id = tab2.id);
```

Basically, these three queries are identical and treated by the planner in the same way. The first query consists of implicit joins. The last one consists only of explicit joins. Internally, the planner will inspect those requests and order joins accordingly to ensure the best runtime possible. The question now is: how many explicit joins will PostgreSQL plan implicitly? This is exactly what you can tell the planner by setting the `join_collapse_limit` variable. The default value is reasonably good for normal queries. However, if your query contains a very high number of joins, playing around with this setting can reduce planning time considerably. Reducing planning time can be essential to maintain good throughput.

To see how the `join_collapse_limit` variable changes the plan, I have written a simple query:

```
test=# EXPLAIN WITH x AS (SELECT * FROM generate_series(1, 1000) AS id)
       SELECT   *
       FROM     x AS a JOIN x AS b ON (a.id = b.id)
                JOIN x AS c ON (b.id = c.id)
                JOIN x AS d ON (c.id = d.id)
                JOIN x AS e ON (d.id = e.id)
                JOIN x AS f ON (e.id = f.id);
```

Try to run the query with different settings and see how the plan changes. Unfortunately, the plan is too long to copy it here so I cannot include the actual changes in this section.

Enabling and disabling optimizer settings

So far, the most important optimizations performed by the planner have been discussed in more or less detail. PostgreSQL has become very smart over the years. Still it can happen that something goes south and users have to convince the planner to do the right thing.

To modify plans, PostgreSQL offers a couple of runtime variables, which will have a significant impact on planning. The idea is to give the end user the chance to make certain types of nodes in the plan more expensive than others. What does that mean in practice? Here is a simple plan:

```
test=# explain  SELECT   *
       FROM     generate_series(1, 100) AS a,
                generate_series(1, 100) AS b
       WHERE    a = b;
                         QUERY PLAN
-----------------------------------------------------------------
 Merge Join  (cost=119.66..199.66 rows=5000 width=8)
   Merge Cond: (a.a = b.b)
```

```
   ->  Sort  (cost=59.83..62.33 rows=1000 width=4)
         Sort Key: a.a
         ->  Function Scan on generate_series a
         (cost=0.00..10.00 rows=1000 width=4)
   ->  Sort  (cost=59.83..62.33 rows=1000 width=4)
         Sort Key: b.b
         ->  Function Scan on generate_series b
         (cost=0.00..10.00 rows=1000 width=4)
(8 rows)
```

The plan shows that PostgreSQL reads the data from the function and sorts both results. Then a merge join is performed.

However, what if a merge join is not the fastest way to run the query? In PostgreSQL there is no way to put planner hints into comments as you could do in Oracle. Instead you can ensure that certain operations are simply considered to be expensive. SET enable_mergejoin TO off command will simply make merging too expensive:

```
test=# SET enable_mergejoin TO off;
SET
test=# explain  SELECT  *
        FROM    generate_series(1, 100) AS a,
                generate_series(1, 100) AS b
        WHERE   a = b;
                          QUERY PLAN
-----------------------------------------------------------------
 Hash Join  (cost=22.50..210.00 rows=5000 width=8)
   Hash Cond: (a.a = b.b)
   ->  Function Scan on generate_series a
         (cost=0.00..10.00 rows=1000 width=4)
   ->  Hash  (cost=10.00..10.00 rows=1000 width=4)
         ->  Function Scan on generate_series b
         (cost=0.00..10.00 rows=1000 width=4)
(5 rows)
```

Because, merging is too expensive, PostgreSQL decided to try a hash join. As you can see, the costs are a bit higher but the plan is still taken as merging is not desired anymore.

What happens if hash joins are turned off as well?

```
test=# SET enable_hashjoin TO off;
SET
test=# explain  SELECT  *
        FROM    generate_series(1, 100) AS a,
                generate_series(1, 100) AS b
        WHERE   a = b;
                          QUERY PLAN
```

```
-------------------------------------------------------------------
 Nested Loop   (cost=0.01..22510.01 rows=5000 width=8)
   Join Filter: (a.a = b.b)
   ->  Function Scan on generate_series a
         (cost=0.00..10.00 rows=1000 width=4)
   ->  Function Scan on generate_series b
         (cost=0.00..10.00 rows=1000 width=4)
 (4 rows)
```

PostgreSQL will again try something else and come up with a nested loop. The costs of a nested loop are already staggering but the planner starts to run out of options.

What happens if nested loops are turned off as well?

```
test=# SET enable_nestloop TO off;
SET
test=# explain   SELECT   *
          FROM      generate_series(1,  100) AS a,
                    generate_series(1,  100) AS b
          WHERE     a = b;
                              QUERY PLAN
-------------------------------------------------------------------
 Nested Loop   (cost=10000000000.00..10000022510.00
                   rows=5000 width=8)
   Join Filter: (a.a = b.b)
   ->  Function Scan on generate_series a
         (cost=0.00..10.00 rows=1000 width=4)
   ->  Function Scan on generate_series b
         (cost=0.00..10.00 rows=1000 width=4)
 (4 rows)
```

PostgreSQL will still perform a nested loop. The important part here is that off does not really mean off—it just means *treat as a very expensive thing*. This is important because otherwise the query could not be performed.

Which settings are there to influence the planner? The following switches are available:

- enable_bitmapscan = on
- enable_hashagg = on
- enable_hashjoin = on
- enable_indexscan = on
- enable_indexonlyscan = on
- enable_material = on
- enable_mergejoin = on
- enable_nestloop = on

- `enable_seqscan = on`
- `enable_sort = on`
- `enable_tidscan = on`

While those settings can definitely be beneficial, I want to point out that those tweaks should be handled with care. Only use them to speedup individual queries and do not turn off things globally. Things can turn against you fairly quickly and destroy performance. Therefore it really makes sense to think twice before changing these parameters.

Understanding genetic query optimization

The result of the planning process is key to achieving superior performance. As shown in this chapter, planning is far from trivial and involves various complex calculations. The more tables are touched by a query, the more complicated planning will become. The more tables there are, the mores choices the planner will have. Logically, planning time will increase. At some point planning will take so long that performing the classical exhaustive search is not feasible anymore. On top of that, the errors made during planning are so great anyway that finding the theoretically best plan does not necessarily lead to the best plan in terms of runtime.

The **genetic query optimization (GEQO)** can come to the rescue. What is GEQO? The idea is actually stolen from nature and resembles the natural process of evolution.

PostgreSQL will approach the problem just like a traveling salesman problem and encode the possible joins as integer strings. An example, *4-1-3-2* means: first join *4* and *1*, then *3*, and then *2*. The numbers represent the relation's IDs. At the beginning, the genetic optimizer will generate a random set of plans. Those plans are then inspected. The bad ones are discarded and new ones are generated based on the genes of the good ones. This way, potentially even better plans are generated. The process can be repeated as often as desired. At the end of the day, we are left with a plan which is expected to be a lot better than just using a random plan.

The GEQO can be turned on and off by adjusting the `geqo` variable:

```
test=# SHOW geqo;
 geqo
------
 on
(1 row)

test=# SET geqo TO off;
SET
```

By default, the `geqo` variable kicks in if a statement exceeds a certain level of complexity, which is controlled by the following variable:

```
test=# SHOW geqo_threshold ;
 geqo_threshold
-----------------
 12
(1 row)
```

If your queries are so large that you start to reach this threshold, it certainly makes sense to play with this setting to see how plans are changed by the planner if you change those variables.

As a general rule, however, I would say that you should try to avoid GEQO as long as you can and try to fix things first by trying to somewhat fix the join order using the `join_collapse_limit` variable. Note that every query is different so it certainly helps to experiment and gain more experience by learning how the planner behaves under which circumstances.

> If you want to see what a really crazy join is, consider checking out the following talk I have given in Madrid at: `http://de.slideshare.net/hansjurgenschonig/postgresql-joining-1-million-tables`.

Partitioning data

Given default 8,000 blocks, PostgreSQL can store up to 32 TB of data inside a single table. If you compile PostgreSQL with 32,000 blocks, you can even put up to 128 TB into a single table. However, large tables like that are not necessarily too convenient anymore and it can make sense to partition tables to make processing easier and in some cases a bit faster.

Starting with PostgreSQL 10.0, we will most likely have improved partitioning, which will offer end users significantly easier handling of data partitioning.

At the time this chapter was written, PostgreSQL 10.0 had not been released yet and therefore the old means of partitioning are covered.

Creating partitions

Before digging deeper into the advantages of partitioning, I want to show how partitions can be created. The entire thing starts with a parent table:

```
test=# CREATE TABLE t_data (id serial, t date, payload text);
CREATE TABLE
```

In this example, the parent table has three columns. The date column will be used for partitioning but more on that a bit later.

Now that the parent table is in place, the child tables can be created. This is how it works:

```
test=# CREATE TABLE t_data_2016 () INHERITS (t_data);
CREATE TABLE
test=# \d t_data_2016
                  Table "public.t_data_2016"
 Column  |  Type   |                    Modifiers
---------+---------+--------------------------------------------------
 id      | integer | not null default
                      nextval('t_data_id_seq'::regclass)
 t       | date    |
 payload | text    |
Inherits: t_data
```

The table is called t_data_2016 and inherits from t_data. () means that no extra columns are added to the child table. As you can see, inheritance means that all columns from the parents are available in the child table. Also note that the id column will inherit the sequence from the parent so that all children can share the very same numbering.

Let's create more tables:

```
test=# CREATE TABLE t_data_2015 () INHERITS (t_data);
CREATE TABLE
test=# CREATE TABLE t_data_2014 () INHERITS (t_data);
CREATE TABLE
```

So far, all the tables are identical and just inherit from the parent. However, there is more: child tables can actually have more columns than parents. Adding more fields is simple:

```
test=# CREATE TABLE t_data_2013 (special text) INHERITS (t_data);
CREATE TABLE
```

In this case, the `special` column has been added. It has no impact on the parent but just enriches the children and makes them capable of holding more data.

After creating a handful of tables, a row can be added:

```
test=# INSERT INTO t_data_2015 (t, payload)
    VALUES ('2015-05-04', 'some data');
INSERT 0 1
```

The most important thing now is that the parent table can be used to find all the data in the child tables:

```
test=# SELECT * FROM t_data;
 id |     t      |  payload
----+------------+-----------
  1 | 2015-05-04 | some data
(1 row)
```

Querying the parent allows you to gain access to everything below the parent in a simple and efficient manner.

To understand how PostgreSQL does partitioning, it makes sense to take a look at the plan:

```
test=# EXPLAIN SELECT * FROM t_data;
                             QUERY PLAN
---------------------------------------------------------------------
 Append  (cost=0.00..84.10 rows=4411 width=40)
   ->  Seq Scan on t_data  (cost=0.00..0.00 rows=1 width=40)
   ->  Seq Scan on t_data_2016
         (cost=0.00..22.00 rows=1200 width=40)
   ->  Seq Scan on t_data_2015
         (cost=0.00..22.00 rows=1200 width=40)
   ->  Seq Scan on t_data_2014
         (cost=0.00..22.00 rows=1200 width=40)
   ->  Seq Scan on t_data_2013
         (cost=0.00..18.10 rows=810 width=40)
(6 rows)
```

Actually, the process is quite simple. PostgreSQL will simply unify all tables and show us all the content from all the tables inside and below the partition we are looking at. Note that all tables are independent and are just connected logically through the system catalog.

Applying table constraints

What happens if filters are applied?

```
test=# EXPLAIN SELECT * FROM t_data WHERE t = '2016-01-04';
                          QUERY PLAN
-------------------------------------------------------------------
 Append  (cost=0.00..95.12 rows=23 width=40)
   ->  Seq Scan on t_data  (cost=0.00..0.00 rows=1 width=40)
         Filter: (t = '2016-01-04'::date)
   ->  Seq Scan on t_data_2016  (cost=0.00..25.00 rows=6 width=40)
         Filter: (t = '2016-01-04'::date)
   ->  Seq Scan on t_data_2015  (cost=0.00..25.00 rows=6 width=40)
         Filter: (t = '2016-01-04'::date)
   ->  Seq Scan on t_data_2014  (cost=0.00..25.00 rows=6 width=40)
         Filter: (t = '2016-01-04'::date)
   ->  Seq Scan on t_data_2013  (cost=0.00..20.12 rows=4 width=40)
         Filter: (t = '2016-01-04'::date)
(11 rows)
```

PostgreSQL will apply the filter to all the partitions in the structure. It does not know that the table name is somehow related to the content of the tables. To the database, names are just names and have nothing to do with what you are looking for. This makes sense, of course, as there is no mathematical justification for doing anything else.

The point now is: how can we teach the database that the 2016 table only contains 2016 data, the 2015 table only contains 2015 data, and so on? Table constraints are here to do exactly that. They teach PostgreSQL about the content of those tables and therefore allow the planner to make smarter decisions than before. The feature is called **constraint exclusion** and helps dramatically to speedup queries in many cases.

The following listing shows how table constraints can be created:

```
test=# ALTER TABLE t_data_2013
    ADD CHECK (t < '2014-01-01');
ALTER TABLE
test=# ALTER TABLE t_data_2014
    ADD CHECK (t >= '2014-01-01' AND t < '2015-01-01');
ALTER TABLE
test=# ALTER TABLE t_data_2015
    ADD CHECK (t >= '2015-01-01' AND t < '2016-01-01');
ALTER TABLE
test=# ALTER TABLE t_data_2016
    ADD CHECK (t >= '2016-01-01' AND t < '2017-01-01');
ALTER TABLE
```

For each table a CHECK constraint can be added.

> **TIP**
>
> Note that PostgreSQL will only create the constraint if all the data in those tables is perfectly correct and if every single row satisfies the constraint. In contrast to MySQL, constraints in PostgreSQL are taken seriously and honored under any circumstances.

In PostgreSQL, those constraints can overlap—this is not forbidden and can make sense in some cases. However, it is usually better to have non-overlapping constraints because PostgreSQL has the option to prune more tables.

Here is what happens after adding those table constraints:

```
test=# EXPLAIN SELECT *
    FROM        t_data
    WHERE       t = '2016-01-04';
                            QUERY PLAN
------------------------------------------------------------------
 Append  (cost=0.00..25.00 rows=7 width=40)
    ->  Seq Scan on t_data  (cost=0.00..0.00 rows=1 width=40)
          Filter: (t = '2016-01-04'::date)
    ->  Seq Scan on t_data_2016  (cost=0.00..25.00 rows=6 width=40)
          Filter: (t = '2016-01-04'::date)
(5 rows)
```

The planner will be able to remove many of the tables from the query and only keep those which potentially contain the data. The query can greatly benefit from a shorter and more efficient plan. Especially if those tables are really large, removing them can boost speed considerably.

Modifying inherited structures

Once in a while data structures have to be modified. The ALTER TABLE clause is here to do exactly that. The question is: how can partitioned tables be modified?

Basically, all you have to do is tackle the parent table and add or remove columns. PostgreSQL will automatically propagate those changes through to the child tables and ensure that changes are made to all the relations as follows:

```
test=# ALTER TABLE t_data ADD COLUMN x int;
ALTER TABLE
test=# \d t_data_2016
                    Table "public.t_data_2016"
 Column  |  Type   |                    Modifiers
---------+---------+---------------------------------------------------------
 id      | integer | not null default
                     nextval('t_data_id_seq'::regclass)
 t       | date    |
 payload | text    |
 x       | integer |
Check constraints:
    "t_data_2016_t_check"
    CHECK (t >= '2016-01-01'::date AND t < '2017-01-01'::date)
Inherits: t_data
```

As you can see, the column is added to the parent and automatically added to the child table here.

Note that this works for columns, and so on. Indexes are a totally different story. In an inherited structure, every table has to be indexed separately. If you add an index to the parent table, it will only be present on the parent—it won't be deployed on those child tables. Indexing all those columns in all those tables is your task and PostgreSQL is not going to make those decisions for you. Of course, this can be seen as a feature or as a limitation. On the upside, you could say that PostgreSQL gives you all the flexibility to index things separately and therefore potentially more efficiently. However, people might also argue that deploying all those indexes one by one is a lot more work.

Moving tables in and out of partitioned structures

Suppose you have an inherited structure. Data is partitioned by date and you want to provide the most recent years to the end user. At some point, you might want to remove some data from the scope of the user without actually touching it. You might want to put data into some sort of archive or so.

PostgreSQL provides a simple means to achieve exactly that. First a new parent can be created:

```
test=# CREATE TABLE t_history (LIKE t_data);
CREATE TABLE
```

The `LIKE` keyword allows you to create a table which has exactly the same layout as the `t_data table`. In case you have forgotten which columns `t_data` table actually has, this might come in handy as it saves you a lot of work. It is also possible to include indexes, constraints, and defaults.

Then the table can be moved away from the old parent table and put below the new one. Here is how it works:

```
test=# ALTER TABLE t_data_2013 NO INHERIT t_data;
ALTER TABLE
test=# ALTER TABLE t_data_2013 INHERIT t_history;
ALTER TABLE
```

The entire process can of course be done in a single transaction to assure that the operation stays atomic.

Cleaning up data

One advantage of partitioned tables is the ability to clean up data quickly. Suppose that we want to delete an entire year. If data is partitioned accordingly, a simple `DROP  TABLE` clause can do the job:

```
test=# DROP TABLE t_data_2014;
DROP TABLE
```

As you can see, dropping a child table is easy. But what about the parent table? There are depending objects and therefore PostgreSQL naturally errors out to make sure that nothing unexpected happens:

```
test=# DROP TABLE t_data;
ERROR:  cannot drop table t_data because other objects depend on it
DETAIL:  default for table t_data_2013 column id depends on
    sequence t_data_id_seq
table t_data_2016 depends on table t_data
table t_data_2015 depends on table t_data
HINT:  Use DROP ... CASCADE to drop the dependent objects too.
```

The DROP TABLE clause will warn us that there are depending objects and refuse to drop those tables. The CASCADE clause is needed to force PostgreSQL to actually remove those objects along with the parent table:

```
test=# DROP TABLE t_data CASCADE;
NOTICE:  drop cascades to 3 other objects
DETAIL:  drop cascades to default for table t_data_2013 column id
drop cascades to table t_data_2016
drop cascades to table t_data_2015
DROP TABLE
```

Adjusting parameters for good query performance

Writing good queries is the first step to reaching good performance. Without a good query, you will most likely suffer from bad performance. Writing good and intelligent code will therefore give you the greatest edge possible. Once your queries have been optimized from a logical and semantical point of view, good memory settings can provide you with a final nice speedup. In this section, you will learn what more memory can do for you and how PostgreSQL can use it for your benefit.

To demonstrate things, I have compiled a simple example:

```
test=# CREATE TABLE t_test (id serial, name text);
CREATE TABLE
test=# INSERT INTO t_test (name) SELECT 'hans'
   FROM generate_series(1, 100000);
INSERT 0 100000
test=# INSERT INTO t_test (name) SELECT 'paul'
   FROM generate_series(1, 100000);
INSERT 0 100000
```

1 million rows containing hans will be added to the table. Then 1 million rows containing paul are loaded. All together there will be 2 million unique IDs but just two different names.

Let us run a simple query now using PostgreSQL's default memory settings:

```
test=# SELECT name, count(*) FROM t_test GROUP BY 1;
 name | count
------+--------
 hans | 100000
 paul | 100000
(2 rows)
```

Two rows will be returned, which should not come as a surprise. The important thing here is not the result but what PostgreSQL is doing behind the scenes:

```
test=# EXPLAIN ANALYZE SELECT name, count(*)
    FROM  t_test
    GROUP BY 1;
                            QUERY PLAN
-----------------------------------------------------------------
 HashAggregate  (cost=4082.00..4082.01 rows=1 width=13)
    (actual time=51.448..51.448 rows=2 loops=1)
                Group Key: name
    ->  Seq Scan on t_test
            (cost=0.00..3082.00 rows=200000 width=5)
            (actual time=0.007..14.150 rows=200000 loops=1)
 Planning time: 0.032 ms
 Execution time: 51.471 ms
(5 rows)
```

PostgreSQL figured out that the number of groups is actually very small. Therefore, it creates a hash and adds one hash entry per group and starts to count. Due to the low number of groups, the hash is really small and PostgreSQL can quickly do the count by incrementing the numbers for each group.

What happens if we group by `id` and not by `name`? The number of groups will skyrocket:

```
test=# EXPLAIN ANALYZE SELECT id, count(*)
    FROM t_test
    GROUP BY 1;
    QUERY PLAN
-----------------------------------------------------------------
 GroupAggregate (cost=23428.64..26928.64 rows=200000 width=12)
 (actual time=97.128..154.205 rows=200000 loops=1)
 Group Key: id
 -> Sort (cost=23428.64..23928.64 rows=200000 width=4)
 (actual time=97.120..113.017 rows=200000 loops=1)
 Sort Key: id
 Sort Method: external sort Disk: 2736kB
 -> Seq Scan on t_test
 (cost=0.00..3082.00 rows=200000 width=4)
```

```
(actual time=0.017..19.469 rows=200000 loops=1)
Planning time: 0.128 ms
Execution time: 160.589 ms
(8 rows)
```

PostgreSQL figured that the number of groups is now a lot larger and quickly changes its strategy. The problem is that a hash containing so many entries does not fit into memory:

```
test=# SHOW work_mem ;
 work_mem
----------
 4MB
(1 row)
```

The `work_mem` variable governs the size of the hash used by the GROUP BY clause. As there are too many entries, PostgreSQL has to find a strategy, which does not require holding the entire dataset in memory. The solution is to sort the data by ID and group it. Once the data is sorted, PostgreSQL can move down the list and form one group after the other. If the first type of value is counted, the partial result is read and can be emitted. Then the next group can be processed. Once the value in the sorted list changes when moving down, it will never show up again, thus the system knows that a partial result is ready.

To speedup the query, a higher value for the `work_mem` variable can be set on the fly (and, of course, globally):

```
test=# SET work_mem TO '1 GB';
SET
```

The plan will now again feature a fast and efficient hash aggregate:

```
test=# EXPLAIN ANALYZE SELECT id, count(*) FROM t_test GROUP BY 1;
 QUERY PLAN
--------------------------------------------------------------------
 HashAggregate (cost=4082.00..6082.00 rows=200000 width=12)
 (actual time=76.967..118.926 rows=200000 loops=1)
 Group Key: id
 -> Seq Scan on t_test
 (cost=0.00..3082.00 rows=200000 width=4)
 (actual time=0.008..13.570 rows=200000 loops=1)
 Planning time: 0.073 ms
 Execution time: 126.456 ms
(5 rows)
```

PostgreSQL knows (or at least assumes) that data will fit into memory and switch to the faster plan. As you can see, the execution time is lower. The query won't be as fast as in the GROUP BY name case because many more hash values have to be calculated but you will be able to see a nice and reliable benefit in the vast majority of all cases.

Speeding up sorting

The work_mem variable does not only speedup grouping. It can also have a very nice impact on simple things such as sorting, which is an essential mechanism mastered by every database system in the world.

The following query shows a simple operation using the default setting of 4 MB:

```
test=# SET work_mem TO default;
SET
test=# EXPLAIN ANALYZE SELECT * FROM t_test ORDER BY name, id;
 QUERY PLAN
----------------------------------------------------------------
 Sort (cost=24111.14..24611.14 rows=200000 width=9)
 (actual time=219.298..235.008 rows=200000 loops=1)
 Sort Key: name, id
 Sort Method: external sort Disk: 3712kB
 -> Seq Scan on t_test
 (cost=0.00..3082.00 rows=200000 width=9)
 (actual time=0.006..13.807 rows=200000 loops=1)
 Planning time: 0.064 ms
 Execution time: 241.375 ms
(6 rows)
```

PostgreSQL needs 13.8 milliseconds to read the data and over 200 milliseconds to sort the data. Due to the low amount of memory available, sorting has to be performed using temporary files. The external sort Disk method needs only small amounts of RAM but has to send intermediate data to a comparatively slow storage device, which of course leads to poor throughput.

Increasing the `work_mem` variable setting will make PostgreSQL use more memory for sorting:

```
test=# SET work_mem TO '1 GB';
SET
test=# EXPLAIN ANALYZE SELECT * FROM t_test ORDER BY name, id;
 QUERY PLAN
-----------------------------------------------------------------
 Sort (cost=20691.64..21191.64 rows=200000 width=9)
 (actual time=36.481..47.899 rows=200000 loops=1)
 Sort Key: name, id
 Sort Method: quicksort Memory: 15520kB
 -> Seq Scan on t_test
 (cost=0.00..3082.00 rows=200000 width=9)
 (actual time=0.010..14.232 rows=200000 loops=1)
 Planning time: 0.037 ms
 Execution time: 55.520 ms
(6 rows)
```

As there is enough memory now, the database will do all the sorting in memory and therefore speedup the process dramatically. The sort takes just 33 milliseconds now, which is a seven times improvement compared to the query we had previously. More memory will lead to faster sorting and speedup the system.

Up to now, you have already seen two mechanisms to sort data: `external sort Disk` and `quicksort Memory`. In addition to those two mechanisms, there is also a third algorithm, which is `top-N heapsort Memory`. It can be used to only provide you with the top-*N* rows:

```
test=# EXPLAIN ANALYZE SELECT *
 FROM t_test
 ORDER BY name, id
 LIMIT 10;
 QUERY PLAN
-----------------------------------------------------------------
 Limit (cost=7403.93..7403.95 rows=10 width=9)
 (actual time=31.837..31.838 rows=10 loops=1)
 -> Sort (cost=7403.93..7903.93 rows=200000 width=9)
 (actual time=31.836..31.837 rows=10 loops=1)
 Sort Key: name, id
 Sort Method: top-N heapsort Memory: 25kB
 -> Seq Scan on t_test
 (cost=0.00..3082.00 rows=200000 width=9)
 (actual time=0.011..13.645 rows=200000 loops=1)
 Planning time: 0.053 ms
 Execution time: 31.856 ms
(7 rows)
```

The algorithm is lightning fast and the entire query will be done in just over 30 milliseconds. The sorting part is now only 18 milliseconds and is therefore almost as fast as reading the data in the first place.

Note that the `work_mem` variable is allocated per operation. It can theoretically happen that a query needs the `work_mem` variable more than once. It is not a global setting—it is really per operation. Therefore you have to set it in a careful way.

There is one thing you should keep in mind: many books claim that setting the `work_mem` variable too high on an OLTP system might cause your server to run out of memory. Yes, if 1,000 people sort 100 MB at the same time, this can result in memory failures. However, do you expect the disk to be able to handle that? I doubt it. The solution can only be: stop doing stupid things. Sorting 100 MB 1,000 times concurrently is not what should happen in an OLTP system anyway. Consider deploying proper indexes, write better queries, or simply rethink your requirement. Under any circumstances, sorting so much data so often concurrently is a bad idea—stop it before those things stop your application.

Speedup administrative tasks

There are more operations which actually have to do some sorting or memory allocation of any kind. The administrative ones such as the CREATE INDEX clause do not rely on the `work_mem` variable but use the `maintenance_work_mem` variable instead. Here is how it works:

```
test=# SET maintenance_work_mem TO '1 MB';
SET
test=# \timing
Timing is on.
test=# CREATE INDEX idx_id ON t_test (id);
CREATE INDEX
Time: 104.268 ms
```

As you can see, creating an index on 2 million rows takes around 100 milliseconds, which is really slow. Therefore, the `maintenance_work_mem` variable can be used to speedup sorting, which is essentially what the CREATE INDEX clause does:

```
test=# SET maintenance_work_mem TO '1 GB';
SET
test=# CREATE INDEX idx_id2 ON t_test (id);
CREATE INDEX
Time: 46.774 ms
```

The speed has now doubled just because sorting has been improved so much.

There are more administrative jobs which can benefit from more memory. The most prominent ones are the VACUUM clause (to clean out indexes) and ALTER TABLE clause. The rules for the maintenance_work_mem variable are the same as for the work_mem variable. The setting is per operation and only the required memory is allocated on the fly.

Summary

In this chapter, a number of query optimizations have been discussed. You have learned about the optimizer and about various internal optimizations such as constant folding, view inlining, joins, and a lot more. All those optimizations contribute to good performance and help to speed things up considerably.

After this introduction to optimizations, the next chapter will be about stored procedures. You will see the options PostgreSQL has to handle user-defined code.

7
Writing Stored Procedures

In the previous chapter, you learned a lot about the optimizer as well as optimizations going on in the system. This chapter is going to be about stored procedures and how to use them efficiently and easily. You will learn what a stored procedure is made of, which languages are available, and how you can speed up things nicely. On top of that, you will be introduced to some of the more advanced features of PL/pgSQL.

The following things will be covered:

- Deciding on the right language
- How stored procedures are executed
- Advanced features of PL/pgSQL
- Packaging up extensions
- Optimizing for good performance
- Configuring function parameters

At the end of the chapter, you will be able to write good and efficient procedures.

Understanding stored procedure languages

When it comes to stored procedures, PostgreSQL differs quite significantly from other database systems. Most database engines force you to use a certain programming language to write server-side code. Microsoft SQL Server offers Transact-SQL while Oracle encourages you to use PL/SQL. PostgreSQL does not force you to use a certain language but allows you to decide on what you know best and what you like best.

The reason PostgreSQL is so flexible is actually quite interesting too in a historical sense. Many years ago, one of the most well-known PostgreSQL developers (Jan Wieck), who had written countless patches back in its early days, came up with the idea of using TCL as the server-side programming language. The trouble was simple—nobody wanted to use TCL and nobody wanted to have this stuff in the database engine. The solution to the problem was to make the language interface so flexible that basically any language can be integrated with PostgreSQL easily. Then, the CREATE LANGUAGE clause was born:

```
test=# h CREATE LANGUAGE
Command:     CREATE LANGUAGE
Description: define a new procedural language
Syntax:
CREATE [ OR REPLACE ] [ PROCEDURAL ] LANGUAGE name
CREATE [ OR REPLACE ] [ TRUSTED ] [ PROCEDURAL ] LANGUAGE name
    HANDLER call_handler [ INLINE inline_handler ]
            [ VALIDATOR valfunction ]
```

Nowadays, many different languages can be used to write stored procedures. The flexibility added to PostgreSQL back in the early days has really paid off, and so you can choose from a rich set of programming languages.

How exactly does PostgreSQL handle languages? If you take a look at the syntax of the CREATE LANGUAGE clause, you will see a couple of keywords:

- HANDLER: This function is actually the glue between PostgreSQL and any external language you want to use. It is in charge of mapping PostgreSQL data structures to whatever is needed by the language and helps to pass the code around.
- VALIDATOR: This is the policeman of the infrastructure. If it is available, it will be in charge of delivering tasty syntax errors to the end user. Many languages are able to parse the code before actually executing it. PostgreSQL can use that and tell you whether a function is correct or not when you create it. Unfortunately, not all languages can do this, so in some cases, you will still be left with problems showing up at runtime.
- INLINE: If it is present, PostgreSQL will be able to run anonymous code blocks in this function.

The anatomy of a stored procedure

Before actually digging into a specific language, I want to talk a bit about the anatomy of a typical stored procedure. For demo purposes, I have written a function that just adds up two numbers:

```
test=# CREATE OR REPLACE FUNCTION mysum(int, int)
RETURNS int AS
'
   SELECT $1 + $2;
' LANGUAGE 'sql';
CREATE FUNCTION
```

The first thing you can see is that the procedure is written in SQL. PostgreSQL has to know which language we are using, so we have to specify that in the definition. Note that the code of the function is passed to PostgreSQL as a string (`'`). That is somewhat noteworthy because it allows a function to become a black box to the execution machinery. In other database engines, the code of the function is not a string but is directly attached to the statement. This simple abstraction layer is what gives the PostgreSQL function manager all its power.

Inside the string, you can basically use all that the programming language of your choice has to offer. In my example, I am simply adding up two numbers passed to the function. For this example, two integer variables are in use. The important part here is that PostgreSQL provides you with function overloading. In other words, the `mysum(int, int)` function is not the same as the `mysum(int8, int8)` function. PostgreSQL sees these things as two distinct functions. Function overloading is a nice feature; however, you have to be very careful not to accidentally deploy too many functions if your parameter list happens to change from time to time. Always make sure that functions that are not needed anymore are really deleted.

> The `CREATE OR REPLACE FUNCTION` clause will not change the parameter list. You can, therefore, use it only if the signature does not change. It will either error out or simply deploy a new function.

Let's run the function:

```
test=# SELECT mysum(10, 20);
 mysum
-------
    30
(1 row)
```

The result is not really surprising.

Introducing dollar quoting

Passing code to PostgreSQL as a string is very flexible. However, using single quotes can be an issue. In many programming languages, single quotes show up frequently. To be able to use quotes, people have to escape them when passing the string to PostgreSQL. For many years this has been the standard procedure. Fortunately, those old times have passed by and new means to pass the code to PostgreSQL are available:

```
test=# CREATE OR REPLACE FUNCTION mysum(int, int)
RETURNS int AS
$$
    SELECT $1 + $2;
$$ LANGUAGE 'sql';
CREATE FUNCTION
```

The solution to the problem of quoting strings is called **dollar quoting**. Instead of using quotes to start and end strings, you can simple use $$. Currently, I am only aware of two languages that have assigned a meaning to $$. In Perl as well as in bash scripts, $$ represents the process ID. To overcome even this little obstacle, you can use $ almost anything $ to start and end the string. The following example shows how that works:

```
test=# CREATE OR REPLACE FUNCTION mysum(int, int)
RETURNS int AS
$__$
    SELECT $1 + $2;
$__$ LANGUAGE 'sql';
CREATE FUNCTION
```

All this flexibility allows you to really overcome the problem of quoting once and for all. As long as the start string and the end string match, there won't be any problems left.

Making use of anonymous code blocks

So far, you have learned to write the most simplistic stored procedures possible, and you have learned to execute code. However, there is more to code execution than just full-blown stored procedures. In addition to full-blown procedures, PostgreSQL allows the use of anonymous code blocks. The idea is to run code that is needed only once. This kind of code execution is especially useful to deal with administrative tasks. Anonymous code blocks don't take parameters and are not permanently stored in the database as they don't have a name anyway.

Here is a simple example:

```
test=# DO
$$
    BEGIN
            RAISE NOTICE 'current time: %', now();
    END;
$$ LANGUAGE 'plpgsql';
NOTICE:  current time: 2016-12-12 15:25:50.678922+01
CONTEXT:  PL/pgSQL function inline_code_block line 3 at RAISE
DO
```

In this example, the code only issues a message and quits. Again, the code block has to know which language it uses. The string is again passed to PostgreSQL using simple dollar quoting.

Using functions and transactions

As you know, everything that PostgreSQL exposes in user land is a transaction. The same, of course, applies if you are writing stored procedures. The procedure is always part of the transaction you are in. It is not autonomous—it is just like an operator or any other operation.

Here is an example:

```
test=# SELECT now(), mysum(id, id) FROM   generate_series(1, 3) AS id;
              now              | mysum
------------------------------+-------
 2016-12-12 15:54:32.287027+01 |     2
 2016-12-12 15:54:32.287027+01 |     4
 2016-12-12 15:54:32.287027+01 |     6
(3 rows)
```

All three function calls happen in the same transaction. This is important to understand because it implies that you cannot do too much transactional flow control inside a function. Suppose the second function call commits. What happens in such a case anyway? It cannot work.

However, Oracle has a mechanism that allows for autonomous transactions. The idea is that even if a transaction rolls back, some parts might still be needed and should be kept. The classical example is as follows:

1. Start a function to look up secret data
2. Add a log line to the document that somebody has modified this important secret data
3. Commit the log line but roll back the change
4. You still want to know that somebody attempted to change data

To solve problems like this one, autonomous transactions can be used. The idea is to be able to commit a transaction inside the main transaction independently. In this case, the entry in the log table will prevail while the change will be rolled back.

As of PostgreSQL 9.6, autonomous transactions are not happening. However, I have already seen patches floating around that implement this feature. We will see when these features make it to the core.

To give you an impression of how things will most likely work, here is a code snippet based on the first patches:

```
. . .
AS $$
DECLARE
  PRAGMA AUTONOMOUS_TRANSACTION;
BEGIN
  FOR i IN 0..9 LOOP
    START TRANSACTION;
    INSERT INTO test1 VALUES (i);
    IF i % 2 = 0 THEN
        COMMIT;
    ELSE
        ROLLBACK;
    END IF;
  END LOOP;

  RETURN 42;
END;
$$;
. . .
```

The point in this example is that we can decide on the fly whether to commit or to roll back the autonomous transaction.

Understanding various stored procedure languages

As already stated previously in this chapter, PostgreSQL gives you the power to write stored procedures in various languages. The following options are available and shipped along with the PostgreSQL core:

- SQL
- PL/pgSQL
- PL/Perl and PL/PerlU
- PL/Python
- PL/Tcl and PL/TclU

SQL is the obvious choice to write stored procedures, and it should be used whenever possible as it gives the most freedom to the optimizer. However, if you want to write slightly more complex code, PL/pgSQL might be the language of your choice. It offers flow control and a lot more. In this chapter, some of the more advanced and less known features of PL/pgSQL will be shown (this chapter is not meant to be a complete tutorial on PL/pgSQL).

Then the core contains code to run stored procedures in Perl. Basically, the logic is the same here. Code will be passed as a string and executed by Perl. Remember that PostgreSQL does not speak Perl—it merely has the code to pass things on to the external programming language.

Maybe you have noticed that Perl and TCL are available in two flavors: Trusted (PL/Perl and PL/TCL) and Untrusted (PL/PerlU and PL/TCLU). The difference between a trusted and an untrusted language is actually an important one. In PostgreSQL, a language is loaded directly into the database connection. Therefore, the language is able to do quite a lot of nasty stuff. To get rid of security problems, the concept of trusted languages has been invented. The idea is that a trusted language is restricted to the very core of the language. It is not possible to:

- Include libraries
- Open network sockets
- Perform system calls of any kind (opening files and so on)

Perl offers something called taint mode, which is used to implement this feature in PostgreSQL. Perl will automatically restrict itself to trusted mode and error out if a security violation is about to happen. In untrusted mode, everything is possible, and therefore, only the superuser is allowed to run untrusted code.

If you want to run trusted as well as untrusted code, you have to activate both languages: `plperl` and `plperlu` (respectively `pltcl` and `pltclu`).

Python is currently only available as an untrusted language; therefore, administrators have to be very careful when it comes to security in general, as a stored procedure running in untrusted mode can bypass all security mechanisms enforced by PostgreSQL. Just keep in mind that Python is running as part of your database connection and is in no way responsible for security.

Introducing PL/pgSQL

Let's get started with the most awaited topic, and I am sure you will love to know more about it.

In this section, you will be introduced to some of the more advanced features of PL/pgSQL, which are important for writing proper and highly efficient code. Note that this is not a beginner's introduction to programming or PL/pgSQL in general.

Handling quoting

One of the most important things in database programming is quoting. If you are not using proper quoting, you will surely get into trouble with SQL injection and open, unacceptable security holes.

What is SQL injection? Consider the following example:

```
CREATE FUNCTION broken (text)
RETURNS void AS
$$
        DECLARE
                v_sql    text;
        BEGIN
                v_sql := 'SELECT schemaname
                                FROM pg_tables
                                WHERE tablename = ''' || $1 || '''';
                RAISE NOTICE 'v_sql: %', v_sql;
                RETURN;
        END;
```

```
$$ LANGUAGE 'plpgsql';
```

In this example, the SQL code is simply pasted together without ever worrying about security. All I am doing here is using the || operator to concatenate strings. This works fine if people run normal queries:

```
SELECT broken('t_test');
```

However, we have to be prepared for bad people all the time. Consider the following example:

```
SELECT broken(''; DROP TABLE t_test; ');
```

Running the function with this parameter will give us a nice little problem:

```
NOTICE:   v_sql: SELECT schemaname FROM pg_tables
    WHERE tablename = ''; DROP TABLE t_test; '
CONTEXT:   PL/pgSQL function broken(text) line 6 at RAISE
 broken
--------


(1 row)
```

Dropping a table when you just want to do a lookup is not a desirable thing to do. It is definitely not acceptable to make the security of your application depend on the parameters passed to your statements.

To avoid SQL injection, PostgreSQL offers various functions; these should be used at all times to ensure that your security stays intact:

```
test=# SELECT quote_literal(E'o''reilly'),
                  quote_ident(E'o''reilly');
 quote_literal | quote_ident
---------------+-------------
 'o''reilly'   | "o'reilly"
(1 row)
```

The quote_literal function will escape a string in a way that nothing bad can happen anymore. It will add all the quotes around the string and escape problematic characters inside the string. Therefore, there is no longer any need to start and end the string manually.

The second function shown here is `quote_ident`. It can be used to quote object names properly. Note that double quotes are used, which is exactly what is needed to handle table names and alike:

```
test=# CREATE TABLE "Some stupid name" ("ID" int);
CREATE TABLE
test=# d "Some stupid name"
Table "public.Some stupid name"
 Column |  Type   | Modifiers
--------+---------+-----------
 ID     | integer |
```

Normally, all table names in PostgreSQL are lowercase. However, if double quotes are used, object names can contain capitalized letters. In general, it is not a good idea to do this kind of trickery as you have to use double quotes all the time in this case, which can be a bit inconvenient.

After a basic introduction to quoting, it is important to take a look at how NULL values are handled:

```
test=# SELECT quote_literal(NULL);
 quote_literal
---------------


(1 row)
```

If you call `quote_literal` function on a NULL value, it will simply return NULL. There is no need to take care of quoting in this case too.

PostgreSQL provides even more functions to explicitly take care of a NULL value:

```
test=# SELECT  quote_nullable(123),
                  quote_nullable(NULL);
 quote_nullable | quote_nullable
----------------+----------------
 '123'          | NULL
(1 row)
```

It is not only possible to quote strings and object names. It is also possible to use PL/pgSQL onboard means to format and prepare entire queries. The beauty here is that you can use the `format` function to add parameters to a statement. Here is how it works:

```
CREATE FUNCTION simple_format ()
RETURNS text AS
$$
    DECLARE
            v_string        text;
            v_result        text;
    BEGIN
            v_string := format('SELECT schemaname
                            || '' .'' || tablename
                    FROM    pg_tables
                    WHERE %I = $1
                    AND %I = $2', 'schemaname', 'tablename');
            EXECUTE v_string USING 'public', 't_test' INTO v_result;
            RAISE NOTICE 'result: %', v_result;
            RETURN v_string;
    END;
$$ LANGUAGE 'plpgsql';
```

The names of the fields are passed to the `format` function. Finally the `USING` clause of the `EXECUTE` statement is here to add the parameters to the query, which is then executed. Again, the beauty here is that no SQL injection can happen.

Here is what happens:

```
test=# SELECT simple_format ();
NOTICE:   result: public .t_test
CONTEXT:  PL/pgSQL function simple_format() line 12 at RAISE
                        simple_format
-----------------------------------------------------------------
  SELECT schemaname                                              +
                            || ' .' || tablename +
                    FROM    pg_tables                             +
                    WHERE schemaname = $1                         +
                    AND tablename = $2
 (1 row)
```

As you can see, the debug message correctly displays the table including the schema and correctly returns the query.

Managing scopes

After dealing with quoting and basic security (SQL injection) in general, I want to shift your focus to another important topic: scopes.

Just like most popular programming languages I am aware of, PL/pgSQL uses variables depending on their context. Variables are defined in the DECLARE statement of a function. However, PL/pgSQL allows you to nest a DECLARE statement:

```
CREATE FUNCTION scope_test ()
RETURNS int AS
$$
    DECLARE
            i       int     := 0;
    BEGIN
            RAISE NOTICE 'i1: %', i;

            DECLARE
                    i       int;
            BEGIN
                    RAISE NOTICE 'i2: %', i;
            END;
            RETURN i;
    END;
$$ LANGUAGE 'plpgsql';
```

In the DECLARE statement, a variable i is defined and a value is assigned to it. Then, i is displayed. The output will of course be 0. Then a second DECLARE statement starts. It contains an additional incarnation of i, which is not assigned a value. Therefore, the value will be NULL. Note that PostgreSQL will now display the inner i. Here is what happens:

```
test=# SELECT scope_test();
NOTICE:  i1: 0
CONTEXT:  PL/pgSQL function scope_test() line 5 at RAISE
NOTICE:  i2: <NULL>
CONTEXT:  PL/pgSQL function scope_test() line 10 at RAISE
 scope_test
------------
          0
(1 row)
```

As expected, the debug messages will show 0 and NULL.

PostgreSQL allows you to do all kinds of trickery. However, it is strongly recommended to keep your code simple and easy to read.

Understanding advanced error handling

In every programming language, in every program, and in every module, error handling is an important thing. Everything is expected to go wrong once in a while, and therefore it is vital and of key importance to handle errors properly and professionally. In PL/pgSQL, you can use EXCEPTION blocks to handle errors. The idea is that in case the BEGIN block does something wrong, the EXCEPTION block will take care and handle the problem correctly. Just like many other languages such as Java, you can react on different types of errors and catch them separately.

In the following example, the code might run into a division by zero problem. The goal is to catch this error and react accordingly:

```
CREATE FUNCTION error_test1(int, int)
RETURNS int AS
$$
    BEGIN
        RAISE NOTICE 'debug message: % / %', $1, $2;
            BEGIN
                RETURN $1 / $2;
            EXCEPTION
                WHEN division_by_zero THEN
                    RAISE NOTICE 'division by zero detected: %',
                                sqlerrm;
                WHEN others THEN
                    RAISE NOTICE 'some other error: %',
                                sqlerrm;
            END;

            RAISE NOTICE 'all errors handled';
            RETURN 0;
    END;
$$ LANGUAGE 'plpgsql';
```

The BEGIN block can clearly throw an error. However, the EXCEPTION block catches the error we are looking at and also takes care of all other potential problems that can unexpectedly pop up.

Technically, this is more or less the same as a savepoint, and therefore the error does not cause the entire transaction to fail completely. Only the block causing the error will be subject to a mini roll back.

By inspecting the `sqlerrm` variable, you can also have direct access to the error message itself. Let us run the code:

```
test=# SELECT error_test1(9, 0);
NOTICE:   debug message: 9 / 0
CONTEXT:  PL/pgSQL function error_test1(integer,integer) line 3 at RAISE
NOTICE:   division by zero detected: division by zero
CONTEXT:  PL/pgSQL function error_test1(integer,integer) line 9 at RAISE
NOTICE:   all errors handled
CONTEXT:  PL/pgSQL function error_test1(integer,integer) line 14 at RAISE
 error_test1
--------------
            0
(1 row)
```

PostgreSQL catches the exception and shows the message in the EXCEPTION block. PostgreSQL is already kind enough to tell us in which line the error has happened, which makes it a lot easier to debug and fix the code in case it is broken.

In some cases, it can also make sense to raise your own exception. As you might expect, this is easy to do:

```
RAISE unique_violation
    USING MESSAGE = 'Duplicate user ID: ' || user_id;
```

On top of what you have already seen, PostgreSQL offers many predefined error codes and exceptions. The following page contains a complete list of those error messages: `https://www.postgresql.org/docs/9.6/static/errcodes-appendix.html`.

Making use of GET DIAGNOSTICS

Many of you who have used Oracle in the past might be familiar with the GET DIAGNOSTICS clause. The idea behind the GET DIAGNOSTICS clause is to allow users to see what is going on in the system. While the syntax might appear a bit strange to people who are used to modern code, it is still a valuable tool you can use to make your applications better.

From my point of view, there are two main tasks that the GET DIAGNOSTICS clause can be used for:

- Inspecting the row count
- Fetching context information and getting a backtrace

Inspecting the row count is definitely something you will need during everyday programming. Extracting context information will be useful if you want to debug applications.

The following example shows how the GET DIAGNOSTICS clause can be used inside your code:

```
CREATE FUNCTION get_diag()
RETURNS int AS
$$
    DECLARE
            rc              int;

            _sqlstate       text;
            _message        text;
            _context        text;

    BEGIN
            EXECUTE 'SELECT * FROM generate_series(1, 10)';
            GET DIAGNOSTICS rc = ROW_COUNT;
            RAISE NOTICE 'row count: %', rc;

            SELECT rc / 0;
    EXCEPTION
            WHEN OTHERS THEN

                    GET STACKED DIAGNOSTICS
                            _sqlstate = returned_sqlstate,
                            _message = message_text,
                            _context = pg_exception_context;
                    RAISE NOTICE 'sqlstate: %, message: %,
                            context: [%]',
                            _sqlstate, _message,
                            replace(_context, E'n', ' <- ');
            RETURN rc;
    END;
$$ LANGUAGE 'plpgsql';
```

The first thing after declaring those variables is to execute an SQL statement and ask the GET DIAGNOSTICS clause for a row count, which is then displayed in a debug message. Then the function forces PL/pgSQL to error out. Once this happens, I am using the GET DIAGNOSTICS clause to extract information from the server to display it.

Here is what happens:

```
test=# SELECT get_diag();
NOTICE:   row count: 10
CONTEXT:   PL/pgSQL function get_diag() line 12 at RAISE
NOTICE:   sqlstate: 22012,
            message: division by zero,
            context: [SQL statement "SELECT rc / 0"
                    <- PL/pgSQL function get_diag() line 14 at
                          SQL statement]
CONTEXT:   PL/pgSQL function get_diag() line 22 at RAISE
 get_diag
-----------
       10
(1 row)
```

As you can see, the GET DIAGNOSTICS clause gives us quite detailed information about what is going on in the system.

Using cursors to fetch data in chunks

If you execute SQL, the database will calculate the result and send it to your application. Once the entire result set has been sent to the client, the application can continue to do its job. The problem is just: what happens if the result set is so large that it does not fit into the memory anymore? What if the database returns 10 billion rows? The client application usually cannot handle so much data at once and actually it should not. The solution to the problem is a cursor. The idea behind a cursor is that data is generated only when it is needed (when FETCH is called). Therefore, the application can already start to consume data while it is actually being generated by the database. On top of that, the memory required to perform an operation is a lot lower.

When it comes to PL/pgSQL, cursors also play a major role. Whenever you loop over a result set, PostgreSQL will internally use a cursor automatically. The advantage is that the memory consumption of your applications will be reduced dramatically and there is hardly a chance of ever running out of memory due to processing large amounts of data. There are various ways to use cursors. Here is the most simplistic one:

```
CREATE FUNCTION c (int)
RETURNS setof text AS
$$
    DECLARE
            v_rec            record;
    BEGIN
            FOR v_rec IN SELECT tablename FROM pg_tables LIMIT $1
            LOOP
                    RETURN NEXT v_rec.tablename;
            END LOOP;

            RETURN;
    END;
$$ LANGUAGE 'plpgsql';
```

This code is interesting for two reasons. First of all, it is a **set returning function** (**SRF**). It produces an entire column and not just a single row. The way to achieve this is to use setof variable instead of just the datatype. The RETURN NEXT clause will build up the result set until we have reached the end. The RETURN clause will tell PostgreSQL that we want to leave the function and that the result is done.

The second important issue is that looping over the cursor will automatically create an internal cursor. In other words, there is no need to be afraid that you could potentially run out of memory. PostgreSQL will optimize the query in a way that it tries to produce the first 10% of the data (defined by the cursor_tuple_fraction variable) as fast as possible.

Here is what the query will return:

```
test=# SELECT * FROM c(3);
c
---------------
 t_test
 pg_statistic
 pg_type
(3 rows)
```

In this example, there will simply be a list of random tables. If the result differs on your side, this is somewhat expected.

What you have just seen is, in my opinion, the most frequent and most common way to use implicit cursors in PL/pgSQL. The following example shows an older mechanism that many people from Oracle might know:

```
CREATE FUNCTION d (int)
RETURNS setof text AS
$$
    DECLARE
            v_cur               refcursor;
            v_data              text;
    BEGIN
            OPEN v_cur FOR SELECT tablename FROM pg_tables LIMIT $1;

            WHILE true
            LOOP
                    FETCH v_cur INTO v_data;
                    IF FOUND THEN
                            RETURN NEXT v_data;
                    ELSE
                            RETURN;
                    END IF;
            END LOOP;
    END;
$$ LANGUAGE 'plpgsql';
```

In this example, the cursor is explicitly declared and opened. Inside, the loop data is then explicitly fetched and returned to the caller. Basically, the query does exactly the same thing—it is merely a matter of taste which syntax developers actually prefer.

Do you still have the feeling that you don't know enough about cursors yet? There is more; here is a third option to do exactly the same thing:

```
CREATE FUNCTION e (int)
RETURNS setof text AS
$$
    DECLARE
            v_cur CURSOR (param1 int) FOR
                    SELECT tablename FROM pg_tables LIMIT param1;
            v_data              text;
    BEGIN
            OPEN v_cur ($1);

            WHILE true
            LOOP
                    FETCH v_cur INTO v_data;
                    IF FOUND THEN
                            RETURN NEXT v_data;
```

```
                        ELSE
                             RETURN;
                        END IF;
                END LOOP;
        END;
$$ LANGUAGE 'plpgsql';
```

In this case, the cursor is fed with an integer parameter, which comes directly from the function call (`$1`).

Sometimes, a cursor is not used up by the stored procedure itself but returned for later use. In this case, you can return a simple use `refcursor` as the return value:

```
CREATE OR REPLACE FUNCTION cursor_test(c refcursor)
RETURNS refcursor AS                                        $$
BEGIN                                                 OPEN c FOR
SELECT * FROM generate_series(1, 10) AS id;
RETURN c;                                                  END;
$$ LANGUAGE plpgsql;
```

The logic here is quite simple. The name of the cursor is passed to the function. Then the cursor is opened and returned. The beauty here is that the query behind the cursor can be created on the fly and compiled dynamically.

The application can fetch from the cursor just like from any other application. Here is how it works. Note that it works only when a transaction block is used:

```
test=# BEGIN;
BEGIN
test=# SELECT cursor_test('mytest');
 cursor_test
-------------
 mytest
(1 row)

test=# FETCH NEXT FROM mytest;
 id
----
  1
(1 row)

test=# FETCH NEXT FROM mytest;
 id
----
  2
(1 row)
```

Actually, in this section, you learned that cursors will only produce data as it is consumed. This holds true for most queries. However, I have added a little catch to this example; whenever an SRF is used, the entire result has to be materialized. It is not created on the fly, but at once. The reason is that, SQL must be able to re-scan a relation, which is easily possible in the case of a normal table. However, for functions the situation is different. Therefore, an SRF is always calculated and materialized, making the cursor in this example totally useless. In other words, be careful when writing functions—in some cases, danger is hidden in nifty details.

Utilizing composite types

In most other database systems, stored procedures are only used with primitive datatypes such as integer, numeric, varchar, and so on. However, PostgreSQL is very different. You can basically use all datatypes available to you. This includes primitive as well as composite and custom types. There are simply no restrictions as far as datatypes are concerned. To unleash the full power of PostgreSQL, composite types are highly important and are often used by extensions which can be found on the Internet.

The following example shows how a composite type can be passed to a function and how it can be used internally. Finally the composite type will be returned again:

```
CREATE TYPE my_cool_type AS (s text, t text);

CREATE FUNCTION f (my_cool_type)
RETURNS my_cool_type AS
$$
    DECLARE
            v_row              my_cool_type;
    BEGIN
            RAISE NOTICE 'schema: (%) / table: (%)', $1.s, $1.t;
            SELECT  schemaname, tablename INTO v_row
                FROM    pg_tables
                WHERE   tablename = trim($1.t)
                        AND schemaname = trim($1.s)
                LIMIT 1 ;
            RETURN v_row;
    END;
$$ LANGUAGE 'plpgsql';
```

The main issue here is that you can simply use $1.field_name to access the composite type. Returning the type is not hard either. You just have to assemble the composite type variable on the fly and return it just like any other datatype. You can even use arrays or even more complex structures easily.

The following listing shows what PostgreSQL will return:

```
test=# SELECT (f).s, (f).t
          FROM   f ('("public", "t_test")'::my_cool_type);
NOTICE:   schema: (public) / table: ( t_test)
CONTEXT:  PL/pgSQL function f(my_cool_type) line 5 at RAISE
    s   |   t
--------+---------
 public | t_test
(1 row)
```

Writing triggers in PL/pgSQL

Server-side code is especially popular if you want to react on certain events happening in the database. A trigger allows you to call a function if an INSERT, UPDATE, DELETE or a TRUNCATE clause happens on a table. The function called by the trigger can then modify the data changed in your table or simply perform some operation needed.

In PostgreSQL, triggers have become ever more powerful over the years and provide a rich set of features:

```
test=# h CREATE TRIGGER
Command:      CREATE TRIGGER
Description: define a new trigger
Syntax:
CREATE [ CONSTRAINT ] TRIGGER name { BEFORE | AFTER | INSTEAD OF }
          { event [ OR ... ] }
    ON table_name
    [ FROM referenced_table_name ]
    [ NOT DEFERRABLE | [ DEFERRABLE ]
     [ INITIALLY IMMEDIATE | INITIALLY DEFERRED ] ]
    [ FOR [ EACH ] { ROW | STATEMENT } ]
    [ WHEN ( condition ) ]
    EXECUTE PROCEDURE function_name ( arguments )
```

Here, event can be one of:

```
    INSERT
      UPDATE [ OF column_name [, ... ] ]
      DELETE
      TRUNCATE
```

The first thing to observe is that a trigger is always fired for a table of a view and calls a function. A trigger has a name and can happen before or after an event. The beauty of PostgreSQL is that you can have as many triggers on a single table as you want. While this does not come as a surprise to hardcore PostgreSQL users, I want to point out that this is not possible in many expensive commercial database engines still in use around the world.

If there is more than one trigger on the same table, the following rule was introduced many years ago in PostgreSQL 7.3: triggers are fired in alphabetical order. First, all those before triggers happen in alphabetical order. Then PostgreSQL performs the row operation the trigger has been fired for and continues executing the after triggers in alphabetical order. In other words, the execution order of triggers is absolutely deterministic and the number of triggers is basically unlimited.

Triggers can modify data before or after the actual modification has happened. In general, this is a good way to verify data and to error out in case some custom restrictions are violated. The following example shows a trigger that is fired in INSERT clause and which changes data added to the table:

```
CREATE TABLE t_sensor (
        id              serial,
        ts              timestamp,
        temperature     numeric
);
```

Our table just stores a couple of values. The goal now is to call a function as soon as a row is inserted:

```
CREATE OR REPLACE FUNCTION trig_func()
RETURNS trigger AS
$$
        BEGIN
                IF      NEW.temperature < -273
                THEN
                        NEW.temperature := 0;
                END IF;

                RETURN NEW;
        END;
$$ LANGUAGE 'plpgsql';
```

As stated previously, the trigger will always call a function, which allows you to nicely abstract code. The important thing here is that the trigger function has to return `trigger`. To access the row you are about to insert, you can access the NEW variable.

> Note, INSERT and UPDATE triggers always provide a NEW variable. UPDATE and DELETE will offer a variable called OLD. Those variables contain the row you are about to modify.

In my example, the code checks whether the temperature is too low. If it is, the value is not okay; it is dynamically adjusted. To ensure that the modified row can be used, NEW is simply returned. If there is a second trigger called after this one, the next function call will already see the modified row.

In the next step, the trigger can be created:

```
CREATE TRIGGER sensor_trig
    BEFORE INSERT ON t_sensor
    FOR EACH ROW
    EXECUTE PROCEDURE trig_func();
```

Here is what the trigger will do:

```
test=# INSERT INTO t_sensor (ts, temperature)
            VALUES ('2017-05-04 14:43', -300)
            RETURNING *;
 id |          ts         | temperature
----+---------------------+-------------
  1 | 2017-05-04 14:43:00 |           0
(1 row)

INSERT 0 1
```

As you can see, the value has been adjusted correctly. The content of the table shows 0 for the temperature.

If you are using triggers, you should be aware of the fact that a trigger knows a lot about itself. It can access a couple of variables that allow you to write more sophisticated code and to achieve better abstraction.

Let us drop the trigger first:

```
test=# DROP TRIGGER sensor_trig ON t_sensor;
DROP TRIGGER
```

Then a new function can be added:

```
CREATE OR REPLACE FUNCTION trig_demo()
RETURNS trigger AS
$$
        BEGIN
                RAISE NOTICE 'TG_NAME: %', TG_NAME;
                RAISE NOTICE 'TG_RELNAME: %', TG_RELNAME;
                RAISE NOTICE 'TG_TABLE_SCHEMA: %',
                        TG_TABLE_SCHEMA;
                RAISE NOTICE 'TG_TABLE_NAME: %', TG_TABLE_NAME;
                RAISE NOTICE 'TG_WHEN: %', TG_WHEN;
                RAISE NOTICE 'TG_LEVEL: %', TG_LEVEL;
                RAISE NOTICE 'TG_OP: %', TG_OP;
                RAISE NOTICE 'TG_NARGS: %', TG_NARGS;
                -- RAISE NOTICE 'TG_ARGV: %', TG_NAME;

                RETURN NEW;
        END;
$$ LANGUAGE 'plpgsql';
```

All those variables used here are predefined and are available by default. All our code does is it displays them so that we can see the content:

```
CREATE TRIGGER demo_trigger
BEFORE INSERT ON t_sensor
FOR EACH ROW EXECUTE PROCEDURE trig_demo();

test=# INSERT INTO t_sensor (ts, temperature)
        VALUES ('2017-05-04 14:43', -300) RETURNING *;
NOTICE:  TG_NAME: demo_trigger
NOTICE:  TG_RELNAME: t_sensor
NOTICE:  TG_TABLE_SCHEMA: public
NOTICE:  TG_TABLE_NAME: t_sensor
NOTICE:  TG_WHEN: BEFORE
NOTICE:  TG_LEVEL: ROW
NOTICE:  TG_OP: INSERT
NOTICE:  TG_NARGS: 0
 id |         ts          | temperature
----+---------------------+-------------
  2 | 2017-05-04 14:43:00 |        -300
(1 row)

INSERT 0 1
```

What you see here is that the trigger knows its name, the table it has been fired for, and a lot more. If you want to apply similar actions of various tables, those variables help you to avoid duplicate code by just writing a single function, which can then be used for all tables you are interested in.

Introducing PL/Perl

There is a lot more to say about PL/pgSQL. However, as I've only got 40 pages to cover this topic, it is time to move on to the next procedural language. PL/Perl has been adopted by many people as the ideal language to do string crunching. As you might know, Perl is famous for its string manipulation capabilities and therefore, still fairly popular after all these years.

To enable PL/Perl, you have two choices:

```
[postgres@linuxpc ~]$ createlang plperl test
[postgres@linuxpc ~]$ createlang plperlu test
```

You can deploy trusted or untrusted Perl. If you want both, you have to enable both languages.

To show you how PL/Perl works, I have implemented a function that simply parses an e-mail address and returns true or false. Here is how it works:

```
test=# CREATE OR REPLACE FUNCTION verify_email(text)
RETURNS boolean AS
$$
        if      ($_[0] =~ /^[a-z0-9.]+@[a-z0-9.-]+$/)
        {
                return true;
        }
        return false;
$$ LANGUAGE 'plperl';
CREATE FUNCTION
```

A `text` parameter is passed to the function. Inside the function, all those input parameters can be accessed using `$_`. In this example, the regular expression is executed and the function returns.

The function can be called just like any other procedure written in any other language:

```
test=# SELECT verify_email('hs@cybertec.at');
 verify_email
--------------
 t
(1 row)

test=# SELECT verify_email('totally wrong');
 verify_email
--------------
 f
(1 row)
```

Keep in mind that you cannot load packages and so on if you are inside a trusted function. For example, if you want to use the w command to find words, Perl will internally load utf8.pm, which is of course not allowed.

Using PL/Perl for datatype abstraction

As stated in this chapter, functions in PostgreSQL are pretty universal and can be used in many different contexts. If you want to use functions to improve data quality, you can use CREATE DOMAIN clause:

```
test=# h CREATE DOMAIN
Command:     CREATE DOMAIN
Description: define a new domain
Syntax:
CREATE DOMAIN name [ AS ] data_type
    [ COLLATE collation ]
    [ DEFAULT expression ]
    [ constraint [ ... ] ]

where constraint is:

[ CONSTRAINT constraint_name ]
{ NOT NULL | NULL | CHECK (expression) }
```

In this example, the PL/Perl function will be used to create a domain called email, which in turn can be used as a datatype.

The following listing shows how the domain can be created:

```
test=# CREATE DOMAIN email AS text
            CHECK (verify_email(VALUE) = true);
CREATE DOMAIN
```

As mentioned previously, the domain functions just like a normal datatype:

```
test=# CREATE TABLE t_email (id serial, data email);
CREATE TABLE
```

The Perl function ensures that nothing violating our checks can be inserted into the database, as the following example demonstrates successfully:

```
test=# INSERT INTO t_email (data)
            VALUES ('somewhere@example.com');
INSERT 0 1
test=# INSERT INTO t_email (data)
            VALUES ('somewhere_wrong_example.com');
ERROR:  value for domain email violates check
            constraint "email_check"
```

Perl might be a good option to do string crunching, but as always you have to decide whether you want this code in the database directly or not.

Deciding between PL/Perl and PL/PerlU

So far, the Perl code has not opened any security related problems because all I did was regular expressions. The question now is: what if somebody tries to do something nasty inside the Perl function? As stated already, PL/Perl will simply error out:

```
test=# CREATE OR REPLACE FUNCTION test_security()
RETURNS boolean AS
$$
        use strict;
        my $fp = open("/etc/password", "r");

        return false;
$$ LANGUAGE 'plperl';
ERROR:  'open' trapped by operation mask at line 3.
CONTEXT:  compilation of PL/Perl function "test_security"
```

PL/Perl will complain as soon as you try to create the function. An error will be displayed instantly.

If you really want to run untrusted code in Perl, you have to use PL/PerlU:

```
test=# CREATE OR REPLACE FUNCTION first_line()
RETURNS text AS
$$
        open(my $fh, '<:encoding(UTF-8)', "/etc/passwd")
            or elog(NOTICE, "Could not open file '$filename' $!");
```

```
        my $row = <$fh>;
        close($fh);

        return $row;
$$ LANGUAGE 'plperlu';
CREATE FUNCTION
```

Basically, the procedure is the same. It returns a string. However, it is allowed to do everything. The only difference is that the function is marked as `plperlu`.

The result is somewhat unsurprising:

```
test=# SELECT first_line();
          first_line
-----------------------------------
 root:x:0:0:root:/root:/bin/bash+

(1 row)
```

Making use of the SPI interface

Once in a while, your Perl procedure has to do database work. Remember, the function is part of the database connection. Therefore, it is pointless to actually create a database connection. To talk to the database, the PostgreSQL server infrastructure provides the SPI interface, which is a C interface to talk to database internals. All procedural languages that help you to run server-side code use this interface to expose functionality to you. PL/Perl does the same, and in this section, you will learn how to use the Perl wrapper around the SPI interface.

The most important thing you might want to do is simply run SQL and retrieve the number of rows fetched. The `spi_exec_query` function is here to do exactly that. The first parameter passed to the function is the query. The second parameter has the number of rows you actually want to retrieve. For simplicity reasons, I decided to fetch all of them:

```
test=# CREATE OR REPLACE FUNCTION spi_sample(int)
RETURNS void AS
$$
        my $rv = spi_exec_query("
                        SELECT *
                        FROM generate_series(1, $_[0])", $_[0]);
        elog(NOTICE, "rows fetched: " . $rv->{processed});
        elog(NOTICE, "status: " . $rv->{status});

        return;
$$ LANGUAGE 'plperl';
```

SPI will nicely execute the query and display the number of rows. The important thing here is that all stored procedure languages provide a means to send log messages. In the case of PL/Perl, this function is called `elog` and takes two parameters. The first one defines the importance of the message (INFO, NOTICE, WARNING, ERROR, and so on) and the second parameter contains the actual message.

The following message shows what the query returns:

```
test=# SELECT spi_sample(9);
NOTICE:   rows fetched: 9
NOTICE:   status: SPI_OK_SELECT
 spi_sample
------------

(1 row)
```

Using SPI for set returning functions

In many cases, you don't just want to execute some SQL and forget about it. In most cases, a procedure will loop over the result and do something with it. The following example will show how you can loop over the output of a query. On top of that, I decided to beef up the example a bit and make the function return a composite datatype. Working with composite types in Perl is very easy because you can simply stuff the data into a hash and return it. The `return_next` function will gradually build up the result set until the function is terminated with a simple return statement.

The example in this listing generates a table consisting of random values:

```
CREATE TYPE random_type AS (a float8, b float8);

CREATE OR REPLACE FUNCTION spi_srf_perl(int)
RETURNS setof random_type AS
$$
        my $rv = spi_query("SELECT random() AS a, random() AS b
                            FROM generate_series(1, $_[0])");
        while (defined (my $row = spi_fetchrow($rv)))
        {
                elog(NOTICE, "data: " . $row->{a}
                        . " / " . $row->{b});
                return_next({
                        a_col => $row->{a},
                        b_col => $row->{b}
                });
        }
```

```
        return;
$$ LANGUAGE 'plperl';
CREATE FUNCTION
```

First, the `spi_query` function is executed and a loop using the `spi_fetchrow` function is started. Inside the loop, the composite type will be assembled and stuffed into the result set.

As expected, the function will return a set of random values:

```
test=# SELECT * FROM spi_srf_perl(3);
NOTICE:   data: 0.154673356097192 / 0.278830723837018
CONTEXT:   PL/Perl function "spi_srf_perl"
NOTICE:   data: 0.615888888947666 / 0.632620786316693
CONTEXT:   PL/Perl function "spi_srf_perl"
NOTICE:   data: 0.910436692181975 / 0.753427186980844
CONTEXT:   PL/Perl function "spi_srf_perl"
       a_col        |        b_col
--------------------+--------------------
 0.154673356097192 | 0.278830723837018
 0.615888888947666 | 0.632620786316693
 0.910436692181975 | 0.753427186980844
(3 rows)
```

Keep in mind that set returning functions have to be materialized so that the entire result set will be stored in memory.

Escaping in PL/Perl and support functions

So far, we only used integers, so SQL injection or special table names were not an issue. Basically, the following functions are available:

`quote_literal`: It returns a string quote as string literal

`quote_nullable`: It quotes a string

`quote_ident`: It quotes SQL identifiers (object names, and so on)

`decode_bytea`: It decodes a PostgreSQL byte array field

`encode_bytea`: It encodes data and turns it into a byte array

`encode_literal_array`: It encodes an array of literals

`encode_typed_literal`: It converts a Perl variable to the value of the datatype passed as a second argument and returns a string representation of this value

`encode_array_constructor`: It returns the contents of the referenced array as a string in array constructor format

`looks_like_number`: It returns true if a string looks like a number

`is_array_ref`: It returns true if something is an array reference

These functions are always available and can be called directly without having to include any library.

Sharing data across function calls

Sometimes it is necessary to share data across calls. The infrastructure has means to actually do that. In Perl, a hash can be used to store whatever data is needed:

```
CREATE FUNCTION perl_shared(text)
RETURNS int AS
$$
    if      (!defined $_SHARED{$_[0]})
    {
            $_SHARED{$_[0]} = 0;
    }
    else
    {
            $_SHARED{$_[0]}++;
    }

    return $_SHARED{$_[0]};
$$ LANGUAGE 'plperl';
```

The `$_SHARED` variable will be initialized with `0` as soon as we figure out that the key passed to the function is not there yet. For every other call, `1` is added to the counter, leaving us with the following output:

```
test=# SELECT perl_shared('some_key') FROM generate_series(1, 3);
 perl_shared
-------------
           0
           1
           2
(3 rows)
```

In case of a more complex statement, the developer usually does not know in which order the functions will be called. It is important to keep that in mind. In most cases, you cannot rely on an execution order.

Writing triggers in Perl

Every stored procedure language shipped with the core of PostgreSQL allows you to write triggers in that language. The same of course applies to Perl. As the possible length of this chapter is limited, I decided not to include an example of a trigger written in Perl but instead to point you to the official PostgreSQL documentation: `https://www.postgresql.org/docs/9.6/static/plperl-triggers.html`.

Basically, writing a trigger in Perl does not differ from writing one in PL/pgSQL. All predefined variables are in place, and as far as return values are concerned, the rules apply in every stored procedure language.

Introducing PL/Python

If you don't happen to be a Perl expert, PL/Python might be the right thing for you. Python has been part of the PostgreSQL infrastructure for a long time and is therefore a solid, well-tested implementation.

When it comes to PL/Python, there is one thing you have to keep in mind: PL/Python is only available as an untrusted language. From a security point of view, it is important to keep that in mind at all times.

To enable PL/Python, you can run the following line from your command line. `test` is the name of the database you want to use with PL/Python:

```
createlang plpythonu test
```

Once the language is enabled, it is already possible to write code.

Alternatively, you can use `CREATE LANGUAGE` clause of course. Also keep in mind that in order to use server-side languages, PostgreSQL packages containing those languages are needed (`postgresql-plpython-9.6` and so on).

Writing simple PL/Python code

In this section, you will learn to write simple Python procedures. The example discussed here is quite simple: if you are visiting a client by car in Austria, you can deduct 42 euro cents per kilometer as expenses in order to reduce your income tax. So what the function does is to take the number of kilometers and return the amount of money we can deduct from our tax bill. Here is how it works:

```
CREATE OR REPLACE FUNCTION calculate_deduction(km float)
RETURNS numeric AS
$$
        if      km <= 0:
                elog(ERROR, 'invalid number of kilometers')
        else:
                return km * 0.42
$$ LANGUAGE 'plpythonu';
```

The function ensures that only positive values are accepted. Finally, the result is calculated and returned. As you can see, the way a Python function is passed to PostgreSQL does not really differ from Perl or PL/pgSQL.

Using the SPI interface

As with all procedural languages, PL/Python gives you access to the SPI interface. The following example shows how numbers can be added up:

```
CREATE FUNCTION add_numbers(rows_desired integer)
        RETURNS integer AS
$$
        mysum = 0

        cursor = plpy.cursor("SELECT * FROM
                  generate_series(1, %d) AS id" % (rows_desired))

        while True:
                rows = cursor.fetch(rows_desired)
                if not rows:
                        break
                for row in rows:
                        mysum += row['id']
        return mysum
$$ LANGUAGE 'plpythonu';
```

When you try this example out, make sure that the call to cursor is actually a single line. Python is all about indentation, so it does make a difference if your code consists of one or of two lines.

Once the cursor has been created, we can loop over it and add up those numbers. The columns inside those rows can easily be referenced using column names.

Calling the function will return the desired result:

```
test=# SELECT add_numbers(10);
 add_numbers
--------------
          55
(1 row)
```

If you want to inspect the result set of an SQL statement, PL/Python offers various functions to retrieve more information from the result. Again, those functions are wrappers around what SPI offers on the C level.

The following function inspects a result more closely:

```
CREATE OR REPLACE FUNCTION result_diag(rows_desired integer)
        RETURNS integer AS
$$
        rv = plpy.execute("SELECT *
                FROM generate_series(1, %d) AS id" % (rows_desired))
        plpy.notice(rv.nrows())
        plpy.notice(rv.status())
        plpy.notice(rv.colnames())
        plpy.notice(rv.coltypes())
        plpy.notice(rv.coltypmods())
        plpy.notice(rv.__str__())

        return 0
$$ LANGUAGE 'plpythonu';
```

The nrows() function will display the number of rows. The status() function tells us whether everything worked out fine. The colnames() function returns a list of columns. The coltypes() function returns the object IDs of the datatypes in the result set. 23 is the internal number of integer:

```
test=# SELECT typname FROM pg_type WHERE oid = 23;
 typname
----------
 int4
(1 row)
```

Then comes `typmod`. Consider something like `varchar(20)`: the configuration part if the type is what `typmod` is all about.

Finally there is a function to return the entire thing as a string for debugging purposes. Calling the function will return the following result:

```
test=# SELECT result_diag(3);
NOTICE:   3
NOTICE:   5
NOTICE:   ['id']
NOTICE:   [23]
NOTICE:   [-1]
NOTICE:   <PLyResult status=5 nrows=3 rows=[{'id': 1},
                       {'id': 2}, {'id': 3}]>
 result_diag
-------------
           0
(1 row)
```

There are many more functions in the SPI interface that help you to execute SQL.

Handling errors

Once in a while, you might have to catch an error. Of course, this is also possible in Python. The following example shows how this works:

```
CREATE OR REPLACE FUNCTION trial_error()
        RETURNS text AS
$$
    try:
        rv = plpy.execute("SELECT surely_a_syntax_error")
    except plpy.SPIError:
        return "we caught the error"
    else:
        return "all fine"
$$ LANGUAGE 'plpythonu';
```

You can use a normal `try`/`except` block and access `plpy` to treat the error you want to catch. The function can then return normally without destroying your transaction:

```
test=# SELECT trial_error();
     trial_error
---------------------
 we caught the error
(1 row)
```

Remember, PL/Python has full access to the internals of PostgreSQL. Therefore, it can also expose all kinds of errors to your procedure. Here is an example:

```
except spiexceptions.DivisionByZero:
    return "found a division by zero"
except spiexceptions.UniqueViolation:
    return "found a unique violation"
except plpy.SPIError, e:
    return "other error, SQLSTATE %s" % e.sqlstate
```

Catching errors in Python is really easy and can help prevent your functions from failing.

Improving stored procedure performance

So far, you have seen how to write basic stored procedures as well as triggers in various languages. Of course, there are many more languages supported. Some of the most prominent ones are PL/R (R is a powerful statistics package) and PL/v8 (which is based on the Google JavaScript engine). However, those languages are beyond the scope of this chapter (regardless of their usefulness).

In this section, we will focus on improving the performance of a stored procedure. There are a couple of areas in which we can speed up processing:

- Reduce the number of calls
- Use cached plans
- Give hints to the optimizer

In this chapter, all three main areas will be discussed.

Reducing the number of function calls

In many cases, performance is bad because functions are called way too often. I cannot stress this point too much: calling things too often is the main reason for bad performance. When you create a function, you can choose from three types of functions: volatile, stable, and immutable. Here is an example:

```
test=# SELECT random(), random();
      random       |       random
-------------------+-------------------
 0.276252629235387 | 0.710661871358752
(1 row)
```

```
test=# SELECT now(), now();
              now              |              now
-------------------------------+-------------------------------
 2016-12-16 12:57:17.135751+01 | 2016-12-16 12:57:17.135751+01
(1 row)

test=# SELECT pi();
        pi
------------------
 3.14159265358979
(1 row)
```

A volatile function means that the function cannot be optimized away. It has to be executed over and over again. A volatile function can also be the reason why a certain index is not used. By default, every function is considered to be volatile. A stable function will always return the same data within the same transaction. It can be optimized and calls can be removed. The now() function is a good example of a stable function; within the same transaction it returns the same data.

Immutable functions are the gold standard because they allow for most optimizations, which is because they always return the same result given the same input. As a first step to optimizing functions, always make sure that they are marked correctly by adding volatile, stable, or immutable to the end of the definition.

Using cached plans

In PostgreSQL, a query is executed using four stages:

- **The parser**: It checks the syntax
- **Rewrite system**: It take cares of rules, and so on
- **Optimizer/planner**: It optimizes the query
- **Executor**: It executes the plan provided by the planner

If the query is short, the first three steps are relatively time consuming compared to the real execution time. Therefore, it can make sense to cache execution plans. PL/pgSQL basically does all the plan caching for you automatically behind the scenes. You don't have to care. PL/Perl and PL/Python will give you the choice. The SPI interface provides functions to handle and run prepared queries, so the programmer has the choice whether a query should be prepared or not. In the case of long queries, it can actually make sense to use unprepared queries—short queries should usually always be prepared to reduce the internal overhead.

Assigning costs to functions

From the optimizer point of view, a function is basically just like an operator. PostgreSQL will also treat the costs the same way as if it was a standard operator. The problem is just this: adding two numbers is usually cheaper than intersecting coastlines using some PostGIS-provided function. The thing is that the optimizer does not know whether a function is cheap or expensive. Fortunately, we can tell the optimizer to make functions cheaper or more expensive:

```
test=# h CREATE FUNCTION
Command:      CREATE FUNCTION
Description: define a new function
Syntax:
CREATE [ OR REPLACE ] FUNCTION
. . .
    | COST execution_cost
    | ROWS result_rows
. . .
```

The COST parameter indicates how much more expensive than a standard operator your operator really is. It is a multiplier for cpu_operator_cost and not a static value. In general, the default value is 100 unless the function has been written in C.

The second parameter is the ROWS parameter. By default, PostgreSQL assumes that a set returning function will return 1,000 rows because the system has no way to figure out precisely how many rows there will be. The ROWS parameter allows developers to tell PostgreSQL about the expected number of rows.

Using stored procedures

In PostgreSQL, stored procedures can be used for pretty much everything. In this chapter, you have already learned about CREATE DOMAIN clause and so on, but it is also possible to create your own operators, type casts, and even collations.

In this section, you will see how a simple type cast can be created and how it can be used to your advantage. To define the type cast, consider taking a look at CREATE CAST clause:

```
test=# h CREATE CAST
Command:      CREATE CAST
Description: define a new cast
Syntax:
CREATE CAST (source_type AS target_type)
    WITH FUNCTION function_name (argument_type [, ...])
```

```
    [ AS ASSIGNMENT | AS IMPLICIT ]

CREATE CAST (source_type AS target_type)
    WITHOUT FUNCTION
    [ AS ASSIGNMENT | AS IMPLICIT ]

CREATE CAST (source_type AS target_type)
    WITH INOUT
    [ AS ASSIGNMENT | AS IMPLICIT ]
```

Using this stuff is very simple. You simply tell PostgreSQL which procedure it is supposed to call to cast whatever type to your desired datatype.

In standard PostgreSQL, you cannot cast an IP address to Boolean. Therefore, it makes a good example. First the stored procedure has to be defined:

```
CREATE FUNCTION inet_to_boolean(inet)
RETURNS boolean AS
$$
        BEGIN
                RETURN true;
        END;
$$ LANGUAGE 'plpgsql';
```

For simplicity reasons, it returns true. However, you can use any code (of course) in any language to do the actual transformation.

In the next step, it is already possible to define the type cast:

```
CREATE CAST (inet AS boolean)
    WITH FUNCTION inet_to_boolean(inet)
    AS IMPLICIT;
```

The first thing is to tell PostgreSQL that we want to cast inet to boolean. Then the function is listed and we tell PostgreSQL that we prefer an implicit cast.

It is simply a straightforward process and we can test the cast:

```
test=# SELECT '192.168.0.34'::inet::boolean;
 bool
------
 t
(1 row)
```

Basically, the same logic can also be applied to define collations. Again a stored procedure can be used to perform whatever has to be done:

```
test=# h CREATE COLLATION
Command:    CREATE COLLATION
Description: define a new collation
Syntax:
CREATE COLLATION name (
    [ LOCALE = locale, ]
    [ LC_COLLATE = lc_collate, ]
    [ LC_CTYPE = lc_ctype ]
)
CREATE COLLATION name FROM existing_collation
```

Summary

In this chapter, you learned how to write stored procedures. After a theoretical introduction, our attention was focused on some selected features of PL/pgSQL. In addition to that, you learned how to use PL/Perl and PL/Python, which are simply two important languages provided by PostgreSQL. Of course, there are many more languages available. However, due to the limitations of the scope (and length) of this book, those could not be covered in detail. If you want to know more, check out the following website: `https://wik i.postgresql.org/wiki/PL_Matrix`.

In the next chapter, you will learn about PostgreSQL security. You will learn how to manage users and permissions in general. On top of that, you will also learn about network security.

8
Managing PostgreSQL Security

The previous chapter was all about stored procedures and writing server-side code. After introducing you to many important topics, it is now time to shift our focus to PostgreSQL security. You will learn how to secure a server and configure permissions.

The following topics will be covered:

- Configuring network access
- Managing authentication
- Handling users and roles
- Configuring database security
- Managing schemas, tables, and columns
- Row-level security

At the end of the chapter, you will be able to write good and efficient procedures.

Managing network security

Before moving on to real-world, practical examples, I want to briefly shift your attention to the various layers of security we will be dealing with. When dealing with security, it makes sense to keep those levels in mind in order to approach security-related issues in an organized way.

Here is my mental model:

- Bind addresses: `listen_addresses` in `postgresql.conf` file
- Host-based access control: `pg_hba.conf` file
- Instance-level permissions: Users, roles, database creation, login, and replication
- Database-level permissions: Connecting, creating schemas, and so on
- Schema-level permissions: Using schemas and creating objects inside a schema
- Table-level permissions: Selecting, inserting, updating, and so on
- Column-level permissions: Allowing or restricting access to columns
- Row-level security: Restricting access to rows

In order to read a value, PostgreSQL has to ensure that you have sufficient permissions on every level. The entire chain of permissions has to be correct.

Understanding bind addresses and connections

When you configure a PostgreSQL server, one of the first things you have to do is define remote access. By default, PostgreSQL does not accept remote connections. The important thing here is that PostgreSQL does not even reject the connection because it simple does not listen on the port. If you try to connect, the error message will actually come from the operating system because PostgreSQL does not care at all.

Assuming that there is a database server using default configuration on `192.168.0.123`, the following will happen:

```
iMac:~ hs$ telnet 192.168.0.123 5432
Trying 192.168.0.123...
telnet: connect to address 192.168.0.123: Connection refused
telnet: Unable to connect to remote host
```

Telnet tries to create a connection on port `5432` and will instantly be rejected by the remote box. From the outside, it looks as if PostgreSQL was not running at all.

The key to success can be found in the `postgresql.conf` file:

```
# - Connection Settings -

#listen_addresses = 'localhost'
        # what IP address(es) to listen on;
    # comma-separated list of addresses;
    # defaults to 'localhost'; use '*' for all
    # (change requires restart)
```

The `listen_addresses` setting will tell PostgreSQL which addresses to listen on. Technically speaking, those addresses are bind addresses. What does that actually mean? Suppose you have four network cards in your machine. You can listen on, say, three of those IP addresses. PostgreSQL takes requests to those three cards into account and does not listen on the fourth one. The port is simply closed.

> You have to put your server's IP address into `listen_addresses` and not the IPs of the clients.

If you put a `'*'` in, PostgreSQL will listen to every IP assigned to your machine.

> Keep in mind that changing `listen_addresses` requires a PostgreSQL service restart. It cannot be changed on the fly without a restart.

However, there are more settings related to connection management that are highly important to understand:

```
#port = 5432
                # (change requires restart)
max_connections = 100
                # (change requires restart)
# Note:  Increasing max_connections costs ~400 bytes of
#          shared memory per
# connection slot, plus lock space
#            (see max_locks_per_transaction).
#superuser_reserved_connections = 3
                # (change requires restart)
#unix_socket_directories = '/tmp'
                # comma-separated list of directories
                # (change requires restart)
#unix_socket_group = ''
                # (change requires restart)
#unix_socket_permissions = 0777
                # begin with 0 to use octal notation
                # (change requires restart)
```

First of all, PostgreSQL listens to a single TCP port (the default value is 5432). Keep in mind that PostgreSQL will listen on a single port only. Whenever a request comes in, the postmaster will fork and create a new process to handle the connection. By default, up to 100 normal connections are allowed. On top of that, three additional connections are reserved for superusers. This means that you can either have 100 connections plus 3 superusers or 103 superuser connections. Note that those connection-related settings will also need a restart. The reason for this is that a static amount of memory is allocated to shared memory, which cannot be changed on the fly.

Inspecting connections and performance

When I am doing consulting, many people ask whether raising the connection limit will have an impact on performance in general. The answer is: not much (there is always some overhead due to context switches and all that). It basically makes little difference how many connections there are. However, what does make a difference is the number of open snapshots. The more the number of open snapshots (not connections), the more the overhead on the database side. In other words, you can increase max_connections cheaply.

If you are interested in some real-world data, consider taking a look at one of my older blog posts: http://www.cybertec.at/max_connections-performance-impacts/.

Living in a world without TCP

In some cases, you might not want to use a network. It often happens that a database will only talk to a local application anyway. Maybe, your PostgreSQL database has been shipped along with your application, or maybe you just don't want the risk of using a network: In this case, Unix sockets are what you need. Unix sockets are a network-free means of communication. Your application can connect through a Unix socket locally without exposing anything to the outside world.

What you need, however, is a directory. By default, PostgreSQL will use the /tmp command. However, if more than one database server is running per machine, each one will need a separate data directory to live in.

Apart from security, there are various reasons why not using a network might be a good idea. One of these reasons is performance. Using Unix sockets is a lot faster than going through the loopback device (127.0.0.1). If that sounds surprising to you, don't worry--it does to many people. However, the overhead of a real network connection should not be underestimated if you are only running very small queries.

To show you what it really means, I have included a simple benchmark.

I have created a `script.sql` file. This is a simple script that just creates a random number and selects it. So it is the most simplistic statement possible. There is nothing simpler than just fetching a number.

So, let's run this simple benchmark on a normal laptop. To do so, I have written a small thing called `script.sql`. It will be used by the benchmark:

```
[hs@linuxpc ~]$ cat /tmp/script.sql
SELECT 1
```

Then you can simply run `pgbench` to execute the SQL over and over again. The `-f` option allows passing the name of the SQL to the script. `-c 10` means that we want 10 concurrent connections to be active for 5 seconds (`-T 5`). The benchmark is running as the `postgres` user and is supposed to use the `postgres` database, which should be there by default. Note that the following examples will work on RHEL derivatives. Debian-based systems will use different paths:

```
[hs@linuxpc ~]$ /usr/pgsql-9.6/bin/pgbench -f /tmp/script.sql
                -c 10 -T 5
                -U postgres postgres 2> /dev/null
transaction type: /tmp/script.sql
scaling factor: 1
query mode: simple
number of clients: 10
number of threads: 1
duration: 5 s
number of transactions actually processed: 871407
latency average = 0.057 ms
tps = 174278.158426 (including connections establishing)
tps = 174377.935625 (excluding connections establishing)
```

As you can see, no hostname is passed to `pgbench`, so the tool connects locally to the Unix socket and runs the script as fast as possible. On this four-core Intel box, the system was able to achieve around 174,000 transactions per second.

What happens if `-h localhost` is added?

```
[hs@linuxpc ~]$ /usr/pgsql-9.6/bin/pgbench -f /tmp/script.sql
              -h localhost -c 10 -T 5
              -U postgres postgres 2> /dev/null
transaction type: /tmp/script.sql
scaling factor: 1
query mode: simple
number of clients: 10
number of threads: 1
duration: 5 s
number of transactions actually processed: 535251
latency average = 0.093 ms
tps = 107000.872598 (including connections establishing)
tps = 107046.943632 (excluding connections establishing)
```

The throughput will drop like a stone to 107,000 transactions per second. The difference is clearly related to networking overhead.

> Note that by using the `-j` option (the number of threads assigned to pgbench), you can squeeze some more transactions out of your systems. However, it does not change the overall picture of the benchmark in my situation. In other tests, it does because pgbench can be a real bottleneck if you don't provide enough CPU power.

As you can see, networking can not only be a security issue but also a performance issue.

Managing pg_hba.conf

After configuring bind addresses, we can move on to the next level. The `pg_hba.conf` file will tell PostgreSQL how to authenticate people coming over the network. In general, `pg_hba.conf` file entries have the following layout:

```
# local      DATABASE  USER  METHOD   [OPTIONS]
# host       DATABASE  USER  ADDRESS  METHOD   [OPTIONS]
# hostssl    DATABASE  USER  ADDRESS  METHOD   [OPTIONS]
# hostnossl  DATABASE  USER  ADDRESS  METHOD   [OPTIONS]
```

There are four types of rules that can be put into the `pg_hba.conf` file:

- `local`: This can be used to configure local Unix socket connections.
- `host`: This can be used for SSL and non-SSL connections.
- `hostssl`: These are only valid for SSL connections. To make use of this option, SSL must be compiled into the server, which is the case if you are using prepackaged versions of PostgreSQL. In addition to that, `ssl = on` has to be set in the `postgresql.conf` file when the server is started.
- `hostnossl`: This works for non-SSL connections.

A list of rules can be put into the `pg_hba.conf` file. Here is an example:

```
# TYPE   DATABASE     USER        ADDRESS            METHOD
  local    all        all                            trust
  host     all        all         127.0.0.1/32       trust
  host     all        all           ::1/128          trust
```

You can see three simple rules. The `local` record says that `all` users from local Unix sockets for `all` databases are to be trusted. The `trust` method means that no password has to be sent to the server and people can log in directly. The other two rules say that the same applies to connections from localhost `127.0.0.1` and `::1/128`, which is an IPv6 address.

As connecting without a password is certainly not the best of all choices for remote access, PostgreSQL provides various authentication methods that can be used to configure `pg_hba.conf` file flexibly. Here is the list of possible authentication methods:

- `trust`: This allows authentication without providing a password. The desired user has to be available on the PostgreSQL side.
- `reject`: The connection will be rejected.
- `md5 and password`: The connections can be created using a password. `md5` means that the password is sent over the wire encrypted. In the case of `password`, the credentials are sent in plain text, which should not be done on a modern system anymore.
- `GSS and SSPI`: This uses GSSAPI or SSPI authentication. This is only possible for TCP/IP connections. The idea here is to allow for single sign-on.
- `ident`: This obtains the operating system username of the client by contacting the Ident server on the client and checking whether it matches the requested database username.

- `peer`: Suppose you are logged in as `abc` on Unix. If `peer` is enabled, you can only log in to PostgreSQL as `abc`. If you try to change the username, you will be rejected. The beauty is that `abc` won't need a password in order to authenticate. The idea here is that only the database administrator can log in to the database on a Unix system and not somebody else who just has the password or a Unix account on the same machine. This only works for local connections.

- `pam`: It uses the **pluggable authentication module (PAM)**. This is especially important if you want to use a means of authentication that is not provided by PostgreSQL out-of-the-box. To use PAM, create a file called `/etc/pam.d/postgresql` on your Linux system and put the desired PAM modules you are planning to use into the config file. Using PAM, you can even authenticate against less common components. However, it can also be used to connect to active directory and so on.

- `ldap`: This configuration allows you to authenticate using **lightweight directory access protocol (LDAP)**. Note that PostgreSQL will only ask LDAP for authentication; if a user is present only on the LDAP but not on the PostgreSQL side, you cannot log in. Also note that PostgreSQL has to know where your LDAP server is. All of this information has to be stored in `pg_hba.conf` file as outlined in the official documentation: `https://www.postgresql.org/docs/9.6/static/auth-methods.html#AUTH-LDAP`.

- `radius`: The **remote authentication dial-in user service (RADIUS)** is a means to do single sign-on. Again, parameters are passed using configuration options.

- `cert`: This authentication method uses SSL client certificates to perform authentication, and therefore, it is possible only if SSL is used. The advantage here is that no password has to be sent. The `CN` attribute of the certificate will be compared to the requested database username, and if they match, the login will be allowed. A map can be used to allow for user mapping.

Rules can simply be listed one after the other. The important thing here is that the order does make a difference, as shown in the following example:

```
host    all      all      192.168.1.0/24      md5
host    all      all      192.168.1.54/32     reject
```

When PostgreSQL walks through `pg_hba.conf` file, it will use the first rule that matches. So, if our request is coming from `192.168.1.54`, the first rule will always match before we make it to the second one. This means that `192.168.1.54` will be able to log in if the password and user are correct; therefore, the second rule is pointless.

If you want to exclude the IP, make sure that those two rules are swapped.

Handling SSL

PostgreSQL allows you to encrypt the transfer between the server and the client. Encryption is highly beneficial, especially if you are communicating over long distances. SSL offers a simple and secure way to ensure that nobody is able to listen to your communication. In this section, you will learn to set up SSL.

The first thing to do is to set the `ssl` parameter to `on` in the `postgresql.conf` file on server start. In the next step, you can put SSL certificates into the `$PGDATA` directory. If you don't want the certificates to be in some other directory, change the following parameters:

```
#ssl_cert_file = 'server.crt'        # (change requires restart)
#ssl_key_file = 'server.key'         # (change requires restart)
#ssl_ca_file = ''                    # (change requires restart)
#ssl_crl_file = ''                   # (change requires restart)
```

If you want to use self-signed certificates, perform the following steps:

```
openssl req -new -text -out server.req
```

Answer the questions asked by OpenSSL. Make sure you enter the local hostname as common name. You can leave the password empty. This call will generate a key that is passphrase protected; it will not accept a passphrase that is less than four characters long. To remove the passphrase (as you must if you want automatic startup of the server), run the commands:

```
openssl rsa -in privkey.pem -out server.key
rm privkey.pem
```

Enter the old passphrase to unlock the existing key. Now do this to turn the certificate into a self-signed certificate and to copy the key and certificate to where the server will look for them:

```
openssl req -x509 -in server.req -text
    -key server.key -out server.crt
```

At the end, make sure that the files have the right set of permissions:

```
chmod og-rwx server.key
```

Once the proper rules have been put into the `pg_hba.conf` file, you can use SSL to connect to your server. To verify that you are indeed using SSL, consider checking out the `pg_stat_ssl` function. It will tell you for every connection and whether it uses SSL or not, and it will provide some important information about encryption:

```
test=# d pg_stat_ssl
    View "pg_catalog.pg_stat_ssl"
    Column      |   Type    | Modifiers
-------------+----------+-----------
 pid         | integer  |
 ssl         | boolean  |
 version     | text     |
 cipher      | text     |
 bits        | integer  |
 compression | boolean  |
 clientdn    | text     |
```

If the `ssl` field for a process contains true, PostgreSQL does what you expect it to do:

```
postgres=# select * from pg_stat_ssl;
-[ RECORD 1 ]---------------------------
pid         | 20075
ssl         | t
version     | TLSv1.2
cipher      | ECDHE-RSA-AES256-GCM-SHA384
bits        | 256
compression | f
clientdn    |
```

Handling instance-level security

So far, we have configured bind addresses and we have told PostgreSQL which means of authentication to use for which IP ranges. Up to now, the configuration was purely network-related.

In the next step, we can shift our attention to permissions at the instance level. The most important thing to know is that users in PostgreSQL exist at the instance level. If you create a user, it is not just visible inside one database--it can be seen by all the databases. A user might have permissions to access just a single database, but basically users are created at the instance level.

To those of you who are new to PostgreSQL, there is one more thing you should keep in mind--users and roles are the same thing. CREATE ROLE and CREATE USER clauses have different default values (literally, the only difference is that roles do not get the LOGIN attribute by default), but at the end of the day, users and roles are the same. Therefore, CREATE ROLE and CREATE USER clauses support the very same syntax:

```
test=# h CREATE USER
Command:     CREATE USER
Description: define a new database role
Syntax:
CREATE USER name [ [ WITH ] option [ ... ] ]

where option can be:

    SUPERUSER | NOSUPERUSER
  | CREATEDB | NOCREATEDB
  | CREATEROLE | NOCREATEROLE
  | INHERIT | NOINHERIT
  | LOGIN | NOLOGIN
  | REPLICATION | NOREPLICATION
  | BYPASSRLS | NOBYPASSRLS
  | CONNECTION LIMIT connlimit
  | [ ENCRYPTED | UNENCRYPTED ] PASSWORD 'password'
  | VALID UNTIL 'timestamp'
  | IN ROLE role_name [, ...]
  | IN GROUP role_name [, ...]
  | ROLE role_name [, ...]
  | ADMIN role_name [, ...]
  | USER role_name [, ...]
  | SYSID uid
```

Let's discuss those syntax elements one by one. The first thing you see is that a user can be a superuser or a normal user. If somebody is marked as superuser, there are no longer any restrictions that a normal user has to face. A superuser can drop objects (databases and so on) as he wishes.

The next important thing is that it takes permissions on the instance level to create a new database. Note than when somebody creates a database, this user will automatically be the owner of the database. The rule is this: the creator is always automatically the owner of an object (unless specified otherwise as it can be done with the CREATE DATABASE clause). The beauty is that object owners can also drop an object again.

The CREATEROLE/NOCREATEROLE clause defines whether somebody is allowed to create new users/roles or not.

The next important thing is the INHERIT/NOINHERIT clause. If the INHERIT clause is set (which is the default value) a user can inherit permissions from some other user. Using inherited permissions allows using roles as a good way to abstract permissions. For example, you can create a role of bookkeeper and make many other roles inherit from bookkeeper. The idea is that you only have to tell PostgreSQL once what a bookkeeper is allowed to do even if you have many people working in accounting.

The LOGIN/NOLOGIN clause defines whether a role is allowed to log in to the instance. Note that the LOGIN clause is not enough to actually connect to a database. To do that, more permissions are needed. At this point, we are trying to make it into the instance, which is basically the gate to all the databases inside the instance. Let us get back to our example: bookkeeper might be marked as NOLOGIN because you want people to log in with their real name. All your accountants (say joe and jane) might be marked as the LOGIN clause but can inherit all the permissions from the bookkeeper role. A structure like this makes it easy to assure that all bookkeepers will have the same permissions.

If you are planning to run PostgreSQL with streaming replication, you can do all the transaction log streaming as superuser. However, doing that is not recommended from a security point of view. To assure that you don't have to be superuser to stream xlog, PostgreSQL allows you to give replication rights to a normal user, which can then be used to do streaming.

As you will see later in this chapter, PostgreSQL provides a feature called **row level security**. The idea is that you can exclude rows from the scope of a user. If a user is explicitly supposed to bypass RLS, set this value to BYPASSRLS. The default value is NOBYPASSRLS.

Sometimes it makes sense to restrict the number of connections allowed for a user. CONNECTION LIMIT allows you to do exactly that. Note that overall there can never be more connections than defined in the postgresql.conf file (max_connections). However, you can always restrict certain users to a lower value.

By default, PostgreSQL will store passwords in the system table encrypted, which is a good default behavior. However, suppose you are doing a training course. 10 students are attending and everybody is connected to your box. You can be 100% certain that one of those people will forget his or her password once in a while. As your setup is not security critical, you might decide to store the password in plain text so that you can easily look it up and give it to a student. This feature might also come in handy if you are testing software.

Often you already know that somebody will leave your organization fairly soon. The VALID UNTIL clause allows you to automatically lock out a specific user if his or her account has expired.

The IN ROLE clause lists one or more existing roles to which the new role will be immediately added as a new member. It helps to avoid additional manual steps. An alternative to IN ROLE is IN GROUP.

ROLE clause will define roles that are automatically added as members of the new role. ADMIN clause is the same as the ROLE clause but adds the WITH ADMIN OPTION.

Finally, you can use the SYSID clause to set a specific ID for the user (similar to what some Unix administrators do for usernames on the operating system level).

Creating and modifying users

After this theoretical introduction, it is time to actually create users and see how things can be used in a practical example:

```
test=# CREATE ROLE bookkeeper NOLOGIN;
CREATE ROLE
test=# CREATE ROLE joe LOGIN;
CREATE ROLE
test=# GRANT bookkeeper TO joe;
GRANT ROLE
```

The first thing done here is that a role called bookkeeper is created. Note that we don't want people to log in as bookkeeper, so the role is marked as NOLOGIN.

> Note also that NOLOGIN is the default value if you use the CREATE ROLE clause. If you prefer the CREATE USER clause, the default setting is LOGIN.

Then, the joe role is created and marked as LOGIN. Finally, the bookkeeper role is assigned to the joe role so that he can do everything a bookkeeper is actually allowed to do.

Once the users are in place, we can test what we have so far:

```
[hs@zenbook ~]$ psql test -U bookkeeper
psql: FATAL:  role "bookkeeper" is not permitted to log in
```

As expected, the bookkeeper role is not allowed to log into the system. What happens if the joe role tries?

```
[hs@zenbook ~]$ psql test -U joe
. . .
test=>
```

This will actually work as expected. However, note that the Command Prompt has changed. This is just a way for PostgreSQL to show you that you are not logged in as a superuser.

Once a user has been created it might be necessary to modify it. One thing you might want to change is the password. In PostgreSQL, users are allowed to change their own passwords. Here is how it works:

```
test=> ALTER ROLE joe PASSWORD 'abc';
ALTER ROLE
test=> SELECT current_user;
 current_user
---------------
 joe
(1 row)
```

ALTER ROLE clause (or ALTER USER) will allow you to change most settings which can be set during user creation. However, there is even more to managing users. In many cases, you want to assign special parameters to a user. ALTER USER clause gives you the means to do that:

```
ALTER ROLE { role_specification | ALL }
    [ IN DATABASE database_name ]
            SET configuration_parameter { TO | = } { value | DEFAULT }
ALTER ROLE { role_specification | ALL }
    [ IN DATABASE database_name ]
            SET configuration_parameter FROM CURRENT
ALTER ROLE { role_specification | ALL }
    [ IN DATABASE database_name ] RESET configuration_parameter
ALTER ROLE { role_specification | ALL }
    [ IN DATABASE database_name ] RESET ALL
```

The syntax is fairly simple and pretty straightforward. To show you why this is really useful, I have added a real-world example. Let us suppose that, Joe happens to live on the island of Mauritius. When he logs in, he wants to be in his time zone even if his database server is located in Europe:

```
test=> ALTER ROLE joe SET TimeZone = 'UTC-4';
ALTER ROLE
test=> SELECT now();
              now
-------------------------------
 2017-01-09 20:36:48.571584+01
(1 row)

test=> q
[hs@zenbook ~]$ psql test -U joe
...
test=> SELECT now();
              now
-------------------------------
 2017-01-09 23:36:53.357845+04
(1 row)
```

ALTER ROLE clause will modify the user. As soon as Joe reconnects, the time zone will already be set for him.

> Note that the time zone is not changed immediately. You should either reconnect or use SET ... TO DEFAULT clause.

The important thing here is that this is also possible for some memory parameters such as work_mem and so on, which have already been covered earlier in this book.

Defining database-level security

After configuring users at the instance level, it is possible to dig deeper and see what can be done at the database level. The first major question that arises is: we explicitly allowed Joe to log in to the database instance. But who or what allowed Joe to actually connect to one of the databases? Maybe, you don't want Joe to access all the databases in your system. Restricting access to certain databases is exactly what you can achieve on this level.

For databases, the following permissions can be set using GRANT clause:

```
GRANT { { CREATE | CONNECT | TEMPORARY | TEMP } [, ...]
    | ALL [ PRIVILEGES ] }
    ON DATABASE database_name [, ...]
    TO role_specification [, ...] [ WITH GRANT OPTION ]
```

There are two major permissions on the database level that deserve really close attention:

- CREATE: It allows somebody to create a schema inside the database. Note that CREATE clause does not allow for the creation of tables; it is about schemas. In PostgreSQL, a table resides inside a schema, so you have to get to the schema level first to be able to create a table.
- CONNECT: It allows somebody to connect to a database.

The question now... Nobody has explicitly assigned CONNECT permissions to the joe role. So where do those permissions actually come from? The answer is this: there is a thing called public, which is similar to Unix world. If the world is allowed to do something, so is Joe, who is part of the general public.

The main thing is that public is not a role in the sense that it can be dropped and renamed. You can simply see it as the equivalent for everybody on the system.

So, to ensure that not everybody can connect to any database at any time, CONNECT may have to be revoked from the general public. To do so, you can connect as superuser and fix the problem:

```
[hs@zenbook ~]$ psql test -U postgres
...
test=# REVOKE ALL ON DATABASE test FROM public;
REVOKE
test=# q
[hs@zenbook ~]$ psql test -U joe
psql: FATAL:  permission denied for database "test"
DETAIL:  User does not have CONNECT privilege.
```

As you can see, the joe role is not allowed to connect anymore. At this point only superusers have access to test.

In general, it is a good idea to already revoke permissions from the postgres database even before other databases are created. The idea behind this concept is that those permissions won't be in all those newly created databases anymore. If somebody needs access to a certain database, rights have to be explicitly granted. Rights are not automatically there anymore.

If you want to allow the `joe` role to connect to the `test` database, try the following line as superuser:

```
[hs@zenbook ~]$ psql test -U postgres
    . . .
test=# GRANT CONNECT ON DATABASE test TO bookkeeper;
GRANT
test=# q
[hs@zenbook ~]$ psql test -U joe
. . .
test=>
```

Basically there are two choices here:

- You can allow the `joe` role directly so that only the `joe` role will be able to connect.
- Alternatively, you can grant permissions to the `bookkeeper` role. Remember, the `joe` role will inherit all the permissions from the `bookkeeper` role, so if you want all accountants to be able to connect to the database, assigning permissions to the `bookkeeper` role seems like an attractive idea.

If you grant permissions to the `bookkeeper` role, it is not risky because the role is not allowed to log in to the instance in the first place; so it purely serves as a source of permissions.

Adjusting schema-level permissions

Once you are done configuring the database level, it makes sense to take a look at the schema level.

Before actually taking a look at schema, I want to run a small test:

```
test=> CREATE DATABASE test;
ERROR:  permission denied to create database
test=> CREATE USER xy;
ERROR:  permission denied to create role
test=> CREATE SCHEMA sales;
ERROR:  permission denied for database test
```

As you can see, Joe is having a bad day and basically nothing but connecting to the database is allowed.

However, there is a small exception, and it comes as a surprise to many people:

```
test=> CREATE TABLE t_broken (id int);
CREATE TABLE
test=> d
              List of relations
  Schema |          Name         | Type  | Owner
 --------+-----------------------+-------+-------
  public | t_broken              | table | joe
 (1 rows)
```

By default, public is allowed to work with the public schema, which is always around. If you are seriously interested in securing your database, make sure that this problem is taken care of. Otherwise, normal users will potentially spam your public schema with all kinds of tables and your entire setup might suffer. Also keep in mind that if somebody is allowed to create an object, this person is also its owner. Ownership means that there are automatically all permissions available to the creator (this includes the destruction of the object).

To take away those permissions from public, run the following line as superuser:

```
test=# REVOKE ALL ON SCHEMA public FROM public;
REVOKE
```

From now on, nobody can put things into your public schema without permissions anymore:

```
[hs@zenbook ~]$ psql test -U joe
. . .
test=> CREATE TABLE t_data (id int);
ERROR:  no schema has been selected to create in
LINE 1: CREATE TABLE t_data (id int);
```

As you can see, the command will fail. The important thing here is the error message you will get; PostgreSQL does not know where to put these tables. By default, it will try to put the table into one of the following schemas:

```
test=> SHOW search_path ;
    search_path
 -----------------
  "$user", public
 (1 row)
```

As there is no schema called joe, it is not an option and PostgreSQL will try the public schema. As there are no permissions, it will complain that it does not know where to put the table.

If the table is explicitly prefixed, the situation will change instantly:

```
test=> CREATE TABLE public.t_data (id int);
ERROR:  permission denied for schema public
LINE 1: CREATE TABLE public.t_data (id int);
```

In this case, you will get the error message you expect. PostgreSQL denies access to the public schema.

The next logical question now is: which permissions can be set at the schema level to give some more power to `joe` role?

```
GRANT { { CREATE | USAGE } [, ...] | ALL [ PRIVILEGES ] }
    ON SCHEMA schema_name [, ...]
    TO role_specification [, ...] [ WITH GRANT OPTION ]
```

`CREATE` means that somebody can put objects into a schema. `USAGE` means that somebody is allowed to enter the schema. Note that entering the schema does not mean that something inside the schema can actually be used--those permissions have not been defined yet. Basically, this just means the user can see the system catalog for this schema.

To allow `joe` role to access the table he has created previously, the following line will be necessary (executed as superuser):

```
test=# GRANT USAGE ON SCHEMA public TO bookkeeper;
GRANT
```

The `joe` role is now able to read his table as expected:

```
[hs@zenbook ~]$ psql test -U joe
test=> SELECT count(*) FROM t_broken;
 count
-------
     0
(1 row)
```

The `joe` role is also able to add and modify rows because he happens to be the owner of the table. However, although he can do quite a lot of things already, the `joe` role is not yet almighty. Consider the following statement:

```
test=> ALTER TABLE t_broken RENAME TO t_useful;
ERROR:  permission denied for schema public
```

Let us take a closer look at the actual error message. As you can see, the message complains about permissions on the schema, not about permissions on the table itself (remember, `joe` role owns the table). To fix the problem, it has to be tackled on the schema and not on the table level. Run the following line as superuser:

```
test=# GRANT CREATE ON SCHEMA public TO bookkeeper;
GRANT
```

`joe` role can now change the name of his table to a more useful name:

```
[hs@zenbook ~]$ psql test -U joe
test=> ALTER TABLE t_broken RENAME TO t_useful;
ALTER TABLE
```

Keep in mind that this is necessary if DDLs are used. In my daily work as a PostgreSQL support service provider, I have seen a couple of issues where this turned out to be a problem.

Working with tables

After taking care of bind addresses, network authentication, users, databases, and schemas, you finally made it to the database level. The following snippet shows which permissions can be set for a table:

```
GRANT { { SELECT | INSERT | UPDATE | DELETE | TRUNCATE
              | REFERENCES | TRIGGER }
    [, ...] | ALL [ PRIVILEGES ] }
    ON { [ TABLE ] table_name [, ...]
           | ALL TABLES IN SCHEMA schema_name [, ...] }
    TO role_specification [, ...] [ WITH GRANT OPTION ]
```

Let me explain those permissions one by one:

- `SELECT`: allows you to read a table.
- `INSERT`: allows you to add rows to the table (this also includes copy and so on--it is not only about the `INSERT` clause). Note that if you are allowed to insert you are not automatically allowed to read. `SELECT` and `INSERT` clauses are needed to be able to read the data you have inserted.
- `UPDATE`: modifies the content of a table.
- `DELETE`: is used to remove rows from a table.

- TRUNCATE: allows you to use the TRUNCATE clause. Note that the DELETE and TRUNCATE clauses are two separate permissions because TRUNCATE clause will lock the table, which is not done by the DELETE clause (not even if there is no WHERE condition).
- REFERENCES: allows the creation of foreign keys. It is necessary to have this privilege on both the referencing and referenced columns otherwise the creation of the key won't work.
- TRIGGER: allows for the creation of triggers.

> The nice thing about the GRANT clause is that you can set permissions on all tables in a schema at the same time.

It greatly simplifies the process of adjusting permissions. It is also possible to use the WITH GRANT OPTION clause. The idea is to ensure that normal users can pass on permissions to others, which has the advantage of being able to reduce the workload of administrators quite a bit. Just imagine a system that provides access to hundreds of users--it can start to be a lot of work to manage all those people, and therefore administrators can appoint people managing a subset of the data themselves.

Handling column-level security

In some cases, not everybody is allowed to see all the data. Just imagine a bank. Some people might see the entire information about a bank account, while others might be limited to only a subset of the data. In a real-world situation, somebody might not be allowed to read the balance column or somebody might not see the interest rates of people's loans.

Another example would be that people are allowed to see people's profiles but not their pictures or some other private information. The question now is: how can column-level security be used?

To demonstrate that, I will add a column to the existing table belonging to the joe role:

```
test=> ALTER TABLE t_useful ADD COLUMN name text;
ALTER TABLE
```

The table now consists of two columns. The goal of the example is to ensure that a user can see only one of those columns:

```
test=> d t_useful
    Table "public.t_useful"
 Column |  Type   | Modifiers
--------+---------+-----------
 id     | integer |
 name   | text    |
```

Let us create a user and give it access to the schema containing our table:

```
test=# CREATE ROLE paul LOGIN;
CREATE ROLE
test=# GRANT CONNECT ON DATABASE test TO paul;
GRANT
test=# GRANT USAGE ON SCHEMA public TO paul;
GRANT
```

Do not forget to give CONNECT rights to the new guy because earlier in the chapter, CONNECT has been revoked from the public. Explicit granting is therefore absolutely necessary to ensure that we can even get to the table.

The SELECT permissions can be given to paul role:

```
test=# GRANT SELECT (id) ON t_useful  TO paul;
GRANT
```

Basically, this is already enough. It is already possible to connect to the database as user paul and read the column:

```
[hs@zenbook ~]$ psql test -U paul
. . .
test=> SELECT id FROM t_useful;
 id
----
(0 rows)
```

If you are using column-level permissions, there is an important thing to keep in mind: you should stop using SELECT * as it does not work anymore:

```
test=> SELECT * FROM t_useful;
ERROR:  permission denied for relation t_useful
```

* still means *all columns*, but as there is no way to access all columns, things will error out instantly.

Configuring default privileges

So far, a lot of stuff has already been configured. The trouble naturally arising now is: what happens if new tables are added to the system? It can be quite painful and risky to process these tables one by one and to set proper permissions. Wouldn't it be nice if those things would just happen automatically? This id exactly what the ALTER DEFAULT PRIVILEGES clause does. The idea is to give users an option to make PostgreSQL automatically set the desired permissions as soon as an object comes into existence. It cannot happen anymore that somebody simply forgets to set those rights.

The following listing shows the first part of the syntax specification:

```
test=# h ALTER DEFAULT PRIVILEGES
Command:     ALTER DEFAULT PRIVILEGES
Description: define default access privileges
Syntax:
ALTER DEFAULT PRIVILEGES
    [ FOR { ROLE | USER } target_role [, ...] ]
    [ IN SCHEMA schema_name [, ...] ]
    abbreviated_grant_or_revoke

where abbreviated_grant_or_revoke is one of:

GRANT { { SELECT | INSERT | UPDATE | DELETE
      | TRUNCATE
      | REFERENCES | TRIGGER }
    [, ...] | ALL [ PRIVILEGES ] }
    ON TABLES
    TO { [ GROUP ] role_name | PUBLIC } [, ...] [ WITH GRANT OPTION ]
...
```

Basically, the syntax works similar to the GRANT clause and is therefore easily and intuitively to use. To show you how it works, I compiled a simple example. The idea is that if the joe role creates a table, the paul role will automatically be able to use it:

```
test=# ALTER DEFAULT PRIVILEGES FOR ROLE joe
    IN SCHEMA public
    GRANT ALL ON TABLES TO paul;
ALTER DEFAULT PRIVILEGES
```

Let me connect as the joe role now and create a table:

```
[hs@zenbook ~]$ psql test -U joe
...
test=> CREATE TABLE t_user (id serial, name text, passwd text);
CREATE TABLE
```

Connecting as the `paul` role will prove that the table has been assigned to the proper set of permissions:

```
[hs@zenbook ~]$ psql test -U paul
. . .
test=> SELECT * FROM t_user;
 id | name | passwd
----+------+--------
(0 rows)
```

Digging into row-level security - RLS

Up to this point, a table has always been shown as a whole. When the table contained 1 million rows, it was possible to retrieve 1 million rows from it. If somebody had the rights to read a table, it was all about the entire table. In many cases, this is not enough. Often it is desirable that a user is not allowed to see all the rows.

Consider the following real-world example: an accountant is doing accounting work for many people. The table containing tax rates should really be visible to everybody as everybody has to pay the same rates. However, when it comes to the actual transactions, you might want to ensure that everybody is only allowed to see his or her own transactions. Person *A* should not be allowed to see person *B*'s data. In addition to that, it might also make sense that the boss of a division is allowed to see all the data in his part of the company.

Row-level security has been designed to do exactly this and enables you to build multi-tenant systems in a fast and simple way. The way to configure those permissions is to come up with policies. The CREATE POLICY command is here to provide you with a means to write those rules:

```
test=# h CREATE POLICY
Command:      CREATE POLICY
Description: define a new row level security policy for a table
Syntax:
CREATE POLICY name ON table_name
    [ FOR { ALL | SELECT | INSERT | UPDATE | DELETE } ]
    [ TO { role_name | PUBLIC | CURRENT_USER | SESSION_USER } [, ...] ]
    [ USING ( using_expression ) ]
    [ WITH CHECK ( check_expression ) ]
```

To show you how a policy can be written, I will first log in as superuser and create a table containing a couple of entries:

```
test=# CREATE TABLE t_person (gender text, name text);
CREATE TABLE
test=# INSERT INTO t_person VALUES
     ('male', 'joe'), ('male', 'paul'), ('female', 'sarah'), (NULL, 'R2-
D2');
INSERT 0 4
```

Then access is granted to the joe role:

```
test=# GRANT ALL ON t_person TO joe;
GRANT
```

So far, everything is pretty normal and the joe role will be able to actually read the entire table as there is no RLS in place. But what happens if row-level security is enabled for the table?

```
test=# ALTER TABLE t_person ENABLE ROW LEVEL SECURITY;
ALTER TABLE
```

There is a deny all default policy in place, so the joe role will actually get an empty table:

```
test=> SELECT * FROM t_person;
 gender | name
--------+------
(0 rows)
```

Actually, the default policy makes a lot of sense as users are forced to explicitly set permissions.

Now that the table is under row-level security control, policies can be written (as superuser):

```
test=# CREATE POLICY joe_pol_1
            ON t_person
            FOR SELECT TO joe
            USING (gender = 'male');
CREATE POLICY
```

Logging in as the `joe` role and selecting all the data, will return just two rows:

```
test=> SELECT * FROM t_person;
 gender | name
--------+------
 male   | joe
 male   | paul
(2 rows)
```

Let us inspect the policy I have just created in a more detailed way. The first thing you see is that a policy actually has a name. It is also connected to a table and allows for certain operations (in this case, the SELECT clause). Then comes the USING clause. It basically defines what the `joe` role will be allowed to see. The USING clause is therefore a mandatory filter attached to every query to only select the rows our user is supposed to see.

Now suppose that, for some reason, it has been decided that the `joe` role is also allowed to see robots. There are two choices to achieve our goal. The first option is to simply use the ALTER POLICY clause to change the existing policy:

```
test=> h ALTER POLICY
Command:     ALTER POLICY
Description: change the definition of a row level security policy
Syntax:
ALTER POLICY name ON table_name RENAME TO new_name

ALTER POLICY name ON table_name
    [ TO { role_name | PUBLIC | CURRENT_USER | SESSION_USER } [, ...] ]
    [ USING ( using_expression ) ]
    [ WITH CHECK ( check_expression ) ]
```

The second option is to create a second policy as shown in the next example:

```
test=# CREATE POLICY joe_pol_2
            ON t_person
            FOR SELECT TO joe
            USING (gender IS NULL);
CREATE POLICY
```

The beauty is that those policies are simply connected using an OR condition. Therefore, PostgreSQL will now return three rows instead of two:

```
test=> SELECT * FROM t_person;
 gender | name
--------+-------
 male   | joe
 male   | paul
        | R2-D2
(3 rows)
```

The R2-D2 role is now also included in the result as it matches the second policy.

To show you how PostgreSQL runs the query, I have decided to include an execution plan of the query:

```
test=> explain SELECT * FROM t_person;
                        QUERY PLAN
-----------------------------------------------------
 Seq Scan on t_person  (cost=0.00..21.00 rows=9 width=64)
   Filter: ((gender IS NULL) OR (gender = 'male'::text))
(2 rows)
```

As you can see, both the USING clauses have been added as mandatory filters to the query.

You might have noticed in the syntax definition that there are two types of clauses:

- USING: This clause filters rows that already exist. This is relevant to SELECT and UPDATE clauses, and so on.
- CHECK: This clause filters new rows that are about to be created; so they are relevant to INSERT and UPDATE clauses, and so on.

Here is what happens if we try to insert a row:

```
test=> INSERT INTO t_person VALUES ('male', 'kaarel');
ERROR:  new row violates row-level security policy for table "t_person"
```

As there is no policy for the INSERT clause, the statement will naturally error out. Here is the policy to allow insertions:

```
test=# CREATE POLICY joe_pol_3
            ON t_person
            FOR INSERT TO joe
            WITH CHECK (gender IN ('male', 'female'));
CREATE POLICY
```

The `joe` role is allowed to add males and females to the table, which is shown in the next listing:

```
test=> INSERT INTO t_person VALUES ('female', 'maria');
INSERT 0 1
```

However, there is also a catch; consider the following example:

```
test=> INSERT INTO t_person VALUES ('female', 'maria') RETURNING *;
ERROR:  new row violates row-level security policy for table "t_person"
```

Remember, there is only a policy to select males. The trouble here is that the statement will return a woman, which is not allowed because `joe` role is under a male only policy.

Only for men, will the `RETURNING *` clause actually work:

```
test=> INSERT INTO t_person VALUES ('male', 'max') RETURNING *;
 gender | name
--------+------
 male   | max
(1 row)

INSERT 0 1
```

If you don't want this behavior, you have to write a policy that actually contains a proper `USING` clause.

Inspecting permissions

When all permissions are set, it is sometimes necessary to know who has which permissions. It is vital for administrators to find out who is allowed to do what. Unfortunately, this process is not so easy and requires a bit of knowledge. Usually I am a big fan of command-line usage. However, in the case of the permission system, it can really make sense to use a graphical user interface to do things.

Before I show you how to read PostgreSQL permissions, I will assign rights to the `joe` role so that we can inspect them in the next step:

```
test=# GRANT ALL ON t_person TO joe;
GRANT
```

Retrieving information about permissions can be done using the z command in psql:

```
test=# x
Expanded display is on.
test=# z t_person
Access privileges
-[ RECORD 1 ]-----+-------------------------------------------------------------
----
Schema            | public
Name              | t_person
Type              | table
Access privileges | postgres=arwdDxt/postgres
+
                  | joe=arwdDxt/postgres
Column privileges |
Policies          | joe_pol_1 (r):
+
                  |    (u): (gender = 'male'::text)
+
                  |    to: joe
+
                  | joe_pol_2 (r):
+
                  |    (u): (gender IS NULL)
+
                  |    to: joe
+
                  | joe_pol_3 (a):
+
                  |    (c): (gender = ANY (ARRAY['male'::text,
'female'::text]))+
                  |    to: joe
```

It will return all those policies along with information about Access privileges. Unfortunately, those shortcuts are hard to read and I have the feeling that they are not widely understood by administrators. In our example, the joe role has gotten arwdDxt from postgres. What do those shortcuts actually mean?

- a: appends for the INSERT clause
- r: reads for the SELECT clause
- w: writes for the UPDATE clause
- d: deletes for the DELETE clause

- D: is used for the TRUNCATE clause (when this was introduced, t was already taken)
- x: is used for references
- t: is used for triggers

If you don't know those shortcuts, there is also a second way to make things more readable. Consider the following function call:

```
test=# SELECT * FROM aclexplode('{joe=arwdDxt/postgres}');
 grantor | grantee | privilege_type | is_grantable
---------+---------+----------------+--------------
      10 |   18481 | INSERT         | f
      10 |   18481 | SELECT         | f
      10 |   18481 | UPDATE         | f
      10 |   18481 | DELETE         | f
      10 |   18481 | TRUNCATE       | f
      10 |   18481 | REFERENCES     | f
      10 |   18481 | TRIGGER        | f
(7 rows)
```

As you can see, the set of permissions is returned as a simple table, which makes life really easy.

Reassigning objects and dropping users

After assigning permissions and restricting access, it can happen that users will be dropped from the system. Unsurprisingly, the commands to do that are the DROP ROLE and DROP USER commands:

```
test=# h DROP ROLE
Command:     DROP ROLE
Description: remove a database role
Syntax:
DROP ROLE [ IF EXISTS ] name [, ...]
```

Let us give it a try:

```
test=# DROP ROLE joe;
ERROR:  role "joe" cannot be dropped because some objects
    depend on it
DETAIL:  target of policy joe_pol_3 on table t_person
target of policy joe_pol_2 on table t_person
target of policy joe_pol_1 on table t_person
privileges for table t_person
```

```
owner of table t_user
owner of sequence t_user_id_seq
owner of default privileges on new relations belonging to role joe
    in schema public
owner of table t_useful
```

PostgreSQL will issue error messages because a user can only be removed if everything has been taken away from him. This makes sense for this reason: just suppose somebody owns a table. What should PostgreSQL do with that table? Somebody has to own them.

To reassign tables from one user to the next, consider taking a look at the REASSIGN clause:

```
test=# h REASSIGN
Command:       REASSIGN OWNED
Description: change the ownership of database objects owned
    by a database role
Syntax:
REASSIGN OWNED BY { old_role | CURRENT_USER | SESSION_USER } [, ...]
                TO { new_role | CURRENT_USER | SESSION_USER }
```

The syntax is again quite simple and helps to simplify the process of handing over. Here is an example:

```
test=# REASSIGN OWNED BY joe TO postgres;
REASSIGN OWNED
```

So let us try to drop the joe role again:

```
test=# DROP ROLE joe;
ERROR:  role "joe" cannot be dropped because some objects depend on it
DETAIL:  target of policy joe_pol_3 on table t_person
target of policy joe_pol_2 on table t_person
target of policy joe_pol_1 on table t_person
privileges for table t_person
owner of default privileges on new relations belonging to role joe
    in schema public
```

As you can see, the list of problems has been reduced significantly. What we can do now is resolve all of those problems one after the other and drop the role. There is no shortcut I am aware of. The only way to make that more efficient is to make sure that as few permissions as possible are assigned to real people. Try to abstract as much as you can into roles, which in turn can be used by many people. If individual permissions are assigned to real people, things tend to be easier in general.

Summary

Database security is a wide field and a 30 page chapter can hardly cover all the aspects of PostgreSQL security. Many things such as SELinux, security definer/invoker, and so on were left untouched. However, in this chapter, you learned the most common things you will face as a PostgreSQL developer and DBA. You learned how to avoid the basic pitfalls and how to make your systems more secure.

In the next chapter, you will learn about PostgreSQL streaming replication and incremental backups. The chapter will also cover failover scenarios.

Handling Backup and Recovery

9

In the previous chapter of this book, I tried to teach you all you need to know about securing PostgreSQL in the most simplistic and most beneficial way possible. The topics of this chapter will be backup and recovery. Performing backups should be a regular task and every administrator is supposed to keep an eye on this vital stuff. Fortunately, PostgreSQL provides easy means to create backups.

The following topics will be covered:

- Running `pg_dump`
- Partially dumping data
- Restoring backups
- Making use of parallelism
- Saving global data

At the end of the chapter, you will be able to set up proper backup mechanisms.

Performing simple dumps

If you are running a PostgreSQL setup, there are basically two major methods to perform backups:

- Logical dumps (extract an SQL script representing your data)
- Transaction log shipping

The idea behind transaction log shipping is to archive binary changes made to the database. Most people claim that transaction log shipping is the only real way to do backups. However, in my opinion this is not necessarily true.

Many people rely on pg_dump to simply extract a textual representation of the data. pg_dump is also the oldest method of creating a backup and has been around since the very early days of the project (transaction log shipping was added much later). Every PostgreSQL administrator will get in touch with pg_dump sooner or later so it is important to know how it really works and what it does.

Running pg_dump

The first thing we want to do is to create a simple textual dump:

```
[hs@linuxpc ~]$ pg_dump test > /tmp/dump.sql
```

This is the most simplistic backup you can imagine. pg_dump logs into the local database instance, connects to a database test, and starts to extract all the data, which will be sent to stdout and redirected to the file. The beauty is that standard output gives you all the flexibility of a Unix system. You can easily compress the data using a pipe or do whatever you want.

In some cases, you might want to run pg_dump as a different user. All PostgreSQL client programs support a consistent set of command-line parameters to pass user information. If you just want to set the user, use the -U flag:

```
[hs@linuxpc ~]$ pg_dump -U whatever_powerful_user test > /tmp/dump.sql
```

The following set of parameters can be found in all PostgreSQL client programs:

```
...
Connection options:
  -d, --dbname=DBNAME      database to dump
  -h, --host=HOSTNAME      database server host or
                           socket directory
  -p, --port=PORT          database server port number
  -U, --username=NAME      connect as specified database user
  -w, --no-password        never prompt for password
  -W, --password           force password prompt (should
                           happen automatically)
  --role=ROLENAME          do SET ROLE before dump
...
```

Just pass the information you want to `pg_dump` and if you have enough permissions, PostgreSQL will fetch the data. The important thing here is to see how the program really works. Basically `pg_dump` connects to the database and opens a large *repeatable read* transaction that simply reads all the data. Remember, *repeatable read* ensures that PostgreSQL creates a consistent snapshot of the data, which does not change throughout the transactions. In other words, a dump is always consistent - no foreign keys will be violated. The output is a snapshot of data as it was when the dump started. Consistency is a key factor here. It also implies that changes made to the data while the dump is running won't make it to the backup anymore.

> A dump simply reads everything - therefore, there are no separate permissions to be able to dump something. As long as you can read it, you can back it up.

Also note that the backup is by default in a textual format. It means that you can safely extract data from say, Solaris, and move it to some other CPU architecture. In the case of binary copies, that is clearly not possible as the on-disk format depends on your CPU architecture.

Passing passwords and connection information

If you take a close look at the connection parameters shown in the previous section, you will notice that there is no way to pass a password to `pg_dump`. You can enforce a password prompt but you cannot pass the parameter to `pg_dump` using a command-line option. The reason for that is simple: the password might show up in the process table and might therefore be visible to other people. Therefore, this is not supported. The question now is: if `pg_hba.conf` on the server enforces a password, how can the client program provide it?

There are various means of doing that:

- Making use of environment variables
- Making use of `.pgpass`
- Using service files

In this section, you will learn about all three methods.

Using environment variables

One way to pass all kinds of parameters is to use environment variables. If information is not explicitly passed to pg_dump, it will look for the missing information in predefined environment variables. A list of all potential settings can be found here: https://www.post gresql.org/docs/9.6/static/libpq-envars.html.

The following overview shows some environment variables commonly needed for backups:

- PGHOST: It tells the system which host to connect to
- PGPORT: It defines the TCP port to be used
- PGUSER: It tells a client program about the desired user
- PGPASSWORD: It contains the password to be used
- PGDATABASE: It is the name of the database to connect to

The advantage of those environments is that the password won't show up in the process table. However, there is more. Consider the following example:

```
psql -U ... -h ... -p ... -d ...
```

Suppose you are a system administrator: do you really want to type a long line like that a couple of times every day? If you are working with the very same host again and again, just set those environment variables and connect with plain SQL:

```
[hs@linuxpc ~]$ export PGHOST=localhost
[hs@linuxpc ~]$ export PGUSER=hs
[hs@linuxpc ~]$ export PGPASSWORD=abc
[hs@linuxpc ~]$ export PGPORT=5432
[hs@linuxpc ~]$ export PGDATABASE=test
[hs@linuxpc ~]$ psql
psql (9.6.1)
Type "help" for help.
```

As you can see, there are no command-line parameters anymore. Just type psql and you are in.

> **TIP**
>
> All applications based on the standard C library (libpq) will understand those environment variables so you cannot only use them for psql and pg_dump but for many other applications.

Making use of .pgpass

A very common way to store login information is the use of `.pgpass` files. The idea is simple: put a file called `.pgpass` into your home directory and put your login information there. The format is simple:

```
hostname:port:database:username:password
```

An example would be:

```
192.168.0.45:5432:mydb:xy:abc
```

PostgreSQL offers some nice additional functionality: most fields can contain `*`. Here is an example:

```
*:*:*:xy:abc
```

This means that on every host, on every port, for every database the user called `xy` will use `abc` as the password. To make PostgreSQL use the `.pgpass` file, make sure that the right file permissions are in place:

```
chmod 0600 ~/.pgpass
```

`.pgpass` can also be used on a Windows system. In this case, the file can be found in the `%APPDATA%postgresqlpgpass.conf` path.

Using service files

However, there is not just the `.pgpass` file. You can also make use of service files. Here is how it works. If you want to connect to the very same servers over and over again, you can create a `.pg_service.conf` file. It will hold all the connection information you need.

Here is an example of a `.pg_service.conf` file:

```
Mac:~ hs$ cat .pg_service.conf

# a sample service
[hansservice]
host=localhost
port=5432
dbname=test
user=hs
password=abc

[paulservice]
```

```
host=192.168.0.45
port=5432
dbname=xyz
user=paul
password=cde
```

To connect to one of the services, just set the environment and connect:

```
iMac:~ hs$ export PGSERVICE=hansservice
```

A connection can now be established without passing parameters to psql:

```
iMac:~ hs$ psql
psql (9.6.1)
Type "help" for help.
test=#
```

Alternatively, you can do:

```
psql service=hansservice
```

Extracting subsets of data

Up to now, you have seen how to dump an entire database. However, this is not what you might wish for. In many cases, you might just want to extract a subset of tables or schemas. pg_dump can do that and provides a number of switches:

- -a: It dumps only the data and does not dump the data structure
- -s: It dumps only the data structure but skips the data
- -n: It dumps only a certain schema
- -N: It dumps everything but excludes certain schemas
- -t: It dumps only certain tables
- -T: It dumps everything but certain tables (this can make sense if you want to exclude logging tables and so on)

Partial dumps can be very useful to speed up things considerably.

Handling various data formats

So far you have seen that `pg_dump` can be used to create text files. The problem is that a text file can only be replayed completely. If you have saved an entire database, you can only replay the entire thing. In many cases, this is not what you want. Therefore, PostgreSQL has additional formats that also offer more functionality.

At this point, four formats are supported:

```
-F, --format=c|d|t|p          output file format
                              (custom, directory, tar,
                              plain text (default))
```

You have already seen plain, which is just normal text. On top of that, you can use custom format. The idea behind custom format is to have a compressed dump including a table of contents. Here are two ways to create a custom format dump:

```
[hs@linuxpc ~]$ pg_dump -Fc test > /tmp/dump.fc
[hs@linuxpc ~]$ pg_dump -Fc test -f /tmp/dump.fc
```

In addition to the table of contents, the compressed dump has also one more advantage: it is a lot smaller. The rule of thumb is that a custom format dump is around 90% smaller than the database instance you are about to backup. Of course, this highly depends on the number of indexes and all that but for many database applications this rough estimation will hold true.

Once you have created the backup, you can inspect the backup file:

```
[hs@linuxpc ~]$ pg_restore --list /tmp/dump.fc
;
; Archive created at 2017-01-04 15:44:56 CET
;     dbname: test
;     TOC Entries: 18
;     Compression: -1
;     Dump Version: 1.12-0
;     Format: CUSTOM
;     Integer: 4 bytes
;     Offset: 8 bytes
;     Dumped from database version: 9.6.1
;     Dumped by pg_dump version: 9.6.1
;
; Selected TOC Entries:
;
3103; 1262 16384 DATABASE - test hs
3; 2615 2200 SCHEMA - public hs
3104; 0 0 COMMENT - SCHEMA public hs
1; 3079 13350 EXTENSION - plpgsql
```

```
3105; 0 0 COMMENT - EXTENSION plpgsql
187; 1259 16391 TABLE public t_test hs
...
```

`pg_restore --list` will return the table of contents of the backup.

Using a custom format is already a good idea as the backup will shrink in size. However, there is more: `-Fd` command will create a backup in a directory format. Instead of a single file, you will now get a directory containing a couple of files:

```
[hs@linuxpc ~]$ mkdir /tmp/backup
[hs@linuxpc ~]$ pg_dump -Fd test -f /tmp/backup/
[hs@linuxpc ~]$ cd /tmp/backup/
[hs@linuxpc backup]$ ls -lh
total 86M
-rw-rw-r--. 1 hs hs  85M Jan  4 15:54 3095.dat.gz
-rw-rw-r--. 1 hs hs  107 Jan  4 15:54 3096.dat.gz
-rw-rw-r--. 1 hs hs 740K Jan  4 15:54 3097.dat.gz
-rw-rw-r--. 1 hs hs   39 Jan  4 15:54 3098.dat.gz
-rw-rw-r--. 1 hs hs 4.3K Jan  4 15:54 toc.dat
```

One advantage of the directory format is that you can use more than one core to perform the backup. In the case of a plain or custom format, only one process will be used by pg_dump. The directory format changes that rule. The following example shows how you can tell pg_dump to use four cores (jobs):

```
[hs@linuxpc backup]$ rm -rf *
[hs@linuxpc backup]$ pg_dump -Fd test -f /tmp/backup/ -j 4
```

Note that the more objects you have in your database, the more potential speed up there will be.

Replaying backups

Having a backup is pointless unless you have tried to actually replay it. Fortunately, it is easy to do. In case you have created a plain text backup, you can simply take the SQL file and execute it:

```
psql your_db < your_file.sql
```

A plain text backup is simply a text file containing everything. You can always simply replay a text file.

In case you have decided on a custom format or directory format, you can use `pg_restore` to replay the backup. `pg_restore` allows you to do all kinds of fancy things such as replaying just a part of a database and so on. In most cases, however, you will simply replay the entire database. In my example, I will create an empty database and just replay a custom format dump:

```
[hs@linuxpc backup]$ createdb new_db
[hs@linuxpc backup]$ pg_restore -d new_db -j 4 /tmp/dump.fc
```

Note, that `pg_restore` will add data to an existing database. In case your database is not empty, `pg_restore` might error out but continue.

Again `-j` is used to throw up more than one process. In my example, four cores are used to replay the data (this works only if you are going to replay more than one table).

In case you are using a directory format, you can simply pass the name of the directory instead of the file.

As far as performance is concerned, dumps are a good solution if you are working with small or medium amounts of data. There are two major downsides:

- You will get a snapshot so everything since the last snapshot will be lost
- Rebuilding a dump from scratch is comparatively slow compared to binary copies because all the indexes have to be rebuilt

Therefore, we will take a look at binary backups in Chapter 10, *Making Sense of Backups and Replication*.

Handling global data

In the previous section, you have learned about pg_dump and pg_restore, which are two vital programs when it comes to creating backups. The thing is: pg_dump creates database dumps - it works on the database level. If you want to backup an entire instance, you have to use pg_dumpall or dump all the databases separately. Before we dig into that, it makes sense to see how pg_dumpall works:

```
pg_dumpall > /tmp/all.sql
```

pg_dumpall will connect to one database after the other and send stuff to standard out, where you can process it with Unix. pg_dumpall can be used just like pg_dump. However, it has some downsides. It does not support a custom or directory format and therefore does not offer multicore support - you will be stuck with one thread.

However, there is more to pg_dumpall. Keep in mind that users live on the instance level. If you create a normal database dump, you will get all the permissions but you won't get all the CREATE USER statements. Those globals are not included in a normal dump - they will only be extracted by pg_dumpall.

If you only want the globals, you can run pg_dumpall using the -g option:

```
pg_dumpall -g > /tmp/globals.sql
```

In most cases, you might want to run pg_dumpall -g along with custom or directory format dumps to extract your instances. A simple backup script might look like this:

```
#!/bin/sh

BACKUP_DIR=/tmp/

pg_dumpall -g > $BACKUP_DIR/globals.sql

for x in $(psql -c "SELECT datname FROM pg_database
          WHERE datname NOT IN ('postgres', 'template0', 'template1')"
postgres -A -t)
do
    pg_dump -Fc $x > $BACKUP_DIR/$x.fc
done
```

It will first dump the globals and then loop through the list of databases to extract them one by one in a custom format.

Summary

In this chapter, you have learned about creating backups and dumps in general. So far binary backups have not been covered yet but you are already able to extract textual backups from the server to save and replay your data in the most simplistic way possible.

The next chapter will be about transaction log shipping, streaming replication, and binary backups. You will learn how to use PostgreSQL onboard tools to replicate instances.

10

Making Sense of Backups and Replication

In the previous chapter of this book, you learned a lot about the backup and recovery, which is essential for administration. So far, only logical backups have been covered; I am about to change that in this chapter.

This chapter is all about PostgreSQL's transaction log and what you can do with it to improve your setup and to make things more secure.

The following things will be covered:

- What the transaction log does and why it is needed
- Performing point-in-time-recovery
- Setting up streaming replication
- Replication conflicts
- Monitoring replication
- Synchronous versus asynchronous replication
- Understanding timelines

At the end of the chapter, you will be able to set up transaction log archiving and replication. Keep this in mind: this chapter can never be a comprehensive guide to replication; it is only a short introduction. Full coverage of replication would require around 500 pages. Just for a comparison, *PostgreSQL Replication* by Packt Publishing alone is close to 400 pages.

This chapter will cover the most essential things in a more compact form.

Understanding the transaction log

Every modern database system provides functionality to make sure that the system can survive a crash in case something goes wrong or in case somebody pulls the plug. This is true for filesystems and database systems alike.

PostgreSQL also provides a means to ensure that a crash cannot harm the data integrity or the data itself. It is guaranteed that if the power cuts out, the system will always be able to come back up again and do its job.

The means to provide this kind of security is called **write ahead log** (**WAL**) or xlog. The idea is to not write into the data file directly, but instead write to the log first. Why is that important? Imagine you are writing some data:

```
INSERT INTO data ... VALUES ('12345678');
```

Suppose data was written directly to the data file. If the operation fails somewhere in the middle, the data file would be corrupted. It might contain half written rows, columns without index pointers, missing commit information, and so on. As hardware does not really guarantee atomic writes of large chunks of data, a way has to be found to make this more robust. By writing to the log instead of writing to the file directly, the problem can be solved.

> In PostgreSQL, the transaction log consists of records.

A single write can consist of various records, which all have a checksum and which are chained together. A single transaction might contain B-tree, index, storage manager, commit records, and a lot more. Each type of object has its own WAL entries and ensures that the object can survive a crash. If there is a crash, PostgreSQL will start up and repair the data files based on the transaction log to ensure that no permanent corruption is allowed to happen.

Looking at the transaction log

In PostgreSQL, the WAL can usually be found in the pg_xlog directory in the data directory (unless specified otherwise on initdb directory). Here is what it looks like:

```
[postgres@zenbook pg_xlog]$ pwd
/var/lib/pgsql/9.6/data/pg_xlog
[postgres@zenbook pg_xlog]$ ls -l
```

```
total 688132
-rw-------. 1 postgres postgres 16777216 Jan 19 07:58
000000010000000000000CD
-rw-------. 1 postgres postgres 16777216 Jan 13 17:04
000000010000000000000CE
-rw-------. 1 postgres postgres 16777216 Jan 13 17:04
000000010000000000000CF
-rw-------. 1 postgres postgres 16777216 Jan 13 17:04
000000010000000000000D0
-rw-------. 1 postgres postgres 16777216 Jan 13 17:04
000000010000000000000D1
-rw-------. 1 postgres postgres 16777216 Jan 13 17:04
000000010000000000000D2
```

What you can see is that the transaction log is always a 16 MB file, which consists of 24 digits. The numbering is hexadecimal. As you can see, CF is followed by D0. The files are always a fixed size.

> One thing to notice is that in PostgreSQL, the number of transaction log files is not related to the size of a transaction. You can have a very small set of transaction log files and still run a multi-TB transaction easily.

Understanding checkpoints

As I have mentioned earlier, every change is written to the WAL in binary format (it does not contain SQL). The problem is this: the database server cannot keep writing to the WAL forever as it would consume more and more space over time. So at some point the transaction log has to be recycled. This point is done by a **checkpoint**, which happens automatically in the background. The idea is the following: when data is written, it first goes to the transaction log, and then a dirty buffer is put into shared buffers. Those dirty buffers have to go to disk and are written out to the data files by the background writer or during a checkpoint. As soon as all dirty buffers up to point have been written, the transaction log can be deleted.

> Please never ever delete transaction log files manually. In the event of a crash, your database server will not be able to start up again and the amount of disk space needed will be reclaimed anyway as new transactions come in. Never touch the transaction log manually. PostgreSQL takes care of things on its own, and doing things in there is really just harmful.

Optimizing the transaction log

Checkpoints happen automatically and are triggered by the server. However, there are configuration settings that decide when a checkpoint is initiated. The following parameters in the `postgresql.conf` file are in charge of handling checkpoints:

```
#checkpoint_timeout = 5min            # range 30s-1d
#max_wal_size = 1GB
#min_wal_size = 80MB
```

There are two reasons to initiate a checkpoint: we can run out of time or we can run out of space. The maximum time between two checkpoints is defined by the `checkpoint_timeout` variable. The amount of space provided to store transaction log will vary between the `min_wal_size` and `max_wal_size` variable. PostgreSQL will automatically trigger checkpoints in a way that the amount of space really needed will be between those two numbers.

> **TIP**
>
> The `max_wal_size` variable is a soft limit and PostgreSQL can (under heavy) load temporarily need a bit more space. In other words, if your transaction log is on a separate disk, it makes sense to make sure that there is actually a bit more space available to store the WAL.

How can somebody tune the transaction log in PostgreSQL 9.6 and 10.0? In 9.6, some changes have been made to the background writer and checkpointing machinery. In older versions, there were some use cases where smaller checkpoint distances could actually make sense from a performance point of view. In 9.6 and beyond, this has pretty much changed and wider checkpoint distances are basically always highly favorable because many optimizations can be applied on the database and the OS level to speed things up. The most noteworthy optimization is that blocks are sorted before they are written out, which greatly reduces random I/O on mechanical disks.

But there is more. Large checkpoint distances will actually decrease the amount of WAL created. Yes, that is right—larger checkpoint distances will lead to less WAL.

The reason for that is simple. Whenever a block is touched after a checkpoint for the first time, it has to be sent to the WAL completely. If the block is changed more often, only the changes make it to the log. Larger distances basically cause fewer full-page writes, which in turn reduces the amount of WAL created in the first place. The difference can be quite substantial as can be seen in one of my blog posts: `http://www.cybertec.at/checkpoint-distance-and-amount-of-wal/`.

But there is more. PostgreSQL also allows us to configure whether or not checkpoints should be short and intense or whether they should be spread out over a longer period. The default value is 0.5, which means that the checkpoint should be done in a way that the process has finished between halfway between the current and the next checkpoint:

```
#checkpoint_completion_target = 0.5
```

Increasing this value basically means that the checkpoint is stretched out and less intensive. In many cases, a higher value has proven beneficial to flatten out I/O spikes caused by intense checkpointing.

Transaction log archiving and recovery

After this brief introduction to the transaction log in general, it is time to focus our attention on the process of transaction log archiving. As you have seen, the transaction log contains a sequence of binary changes made to the storage system. So, why not use it to replicate database instances and do a lot of other cool stuff?

Configuring for archiving

The first thing we want to achieve in this chapter is to create a configuration to perform standard **point-in-time-recovery** (**PITR**). There are a couple of advantages of PITR over ordinary dumps:

- You will lose less data because you can restore a certain point in time and not just to the fixed backup point.
- Restoring will be faster because indexes don't have to be created from scratch. They are just copied over and are ready to use.

Configuring for PITR is easy. Just a handful of settings have to be made in postgresql.conf file:

```
wal_level = replica      # used to be "hot_standby" in older versions
max_wal_senders = 5      # at least 2, better at least 2
```

The `wal_level` variable says that the server is supposed to produce enough transaction log to allow for PITR. If the `wal_level` variable is set to `minimal` (which is the default value up to PostgreSQL 9.6), the transaction log will only contain enough information to recover a single node setup—it is not rich enough to handle replication. According to the latest patches, those default values have been changed for PostgreSQL 10.0 so that setting up archiving is even easier.

The `max_wal_senders` variable will allow us to stream WAL from the server. It will allow you to use `pg_basebackup` to create an initial backup instead of traditional file-based copying. The advantage here is that `pg_basebackup` is a lot easier to use.

The idea behind WAL streaming is that the transaction log created is copied to some place where it can be stored safely. Basically, there are two means to transport the WAL:

- Using `pg_receivexlog`
- Using filesystem means to archive

In this section, you will see how to set up the second option. During normal operations, PostgreSQL keeps writing to those WAL files. When `archive_mode = on` in `postgresql.conf` file, PostgreSQL will call the `archive_command` variable for every single file.

A configuration might look like this—first, a directory storing those transaction log files can be created:

```
mkdir /archive
chown postgres.postgres archive
```

The following entries can be changed in the `postgresql.conf` file:

```
archive_mode = on
archive_command = 'cp %p /archive/%f'
```

A restart will enable archiving, but let us configure the `pg_hba.conf` file first to reduce downtime to an absolute minimum.

Note that you can put any command into the `archive_command` variable. Many people use `rsync`, `scp`, and so on to transport their WAL files to a safe location. If your script returns `0`, PostgreSQL will assume that the file has been archived. If anything else is returned, PostgreSQL will try to archive the file again. This is necessary because the database engine has to ensure that no files are lost. To perform the recovery process, not a single file is allowed to go missing.

Confguring the pg_hba.conf file

Now that the `postgresql.conf` file has been configured successfully, it is necessary to configure the `pg_hba.conf` file for streaming. Note that this is only necessary if you are planning to use `pg_basebackup`, which is the state-of-the-art tool to create base backups.

Basically, the options you have in the `pg_hba.conf` file are the same you have already seen in Chapter 8, *Managing PostgreSQL Security*. There is just one major issue to keep in mind:

```
# Allow replication connections from localhost, by a user with the
# replication privilege.
local   replication     postgres                        trust
host    replication     postgres     127.0.0.1/32       trust
host    replication     postgres       ::1/128          trust
```

You can define standard `pg_hba.conf` file rules. The important thing is that the second column says `replication`. Normal rules are not enough—it is really important to add explicit replication permissions. Also keep in mind that you don't have to do this as a superuser. You can create a specific user who is only allowed to do login and replication.

Now that the `pg_hba.conf` file has been configured correctly, PostgreSQL can be restarted.

Creating base backups

After teaching PostgreSQL to archive those WAL files, it is time to create a first backup. The idea is to have a backup and to replay WAL files based on that backup to reach any point in time.

To create an initial backup, you can turn to `pg_basebackup`, which is a command-line tool used to perform backups. Let us call `pg_basebackup` and see how it works:

```
pg_basebackup -D /some_target_dir
         -h localhost
         --checkpoint=fast
         --xlog-method=stream
```

As you can see, I am using four parameters here:

- `-D`: Where do you want the base backup to live? PostgreSQL requires an empty directory. At the end of the backup you will see a copy of the server's data directory there (destination).
- `-h`: Indicates the IP address or the name of the master (source). This is the server you want to backup.
- `--checkpoint=fast`: Usually `pg_basebackup` waits for the master to checkpoint. The reason is that the replay process has to start somewhere. A checkpoint ensures that data has been written up to a certain point and so PostgreSQL can safely jump in there and start the replay process. Basically, it can also be done without `--checkpoint=fast` parameter. However, it might take a while before `pg_basebackup` starts to copy data in this case. Checkpoints can be up to one hour apart, which can already delay your backups unnecessarily.
- `--xlog-method=stream`: By default, `pg_basebackup` connects to the master server and starts copying files over. Now, keep in mind that those files are modified while they are copied. The data reaching the backup is therefore inconsistent. This inconsistency can be repaired during the recovery process using the WAL. The backup itself, however, is not consistent. By adding `--xlog-method=stream` parameter it is possible to create a self-contained backup; it can be started directly without replaying transaction log (this is nice if you just want to clone an instance and not use PITR).

Reducing the bandwidth of a backup

When `pg_basebackup` starts, it tries to finish its work as fast as possible. If you have a good network connection, `pg_basebackup` is definitely able to fetch hundreds of megabytes a second from the remote server. If your server has a weak I/O system it can mean that `pg_basebackup` can suck up all the resources easily and end users might experience bad performance, because their I/O requests are simply too slow.

To control the maximum transfer rate, `pg_basebackup` offers the following:

```
 -r, --max-rate=RATE    maximum transfer rate to transfer data directory
(in kB/s, or use suffix "k" or "M")
```

When you create a base backup, make sure that the disk system on the master can actually stand the load. Adjusting your transfer rate can therefore make a lot of sense.

Mapping tablespaces

pg_basebackup can be called directly if you are using an identical filesystem layout on the target system. If this is not the case, pg_basebackup allows mapping the master's filesystem layout to the desired layout:

```
-T, --tablespace-mapping=OLDDIR=NEWDIR
                relocate tablespace in OLDDIR to NEWDIR
```

> **TIP**
>
> If your system is small, it can be a good idea to keep everything in one tablespace.

This holds true if I/O is not the problem (maybe because you are only managing a couple of GB of data).

Using different formats

pg_basebackup can create various formats. By default, it will put data in an empty directory. Essentially, it will connect to the source server and perform a tar over a network connection and put the data into the desired directory.

The trouble with this approach is that pg_basebackup will create many files, which is not suitable if you want to move the backup to an external backup solution (maybe Tivoli storage manager or some other solution):

```
-F, --format=p|t        output format (plain (default), tar)
```

To create a single file, you can use the -F=t option. By default, it will create a file called base.tar, which can then be managed more easily. The downside, of course, is that you have to inflate the file again before performing PITR.

Testing transaction log archiving

Before we dig into the actual replay process, it makes sense to actually check archiving to make sure it is working perfectly and as expected:

```
[hs@zenbook archive]$ ls -l
total 212996
-rw------- 1 hs hs 16777216 Jan 30 09:04 000000010000000000000001
-rw------- 1 hs hs 16777216 Jan 30 09:04 000000010000000000000002
-rw------- 1 hs hs      302 Jan 30 09:04
```

```
000000010000000000000002.00000028.backup
-rw------- 1 hs hs 16777216 Jan 30 09:20 000000010000000000000003
-rw------- 1 hs hs 16777216 Jan 30 09:20 000000010000000000000004
-rw------- 1 hs hs 16777216 Jan 30 09:20 000000010000000000000005
-rw------- 1 hs hs 16777216 Jan 30 09:20 000000010000000000000006
. . .
```

As soon as serious activity on the database is going on, WAL files should be sent to the archive.

In addition to just checking for files, the following view can be useful:

```
test=# d pg_stat_archiver
          View "pg_catalog.pg_stat_archiver"
        Column        |            Type           | Modifiers
----------------------+---------------------------+-----------
 archived_count       | bigint                    |
 last_archived_wal    | text                      |
 last_archived_time   | timestamp with time zone  |
 failed_count         | bigint                    |
 last_failed_wal      | text                      |
 last_failed_time     | timestamp with time zone  |
 stats_reset          | timestamp with time zone  |
```

The pg_stat_archiver extension is very useful to figure out, if and when archiving has stalled for whatever reason. It will tell you about the number of files already archived (archived_count). You can also see which file was the last one and when it happened. Finally, the pg_stat_archiver extension can tell you when archiving has gone wrong, which is vital information. Unfortunately, the error code or the error message is not shown in the table, but as the archive_command can be an arbitrary command, it is easy to log.

There is one more thing to see in the archive. As described already, it is important to see that those files are actually archived. But there is more: when pg_basebackup extension is called, you will see a .backup file in the stream of WAL files. It is small and contains only some information about the base backup itself—it is purely informative and is not needed by the replay process. However, it gives you some vital clues. When you start to replay transaction log later on, you can delete all WAL files that are older than the .backup file. In this case, our backup file is called 000000010000000000000002.00000028.backup. This means that the replay process starts somewhere within file ...0002 (at position ...28). It also means that we can delete all files older than ...0002. Older WAL files won't be needed for recovery anymore. Keep in mind that you can keep more than just one backup around so I am only referring to the current backup.

Now that archiving works, we can turn our attention to the replay process.

Replaying the transaction log

Let us sum up the process so far. We have adjusted `postgresql.conf` file (`wal_level`, `max_wal_senders`, `archive_mode`, and `archive_command`) and we have allowed for `pg_basebackup` extension in `pg_hba.conf` file. Then the database has been restarted and a base backup has successfully been produced.

Keep in mind that base backups can happen while the database is fully operational—only a brief restart to change the `max_wal_sender` and `wal_level` variables is needed. The backup can happen while the database is fully active.

Now after the system has been working properly, we might face a crash from which we want to recover. Therefore, we can perform PITR to restore as much data as potentially possible. The first thing we've got to do is take the base backup and put it at the desired location.

> **TIP**
> It can be a good idea to save the old database cluster. Even if it is broken, your PostgreSQL support company might need it to track down the reason of the crash. You can still delete it later on once you've got everything up and running again.

Given the preceding filesystem layout, you might want to do something like this:

```
cd /some_target_dir
cp -Rv * /data
```

I am assuming that your new database server will be located in `/data` directory. Make sure that the directory is empty before you copy the base backup over.

In the next step, a file called `recovery.conf` can be created. It will contain all the information concerning the replay process such as the position of the WAL archive, the time you want to reach and all that.

> **TIP**
> In PostgreSQL 10.0, `recovery.conf` file will most likely not exist anymore. Settings are expected to be moved to `postgresql.conf` file. At the time this chapter was written, it has not been totally clear to me yet, what will happen precisely.

Here is a sample `recovery.conf` file:

```
restore_command = 'cp /archive/%f %p'
recovery_target_time = '2019-04-05 15:43:12'
```

After putting `recovery.conf` file into the `$PGDATA` directory, you can simply start up your server. The output might look like this:

```
server starting
LOG:    database system was interrupted; last known up
    at 2017-01-30 09:04:07 CET
LOG:    starting point-in-time recovery to 2019-04-05 15:43:12+02
LOG:    restored log file "000000010000000000000002" from archive
LOG:    redo starts at 0/2000028
LOG:    consistent recovery state reached at 0/20000F8
LOG:    restored log file "000000010000000000000003" from archive
LOG:    restored log file "000000010000000000000004" from archive
LOG:    restored log file "000000010000000000000005" from archive
. . .
LOG:    restored log file "00000001000000000000000E" from archive
cp: cannot stat '/archive/00000001000000000000000F':
    No such file or directory
LOG:    redo done at 0/E7BF710
LOG:    last completed transaction was at log time
    2017-01-30 09:20:47.249497+01
LOG:    restored log file "00000001000000000000000E" from archive
cp: cannot stat '/archive/00000002.history': No such file or directory
LOG:    selected new timeline ID: 2
cp: cannot stat '/archive/00000001.history': No such file or directory
LOG:    archive recovery complete
LOG:    MultiXact member wraparound protections are now enabled
LOG:    database system is ready to accept connections
LOG:    autovacuum launcher started
```

When the server is started there are a couple of messages to look for to ensure that your recovery works perfectly: the first one is `consistent recovery state reached`. This message means that PostgreSQL could replay enough transaction log to bring the database back to a state, which makes it actually usable.

Then PostgreSQL will copy one file after the other and replay it. However, remember we have told `recovery.conf` file to bring us all the way up to 2019. This text is written in 2017 so there is clearly not enough WAL to reach 2019. Therefore, PostgreSQL will error out and tell us about the last completed transaction.

Of course, this is just a showcase, and in real-world examples you will most likely use a date in the past, which you can use to safely recover. However, I wanted to show that it is perfectly feasible to use a date in the future—just be prepared to accept the fact that errors will happen.

After the recovery has finished, the `recovery.conf` file will be renamed `recovery.done` so that you can see what you have done during recovery. All the processes of your database server will be up and running and you will have a ready to use database instance.

Finding the right timestamp

So far, I have silently assumed that you know the timestamp you want to recover to or that you simply want to replay all the transaction log possible to reduce data loss. However, what if you don't want to replay everything? What if you don't know to which point in time to recover to? In everyday life, this is actually a very common scenario. One of your developers has lost some data in the morning and you are supposed to make things fine again. The trouble is this: when is in the morning? Once recovery has ended, it cannot be restarted easily. Once recovery is completed, the system will be promoted, and once it has been promoted you cannot continue to replay WAL.

However, what you can do is pause recovery without promotion, check what is inside the database, and continue.

Doing that is easy. The first thing you have to make sure is that `hot_standby variable` set as `on` in `postgresql.conf` file. This will make sure that the database is readable while it is still in recovery mode. Then you have to adapt the `recovery.conf` file before starting the replay process:

```
recovery_target_action = 'pause'
```

There are various `recovery_target_action` settings. If case you use `pause`, PostgreSQL will pause at the desired time and let you check what has already been replayed. You can adjust the time you want, restart, and try again. Alternatively, you can set the value to `promote` or `shutdown`.

There is a second way to pause transaction log replay. Basically, it can also be used when performing PITR. However, in most cases, it is used with streaming replication. Here is what can be done during WAL replay:

```
postgres=# x
Expanded display is on.
postgres=# df *pause*
List of functions
-[ RECORD 1 ]-------+-------------------------
Schema              | pg_catalog
Name                | pg_is_xlog_replay_paused
Result data type    | boolean
```

```
Argument data types |
Type                 | normal
-[ RECORD 2 ]-------+-----------------------
Schema               | pg_catalog
Name                 | pg_xlog_replay_pause
Result data type     | void
Argument data types |
Type                 | normal

postgres=# df *resume*
List of functions
-[ RECORD 1 ]-------+-----------------------
Schema               | pg_catalog
Name                 | pg_xlog_replay_resume
Result data type     | void
Argument data types |
Type                 | normal
```

You can call the SELECT pg_xlog_replay_pause(); command to halt WAL replay until you call the SELECT pg_xlog_replay_resume(); command.

The idea is to figure out how much WAL has already been replayed and to continue as necessary. However, keep this in mind: once a server has been promoted, you cannot just continue to replay WAL without further precautions.

As you have seen already, it can be pretty tricky to figure out how far you have to recover. Therefore, PostgreSQL provides some means to help. Consider the following real-world example: a midnight, you are running a nightly process that ends at some point that is usually not known. The goal is to recover exactly to the end of the nightly process. The trouble is this: how do you know when the process has ended? In most cases, this is hard to figure out. So why not add a marker to the transaction log:

```
postgres=# SELECT pg_create_restore_point('my_daily_process_ended');
 pg_create_restore_point
-------------------------
 1F/E574A7B8
(1 row)
```

If your process calls this SQL statement as soon as it ends, it will be possible to use this label in the transaction log to recover exactly to this point in time by adding the following directive to the recovery.conf file:

```
recovery_target_name = 'my_daily_process_ended'
```

Use this setting instead of recovery_target_time and the replay process will beam you exactly to the end of the nightly process.

Of course, you can also replay up to a certain transaction ID. However, in real life, this has proven to be difficult as the exact transaction ID is rarely ever known to the administrator, and therefore, there is not much practical value here.

Cleaning up the transaction log archive

So far, data has been written to the archive all the time and no attention has been paid to cleaning out the archive again to free up some space in the filesystem. PostgreSQL cannot do this job for you because it has no idea whether you want to use the archive again. Therefore, you are in charge of cleaning up the transaction log. Of course, you can also use a backup tool—however, it is important to know that PostgreSQL has no chance of doing the cleanup for you.

Suppose we want to clean out old transaction log, which is not needed anymore. Maybe you want to keep several base backups around and clean out all transaction logs that won't be needed anymore to restore one of those backups.

In this case, the `pg_archivecleanup` extension is exactly what you need. You can simply pass the archive directory and the name of the backup file to the `pg_archivecleanup` extension, and it will make sure that files are removed from disk. Using this tool makes life easier for you because you don't have to figure out which transaction log files to keep on your own. Here is how it works:

```
[hs@pgnode01 ~]$ pg_archivecleanup --help
pg_archivecleanup removes older WAL files from PostgreSQL archives.

Usage:
  pg_archivecleanup [OPTION]... ARCHIVELOCATION OLDESTKEPTWALFILE

Options:
  -d               generate debug output (verbose mode)
  -n               dry run, show the names of the files that
                     would be removed
  -V, --version    output version information, then exit
  -x EXT           clean up files if they have this extension
  -?, --help       show this help, then exit

For use as archive_cleanup_command in recovery.conf when standby_mode = on:
  archive_cleanup_command = 'pg_archivecleanup
          [OPTION]... ARCHIVELOCATION %r'
e.g.
  archive_cleanup_command = 'pg_archivecleanup
    /mnt/server/archiverdir %r'
```

```
Or for use as a standalone archive cleaner:
e.g.
  pg_archivecleanup /mnt/server/archiverdir
            000000010000000000000010.00000020.backup
```

The tool can be used easily. It is available on all platforms.

Setting up asynchronous replication

After taking a look at transaction log archiving and PITR we can focus our attention on one of the most widely used features in the PostgreSQL world today: streaming replication. The idea behind streaming replication is simple. After an initial base backup, the secondary can connect to the master and fetch transaction log in real time and apply it. Transaction log replay is not a single operation anymore, but rather a continuous process that is supposed to keep running as long as the cluster exists.

Performing a basic setup

In this section, you will learn how to set up asynchronous replication quickly and easily. The goal is to set up a system consisting of two nodes.

Basically, most of the work has already been done for WAL archiving. However, to make it easy for you I will explain the entire process of setting up streaming because we cannot assume that WAL shipping is really already set up as needed.

The first thing to do is to go to the `postgresql.conf` file and adjust the following parameters:

```
wal_level = replica
max_wal_senders = 5   # or whatever value >= 2
hot_standby = on      # already a sophistication
```

Just like previously, the `wal_level` variable has to be adjusted to ensure that PostgreSQL produces enough transaction logs to sustain a slave. Then we have to configure the `max_wal_senders` variable. When a slave is up and running or when a base backup is created, a WAL sender process will talk to a WAL receiver process on the client side. The `max_wal_senders` setting allows PostgreSQL to create enough processes to serve those clients.

Theoretically, it is enough to have just one WAL sender process. However, it is pretty inconvenient. A base backup that uses the `--xlog-method=stream` parameter will already need two WAL sender processes. If you want to run a slave and perform a base backup at the same time, there are already three processes in use. So, make sure that you allow PostgreSQL to create enough processes to save on pointless restarts.

Then comes the `hot_standby` variable. Basically, a master ignores the `hot_standby` variable and does not take it into consideration. All it does is to make the slave readable during WAL replay. So why do we care? Keep in mind: `pg_basebackup` extension will clone the entire server including its configuration. This means that if you have already set the value on the master, the slaves will automatically get it already when the data directory is cloned.

After setting the `postgresql.conf` file, we can turn our attention to the `pg_hba.conf` file: just allow the slave to perform replication by adding rules. Basically, those rules are the same as you have already seen for PITR.

Then restart the database server as it has been done for PITR already.

Then, the `pg_basebackup` extension can be called on the slave. Before you do that, make sure that the `/target` directory is empty. If you are using RPM packages, ensure that you shut down a potentially running instance and empty the directory (for example, `/var/lib/pgsql/data`):

```
pg_basebackup -D /target
          -h master.example.com
          --checkpoint=fast
          --xlog-method=stream -R
```

Just replace the `/target` directory with your desired destination directory and replace `master.example.com` with the IP or DNS name of your master. The `--checkpoint=fast` parameter will trigger an instant checkpoint. Then there is the `--xlog-method=stream` parameter: it will open two streams. One will copy the data; the other one will fetch the WAL, which is created while the backup is running.

Finally, there is the `-R` flag:

```
-R, --write-recovery-conf
        write recovery.conf after backup
```

The −R flag is a really good feature. The `pg_basebackup` extension has the ability to automatically create the slave configuration. It will add various entries to the `recovery.conf` file:

```
standby_mode = on
primary_conninfo = ' ... '
```

The first setting says that PostgreSQL should keep replaying WAL all the time—if all the transaction log has been replayed, it should wait for new WAL to arrive. The second setting will tell PostgreSQL where the master is. It is a normal database connection.

> **TIP**
>
> Slaves can also connect to other slaves to stream transaction log. It is possible to cascade replication by simply creating base backups from a slave. So *master* really means *source server* in this context.

After running the `pg_basebackup` extension, the services can already be started. The first thing you should check is whether the master shows a WAL sender process:

```
[hs@linuxpc ~]$ ps ax | grep sender
17873 ?        Ss     0:00 postgres: wal sender process
                           ah ::1(57596) streaming 1F/E9000060
```

If there is one, the slave will also carry a WAL receiver process:

```
17872 ?        Ss     0:00 postgres: wal receiver process
                           streaming 1F/E9000060
```

If those processes are there, you are already on the right track and replication is working as expected. Both sides are now talking to each other and WAL flows from the master to the slave.

Improving security

So far, you have seen that data is streamed as superuser. However, it is not a good idea to allow super access from a remote side. Fortunately, PostgreSQL allows you to create a user that is only allowed to consume the transaction log stream but cannot do anything else.

Creating a user just for streaming is easy:

```
test=# CREATE USER repl LOGIN REPLICATION;
CREATE ROLE
```

By assigning replication to the user it is possible to use it just for streaming—everything else is forbidden.

It is highly recommended to not use your superuser account to set up streaming. Simply change the `recovery.conf` file to the newly created user. Not exposing superuser accounts will dramatically improve security (just like giving the replication user a password).

Halting and resuming replication

Once streaming replication has been set up, it works flawlessly without too much administrator intervention. However, in some cases it might make sense to halt replication and to resume it at some later point. Why would anybody want to do that?

Consider the following use case: you are in charge of a master/slave setup, which is running some crappy CMS or some dubious forum software. Suppose you want to update your application from crappy CMS 1.0 to crappy CMS 2.0. Some changes will be executed in your database, which will instantly be replicated to the slave database. What if the upgrade process does something wrong? The error will instantly be replicated to both nodes due to streaming.

To avoid instant replication you can halt replication and resume as needed. In the case of our CMS update we could simply do following things:

- Halt replication.
- Perform the app update on the master.
- Check if your application still works. If yes, resume replication. If not, failover to the replica, which still has the old data.

With this mechanism you can protect your data because you can fall back to the data if it was before the problem. You will learn later in this chapter how to promote a slave to become the new master server.

The main question now is: how can you halt replication? Here is how it works. Execute the following line on the standby:

```
test=# SELECT pg_xlog_replay_pause();
```

This line will halt replication. Note that transaction log will still flow from the master to the slave—only the replay process is halted. Your data is still protected as it is persisted on the slave. In case of a server crash, no data will be lost.

Keep in mind that replay has to be halted on the slave. Otherwise, an error will be thrown by PostgreSQL:

```
ERROR:  recovery is not in progress
HINT:  Recovery control functions can only be executed during recovery.
```

Once replication is resumed, the following line will be needed on the slave:

```
SELECT pg_xlog_replay_resume();
```

PostgreSQL will start to replay xlog again.

Checking replication to ensure availability

One of the core jobs of every administrator is to ensure that replication stays up and running all the time. If replication is down, it is possible that data is lost if the master crashes. Therefore, keeping an eye on replication is absolutely necessary.

Fortunately, PostgreSQL provides system views, which allow you to take a deep look at what is going on. One of those views is `pg_stat_replication`:

```
test=# d pg_stat_replication
        View "pg_catalog.pg_stat_replication"
      Column         |            Type            | Modifiers
--------------------+----------------------------+-----------
 pid                | integer                    |
 usesysid           | oid                        |
 usename            | name                       |
 application_name   | text                       |
 client_addr        | inet                       |
 client_hostname    | text                       |
 client_port        | integer                    |
 backend_start      | timestamp with time zone   |
 backend_xmin       | xid                        |
 state              | text                       |
 sent_location      | pg_lsn                     |
 write_location     | pg_lsn                     |
 flush_location     | pg_lsn                     |
 replay_location    | pg_lsn                     |
 sync_priority      | integer                    |
 sync_state         | text                       |
```

The `pg_stat_replication` view will contain information on the *sender*. I don't want to use the word *master* here because slaves can be connected to some other slave. It is possible to build a tree of servers. In the case of a tree of servers, the master will only have information about the slaves it is directly connected to.

The first thing you will see in this view is the process ID of the WAL sender process. It helps you to identify the process in case something goes wrong (which is usually not the case). Then you will see the username the slave uses to connect to its sending server. The `client_` fields will indicate, where the slaves are. You will be able to extract network information from those fields. Then there is the `backend_start` field: it shows when the slaves started to stream from your server.

Then there is this magical `backend_xmin` field. Suppose you are running a master/slave setup. It is possible to tell the slave to report back its transaction ID to the master. The idea behind that is to delay cleanup on the master so that data is not taken from a transaction running on the slave.

The `state` field informs you about the state of the server. If your system is fine, the field will contain streaming. Otherwise, closer inspection is needed.

The next four fields are really important. The `sent_location` field indicates how much WAL has already reached the other side (accepted by the WAL receiver). You can use it to figure out how much data has already made it to the slave. Then there is the `write_location` field. Once the WAL has been accepted, it is passed on to the OS. The `write_location` field will tell us the WAL position that has safely made it to the OS already. The `flush_location` field will know how much WAL the database has already flushed to disk.

Finally, there is the `replay_location` field. The fact that the WAL has made it to the disk on the standby does not mean that PostgreSQL has already replayed (made visible to the end user) yet. Suppose replication is paused. Data will still flow to the standby. However, it will be applied later. The `replay_location` field will tell you how much data is already visible.

Finally, PostgreSQL tells us whether replication is synchronous or asynchronous.

The question now is how can anybody use this view to gain vital information? One common use case is to check the replication delay. Here is how it works:

```
SELECT    client_addr, pg_current_xlog_location() - sent_location AS diff
FROM      pg_stat_replication;
```

When running this on the master the `pg_current_xlog_location()` function returns the current transaction log position. PostgreSQL has a special datatype for transaction log positions called `pg_lsn`, which even features a couple of operators, which are used here to subtract the slave's from the master's xlog position. The view outlined here therefore returns the difference between two servers in bytes (replication delay).

While the `pg_stat_replication` extension contains information on the sending side, the `pg_stat_wal_receiver` extension will provide you with similar information on the receiving side:

```
test=# d pg_stat_wal_receiver
            View "pg_catalog.pg_stat_wal_receiver"
        Column          |            Type            | Modifiers
------------------------+----------------------------+-----------
 pid                    | integer                    |
 status                 | text                       |
 receive_start_lsn      | pg_lsn                     |
 receive_start_tli      | integer                    |
 received_lsn           | pg_lsn                     |
 received_tli           | integer                    |
 last_msg_send_time     | timestamp with time zone   |
 last_msg_receipt_time  | timestamp with time zone   |
 latest_end_lsn         | pg_lsn                     |
 latest_end_time        | timestamp with time zone   |
 slot_name              | text                       |
 conninfo               | text                       |
```

After the process ID of the WAL receiver process PostgreSQL will provide you with the status of the process. Then the `receive_start_lsn` field will tell you about the transaction log position the WAL receiver started at, while the `receive_start_tli` field will inform us about the timeline used when WAL receiver was started.

The `received_lsn` field contains information about the WAL position, which was already received and flushed to disk. Then we got some information about time as well as information about slots and connections.

In general, many people find it easier to read the `pg_stat_replication` extension than the `pg_stat_wal_receiver` extension and most tools are built around the `pg_stat_replication` extension.

Performing failovers and understanding timelines

Once a master/slave setup has been created, it usually works flawlessly for a very long time. However, everything can fail, and therefore it is important to understand how a failed server can be replaced with a backup system.

PostgreSQL makes failovers and promotion easy. Basically, all you have to do is to use the `pg_ctl` parameter to tell a replica to promote itself:

```
pg_ctl -D data_dir promote
```

The server will disconnect itself from the master and perform the promotion instantly. Remember, the slave might already support thousands of read-only connections while being promoted. One nice feature of PostgreSQL is that all open connections will be turned into read/write connections during promotion—there is not even a need to reconnect.

When promoting a server, PostgreSQL will increment the timeline: if you set up a brand new server, it will be in timeline 1. If a slave is cloned from that server, it will be in the same timeline as its master. So, both boxes will be in timeline 1. If the slave is promoted to an independent master, it will move on to timeline 2.

Timelines are especially important to PITR. Suppose you have created a base backup around midnight. At 12.00 AM, the slave is promoted. At 03.00 PM, something crashes and you want to recover to 02.00 PM. You will start to replay transaction log created after the base backup and follow the xlog stream of your desired server as those two nodes started to diverge at 12.00 AM.

The timeline change will also be visible in the name of the transaction log files. Here is an example of an xlog file in timeline 1:

```
000000010000000000000F5
```

If the timeline switches to 2 the new filename would be as follows:

```
000000020000000000000F5
```

As you can see, xlog files from different timelines could theoretically exist in the same archive directory.

Managing conflicts

So far you have learned a lot about replication already. In the next step, it is important to take a look at replication conflicts. The main question arising straight away is how can a conflict can ever happen in the first place?

Consider the following example:

Master	Slave
	BEGIN;
	SELECT ... FROM tab WHERE ...
	... running ...
DROP TABLE tab;	... conflict happen ...
	... transaction is allowed to continue for 30 seconds ...
	... conflict is resolved or ends before timeout ...

The problem here is that the master does not know that there is a transaction happening on the slave. Therefore, the DROP TABLE command does not block until the reading transaction is gone. If those two transactions happened on the same node, this would of course be the case. However, we are looking at two servers here. The DROP TABLE command will execute normally, and a request to kill those data files on disk will reach the slave through the transaction log. The slave is not in trouble: if the table is removed from disk, the SELECT clause has to die—if the slave waits for the SELECT clause to complete before applying the xlog, it might fall hopelessly behind.

The ideal solution is a compromise that can be controlled using a configuration variable:

```
max_standby_streaming_delay = 30s
        # max delay before canceling queries
            # when reading streaming WAL;
```

The idea is to wait for 30 seconds before resolving the conflict by killing the query on the slave. Depending on your application, you might want to change this variable to a more or less aggressive setting. Note that 30 seconds is for the entire replication stream and not for a single query. It might happen that a single query is killed a lot earlier because some other query has already waited for some time.

While the DROP TABLE command is clearly a conflict, there are some operations that are less obvious. Here is an example:

```
BEGIN;
...
DELETE FROM tab WHERE id < 10000;
COMMIT;
...
VACUUM tab;
```

Let us assume again that there is a long-running SELECT clause happening on the slave.

The DELETE clause is clearly not the problem here as it only flags the row as deleted—it does not actually remove it. Nor is the commit a problem, because it simply marks the transaction as done. Physically, the row is still there.

The problem starts when an operation such as vacuum kicks in. It will destroy the row on disk. Of course, those changes will make it to the xlog and eventually reach the slave, which is again in trouble.

To prevent typical problems caused by standard OLTP workloads, the PostgreSQL development team has introduced a config variable:

```
hot_standby_feedback = off
        # send info from standby to prevent
            # query conflicts
```

If this setting is on, the slave will periodically send the oldest transaction ID to the master. The vacuum will then know that there is an older transaction going on somewhere in the system and defer the cleanup age to a later point when it is safe to clean out those rows. In fact, the hot_standby_feedback parameter causes the same effect as a long transaction on the master.

As you can see, the `hot_standby_feedback` parameter is off by default. Why is that the case? Well, there is a good reason for that: if it is off, a slave does not have a real impact on the master. Transaction log streaming does not consume a lot of CPU power, making streaming replication cheap and efficient. However, if a slave (which might not even be under your control) keeps transactions open for too long, your master might suffer from table bloat due to late cleanup. In a default setup this is less desirable than reduced conflicts.

Having `hot_standby_feedback = on` will usually avoid 99% of all OLTP-related conflicts, which is especially important if your transactions take longer than just a couple of milliseconds.

Making replication more reliable

In this chapter you have already seen that setting up replication is easy and does not require a lot of effort. However, there are always some corner cases which can cause operational challenges. One of those corner cases is all about transaction log retention.

Consider the following scenario:

- A base backup is fetched
- After the backup, nothing happens for one hour
- The slave is started

Keep in mind that the master does not care too much about the existence of the slave. Therefore, the transaction log needed for the slave to start up might not exist on the master anymore as it might have been removed by checkpoints already. The problem is that a re-sync is needed to be able to fire up the slave. In the case of a multi-TB database, this is clearly a problem.

A potential solution to the problem is to use the `wal_keep_segments` setting:

```
wal_keep_segments = 0       # in logfile segments, 16MB each; 0 disables
```

By default, PostgreSQL keeps enough transaction logs around to survive an unexpected crash, but not much more. With the `wal_keep_segments` setting you can tell the server to preserve more data so that a slave can catch up even if it falls behind.

It is important to keep in mind that servers not only fall behind because they are too slow or too busy—in many cases a delay happens because the network is too slow. Suppose you are creating an index on a 1 TB table: PostgreSQL will sort the data, and when the index is actually built it is also sent to the transaction log. Just imagine what it means when hundreds of megabytes of xlog should be sent over a wire, which can maybe only handle 1 gigabit or so. Many gigabytes of data might be the consequence within seconds. Therefore, adjusting the `wal_keep_segments` setting should not focus on the typical delay but on the highest delay tolerable to the administrator (maybe some margin of safety).

Investing in a reasonably high setting for the `wal_keep_segments` setting makes a lot of sense, and I recommend ensuring that there is always enough data around.

An alternative solution to the problem of running out of transaction logs is replication slots, which will be covered later in this chapter.

Upgrading to synchronous replication

So far, asynchronous replication has been covered in reasonable detail. However, asynchronous replication means that a commit on the slave is allowed to happen after the commit on the master. If a master crashes, data that has not made it to the slave yet might be lost even if replication is around.

Synchronous replication is here to solve the problem: if PostgreSQL replicates synchronously, a commit has to be flushed to disk by at least one replica in order to go through on the master. Therefore, synchronous replication basically reduces the odds of data loss quite substantially.

In PostgreSQL, configuring synchronous replication is easy. Basically, just two things have to be done:

- Adjust the `synchronous_standby_names` setting in the `postgresql.conf` file on the master
- Add an `application_name` setting to the `primary_conninfo` parameter in the `recovery.conf` file in the replica

Let us get started with the `postgresql.conf` file on the master:

```
synchronous_standby_names = ''
        # standby servers that provide sync rep
                # number of sync standbys and comma-separated
        # list of application_name
                # from standby(s); '*' = all
```

If you put in `'*'`, all nodes will be considered as synchronous candidates. However, in real-life scenarios it is more likely that only a couple of nodes will be listed. Here is an example:

```
synchronous_standby_names = 'slave1, slave2, slave3'
```

Now we have to change the `recovery.conf` file and add `application_name`:

```
primary_conninfo = '... application_name=slave2'
```

The replica will now connect to the master as `slave2`. The master will check its config and figure that `slave2` is the first one in the list, which makes a viable slave. PostgreSQL will therefore ensure that a commit on the master will only be successful if the slave confirms that the transaction is there.

Let us assume now that `slave2` goes down for some reason: PostgreSQL will try to turn one of the other two nodes into a synchronous standby. The problem is this: what if there is no other server? In this case, PostgreSQL will wait on commit forever if a transaction is supposed to be synchronous. Yes, this is true: PostgreSQL will not continue to commit unless there are at least two viable nodes available. Remember, you have asked PostgreSQL to store data on at least two nodes—if you cannot provide enough hosts at any given point in time, it is your fault. In reality, this means that synchronous replication is best achieved with at least three nodes, as there is always a chance that one host is lost.

Talking about host failures, there is an important thing to note at this point: if a synchronous partner dies while a commit is going in, PostgreSQL will wait for it to return. Alternatively, the synchronous commit can happen with some other potential synchronous partner. The end user might not even notice that the synchronous partners change.

In some cases, storing data on just two nodes might not be enough: maybe you want to improve safety even more and store data on even more nodes. To achieve, that you can make use of the following syntax (in PostgreSQL 9.6 or higher):

```
synchronous_standby_names =
    '4(slave1, slave2, slave3, slave4, slave5, slave6)'
```

In this case, data is supposed to end up on four out of six nodes before the commit is confirmed by the master.

Of course, this comes with a price tag—keep in mind that speed will go down if you add more and more synchronous replicas. There is no such thing as a free lunch. To keep the performance overhead under control, PostgreSQL provides a couple of means, which will be discussed in the following section.

Adjusting durability

In this chapter, you have seen that data is either replicated synchronously or asynchronously. However, this is not a global thing. To ensure good performance, PostgreSQL allows you to configure things in a very flexible way. It is possible to replicate everything synchronously or asynchronously, but in many cases you might want to do things in a more fine-grained way. This is exactly when the `synchronous_commit` setting is needed.

Assuming that synchronous replication has been configured (the `application_name` setting in the `recovery.conf` file as well as the `synchronous_standby_names` setting in the `postgresql.conf` file), the `synchronous_commit` setting will offer the following options:

- `off`: This is basically asynchronous replication. WAL won't be flushed to disk on the master instantly and the master won't wait for the slave to write everything to disk. If the master fails, some data might be lost (up to three times `wal_writer_delay`).
- `local`: The transaction log is flushed to disk on commit on the master. However, the master does not wait on the slave (asynchronous replication).
- `remote_write`: The `remote_write` setting already makes PostgreSQL replicate synchronously. However, only the master saves data to disk. For the slave, it is enough to send the data to the operating system. The idea is to now wait for the second disk flush to speed up things. It is very unlikely that both storage systems crash at exactly the same time. Therefore, the risk of data loss is close to zero.
- `on`: In this case, a transaction is okay if the master and the slave(s) have successfully flushed the transaction to disk. The application will not receive a commit unless data is safely stored on two servers (or more depending on the configuration).

- `remote_apply`: While `on` ensures that data is safely stored on two nodes, it does not guarantee that you can simply load balance right away. The fact that data is flushed on the disk does not ensure that the user can already see the data. For example, if there is a conflict, a slave will halt transaction replay—however, a transaction log is still sent to the slave during a conflict and flushed to disk. In short, it can happen that data is flushed on the slave even if it is not visible to the end user yet. `remote_apply` fixes this problem. It ensures that data must be visible on the replica so that the next read request can be safely executed on the slave, which can already see the changes made to the master and exposes them to the end user.

`remote_apply` is, of course, the slowest way to replicate data because it requires the slave to already expose the data to the end user.

In PostgreSQL, the `synchronous_commit` parameter is not a global value. It can be adjusted on various levels, just like many other settings. You might want to do something like this:

```
test=# ALTER DATABASE test SET synchronous_commit TO off;
ALTER DATABASE
```

Sometimes, only a single database should replicate in a certain way. It is also possible to just synchronously replicate if you are connected as a specific user. Last but not least, it is also possible to tell a single transaction how to commit. By adjusting the `synchronous_commit` parameter on the fly it is possible to even control things on a per-transaction level.

For example, consider the following two scenarios:

- Writing to a log table where you might want to use asynchronous commit because you want to be fast
- Storing a credit card payment where you want to be safe so a synchronous transaction might be the desired thing

As you can see, the very same database might have different requirements depending on which data is modified. Therefore, changing data on the transaction level is very useful and helps to improve speed.

Making use of replication slots

After this introduction to synchronous replication and dynamically adjustable durability I want to focus your attention on a feature called replication slots.

What is the purpose of a replication slot? Let us consider the following example: there is a master and a slave. On the master, a large transaction is executed and the network connection is not fast enough to ship all the data in time. At some point, the master removes its transaction log (checkpoint). If the slave is too far behind, a re-sync is needed. As you have already seen, the `wal_keep_segments` setting can be used to reduce the risk of failing replication. The question is this: what is the best value for the `wal_keep_segments` setting? Sure, more is better, but how much is best?

Replication slots will solve this problem for you: if you are using a replication slot, a master can only recycle the transaction log once it has been consumed by all replicas. The advantage here is that a slave can never fall behind so much that a re-sync is needed. The trouble is, suppose you shut down a replica without telling the master about it. The master would keep a transaction log forever and the disk on the primary server would eventually fill up causing unnecessary downtime.

To reduce the risk for the master, replication slots should only be used in conjunction with proper monitoring and alerting. It is simply necessary to keep an eye on open replication slots, which could potentially cause issues or which might not be in use anymore.

In PostgreSQL there are two types of replication slot:

- Physical replication slots
- Logical replication slots

Physical replication slots can be used for standard streaming replication. They will make sure that data is not recycled too early. Logical replication slots do the same thing. However, they are used for logical decoding. The idea behind logical decoding is to give users a chance to attach to the transaction log and decode it with a plugin. A logical transaction slot is therefore some sort of tail `-f` for database instances. It allows to extract changes made to the database and therefore to the transaction log in any format and for any purpose. In many cases a logical replication slot is used for logical replication.

Handling physical replication slots

To make use of replication slots, changes have to be made to the `postgresql.conf` file:

```
wal_level = logical
max_replication_slots = 5        # or whatever number is needed
```

With physical slots, logical is not yet necessary—replica is enough. However, for logical slots, we need a higher `wal_level` setting. Then the `max_replication_slots` setting has to be changed. Basically, just put in a number that serves your purpose. My recommendation is to add some spare slots so that you can easily attach more consumers without restarting the server along the way.

After a restart, the slot can already be created:

```
test=# x
Expanded display is on.
test=# df *create*physical*slot*
List of functions
-[ RECORD 1 ]-------+------------------------------------------------
-----------------
Schema                   | pg_catalog
Name                     | pg_create_physical_replication_slot
Result data type     | record
Argument data types | slot_name name,
                 immediately_reserve boolean DEFAULT false,
               OUT slot_name name,
              OUT xlog_position pg_lsn
Type                     | normal
```

The `pg_create_physical_replication_slot` function is here to help you create the slot. It can be called with one or two parameters: In case only a slot name is passed, the slot will be active when it is used for the first time. If `true` is passed as the second parameter, the slot will immediately start to conserve transaction log:

```
test=# SELECT *
       FROM pg_create_physical_replication_slot('some_slot_name', true);
   slot_name    | xlog_position
----------------+---------------
 some_slot_name | 0/EF8AD1D8
(1 row)
```

To see which slots are active on the master, consider running the following SQL statement:

```
test=# x
Expanded display is on.
test=# SELECT * FROM pg_replication_slots;
-[ RECORD 1 ]-------+----------------
slot_name           | some_slot_name
plugin              |
slot_type           | physical
datoid              |
database            |
active              | f
active_pid          |
xmin                |
catalog_xmin        |
restart_lsn         | 0/EF8AD1D8
confirmed_flush_lsn |
```

The view will tell us a lot about the slot. It contains information about the type of slot in use, the transaction log positions, and so on.

To make use of the slot, all you have to do is to add it to the `recovery.conf` file:

```
primary_slot_name = 'some_slot_name'
```

Once streaming is restarted, the slot will be used directly and protect replication.

If you don't want your slot anymore, you can drop it easily:

```
test=# df *drop*slot*
List of functions
-[ RECORD 1 ]-------+--------------------------
Schema              | pg_catalog
Name                | pg_drop_replication_slot
Result data type    | void
Argument data types | name
Type                | normal
```

When a slot is dropped there is no distinction between a logical and a physical slot anymore. Just pass the name of the slot to the function and execute it.

> Note that nobody is allowed to use the slot when it is dropped. Otherwise, PostgreSQL will error out (for good reason).

Handling logical replication slots

Logical replication slots are essential to logical replication. Due to space limitations in this chapter it is unfortunately not possible to cover all aspects of logical replication. However, I want to outline some of the basic concepts, which are essential for logical decoding and therefore also to logical replication.

If you want to create a replication slot, here is how it works. The function needed here takes two parameters: the first one will define the name of the replication slot, while the second one carries the plugin used to decode the transaction log. It will determine the format PostgreSQL is going to use to return the data:

```
test=# SELECT *
    FROM pg_create_logical_replication_slot('logical_slot',
'test_decoding');
  slot_name   | xlog_position
--------------+---------------
 logical_slot | 0/EF8AD4B0
(1 row)
```

You can check for the existence of the slot using the same command as earlier again.

To show you what a slot really does, a small test can be created:

```
test=# CREATE TABLE t_demo (id int, name text, payload text);
CREATE TABLE
test=# BEGIN;
BEGIN
test=# INSERT INTO t_demo VALUES (1, 'hans', 'some data');
INSERT 0 1
test=# INSERT INTO t_demo VALUES (2, 'paul', 'some more data');
INSERT 0 1
test=# COMMIT;
COMMIT
test=# INSERT INTO t_demo VALUES (3, 'joe', 'less data');
INSERT 0 1
```

Note that two transactions were executed. The changes made to those transactions can now be extracted from the slot:

```
test=# SELECT pg_logical_slot_get_changes('logical_slot', NULL, NULL);
                                    pg_logical_slot_get_changes
-------------------------------------------------------------------------
--------------------------------------------------
 (0/EF8AF5B0,606546,"BEGIN 606546")
 (0/EF8CCCA0,606546,"COMMIT 606546")
 (0/EF8CCCD8,606547,"BEGIN 606547")
```

```
(0/EF8CCCD8,606547,"table public.t_demo: INSERT: id[integer]:1
    name[text]:'hans' payload[text]:'some data'")
(0/EF8CCD60,606547,"table public.t_demo: INSERT: id[integer]:2
    name[text]:'paul' payload[text]:'some more data'")
(0/EF8CCDE0,606547,"COMMIT 606547")
(0/EF8CCE18,606548,"BEGIN 606548")
(0/EF8CCE18,606548,"table public.t_demo: INSERT: id[integer]:3
    name[text]:'joe' payload[text]:'less data'")
(0/EF8CCE98,606548,"COMMIT 606548")
(9 rows)
```

The format used here depends on the output plugin we have chosen previously. There are various output plugins for PostgreSQL such as `wal2json` and alike.

Note that in case default values are used, the logical stream will contain real values and not just functions. The logical stream has the data that ended up in the underlying tables.

Also keep in mind that the slot does not return data anymore once it is consumed:

```
test=# SELECT pg_logical_slot_get_changes('logical_slot', NULL, NULL);
 pg_logical_slot_get_changes
-----------------------------
(0 rows)
```

The result set on the second call is therefore empty. If you want to fetch data repeatedly, PostgreSQL offers the `pg_logical_slot_peek_changes` function. It works just like the `pg_logical_slot_get_changes` function but assures that data will still be available in the slot.

Using plain SQL is, of course, not the only way to consume transaction log. There is also a tool called the `pg_recvlogical` extension. It can be compared to doing `tail -f` on an entire database instance and to receive the flow of data in real time.

Let us start the `pg_recvlogical` extension:

```
[hs@zenbook ~]$ pg_recvlogical -S logical_slot -P test_decoding
    -d test -U postgres --start -f -
```

In this case, the tool connects to the test database and consumes data from the `logical_slot`. `-f -` means that the stream will be sent to `stdout`.

Let us kill some data:

```
test=# DELETE FROM t_demo WHERE id < random()*10;
DELETE 3
```

The changes will make it into the transaction log. However, by default the database only cares about what the table will look like after the deletion. It knows which blocks have to be touched and all that—it does not know what was previously:

```
BEGIN 606549
table public.t_demo: DELETE: (no-tuple-data)
table public.t_demo: DELETE: (no-tuple-data)
table public.t_demo: DELETE: (no-tuple-data)
COMMIT 606549
```

Therefore, the output is pretty pointless. To fix that, the following line comes to the rescue:

```
test=# ALTER TABLE t_demo REPLICA IDENTITY FULL;
ALTER TABLE
```

If the table is repopulated with data and deleted again, the transaction log stream looks like that:

```
BEGIN 606558
table public.t_demo: DELETE: id[integer]:1 name[text]:'hans'
    payload[text]:'some data'
table public.t_demo: DELETE: id[integer]:2 name[text]:'paul'
    payload[text]:'some more data'
table public.t_demo: DELETE: id[integer]:3 name[text]:'joe'
    payload[text]:'less data'
COMMIT 606558
```

Now all the changes are in.

Use cases of logical slots

There are various use cases of replication slots. The most simplistic use case is the one shown here. Data can be fetched from the server in the desired format and used to audit, debug or simply monitor a database instance.

The next logical step of course is to take this stream of changes and use it for replication. Solutions such as BDR are totally based on logical decoding because changes on the binary level would not work with multi-master replication.

Finally, there is the need to upgrade without downtime. Remember, the binary transaction log stream cannot be used to replicate between different versions of PostgreSQL. Therefore, future versions of PostgreSQL will support a tool called `pglogical`, which helps to upgrade without downtime.

Summary

In this chapter, you have learned about the most important features of PostgreSQL replication, such as streaming replication and replication conflicts. You have learned about PITR as well as about replication slots. Note that a book on replication is never complete unless it spans around 400 pages or so, but you have learned the most important things every administrator should know.

The next chapter will be about useful extensions to PostgreSQL. You will learn about extensions that have been widely adapted by the industry and that provide even more functionality.

11
Deciding on Useful Extensions

In the previous chapter of this book, our attention was focused on replication, transaction log shipping, and logical decoding. After this mostly administration-related stuff, the goal is to aim at a broader topic. In the PostgreSQL world, many things are done through extensions. The advantage of extensions is that functionality can be added without bloating the PostgreSQL core. People can choose from sometimes-competing extensions and find what is best for them.

In this chapter, some of the most widespread extensions for PostgreSQL are discussed. However, before digging deeper into the issue I want to state that this chapter only features a list of extensions that I personally find useful. There are so many modules out there these days that it is impossible to cover them all in a reasonable way. Stuff is published every day and it is sometimes even hard for a professional to be aware of everything out there.

The following main topics will be covered in this chapter:

- How extensions work
- A selection of `contrib` modules
- A quick look at GIS-related modules
- Other useful extensions

Note that only the most important extensions will be covered.

Understanding how extensions work

Before digging into the extensions available out there, it is a good idea to take a look at how extensions work in the first place. Understanding the inner workings of the extension machinery can be quite beneficial.

Let's take a look at the syntax first:

```
test=# \h CREATE EXTENSION
Command:     CREATE EXTENSION
Description: install an extension
Syntax:
CREATE EXTENSION [ IF NOT EXISTS ] extension_name
    [ WITH ] [ SCHEMA schema_name ]
             [ VERSION version ]
             [ FROM old_version ]
             [ CASCADE ]
```

When you want to deploy an extension, simply call CREATE EXTENSION clause. It will check for the extension and load it into your database. Note that the extension will be loaded into a database and not into the entire database instance.

If you are loading an extension, you can decide on the schema you want to use. Many extensions can be relocated so the user has the choice which schema to use. Then it is possible to decide on a specific version of the extension. Often you don't want to deploy the latest version of an extension because your client is running outdated software. In such cases, it might be handy to be able to deploy any version available on the system.

The FROM old_version clause requires some more attention. Back in the old days, PostgreSQL did not support extensions, so a lot of unpackaged code is still around. This option causes the CREATE EXTENSION clause to run an alternative installation script that absorbs the existing objects into the extension, instead of creating new objects. Be careful that the SCHEMA clause specifies the schema containing these preexisting objects. Use it only when you have old modules around.

Finally there is the CASCADE clause. Some extensions depend on other extensions. The CASCADE option will automatically deploy those software packages too. Here is an example:

```
test=# CREATE EXTENSION earthdistance;
ERROR:  required extension "cube" is not installed
HINT:  Use CREATE EXTENSION ... CASCADE to install required extensions too.
```

`earthdistance` is a module that implements great circle distance calculations. As you might know, the shortest distance between two points on earth is not a straight line; but instead a pilot has to adjust his course constantly to find the fastest route to fly from one point to the other. The thing is: the `earthdistance` extension depends on the `cube` extension, which allows you to perform operations on a sphere.

To automatically deploy the dependency, the `CASCADE` clause can be used as just described:

```
test=# CREATE EXTENSION earthdistance CASCADE;
NOTICE:  installing required extension "cube"
CREATE EXTENSION
```

In this case, both extensions will be deployed.

Checking for available extensions

PostgreSQL offers various views to figure out which extensions are there on the system and which ones are actually deployed. One of those views is `pg_available_extensions`:

```
test=# \d pg_available_extensions
View "pg_catalog.pg_available_extensions"
      Column         | Type | Modifiers
-------------------+------+-----------
 name              | name |
 default_version   | text |
 installed_version | text |
 comment           | text |
```

It contains a list of all extensions available, including their names, their default version, and the version currently installed. To make it easier to the end user, there is also a description available, telling us more about the extension.

The following listing contains two lines taken from `pg_available_extensions`:

```
test=# \x
Expanded display is on.
test=# SELECT * FROM pg_available_extensions LIMIT 2;
-[ RECORD 1 ]-----+-------------------------------------------------------
-----
name              | earthdistance
default_version   | 1.1
installed_version | 1.1
comment           | calculate great-circle distances on the surface of the
Earth
-[ RECORD 2 ]-----+-------------------------------------------------------
```

```
-----
name              | plpgsql
default_version   | 1.0
installed_version | 1.0
comment           | PL/pgSQL procedural language
```

As you can see, the earthdistance and plpgsql extensions are both enabled in my database. The plpgsql extension is there by default and earthdistance has just been added before along with cube. The beauty of this view is that you can quickly get an overview of what is installed and what can be installed.

However, in some cases, extensions are available in more than just one version. To find out more about versioning, consider checking out the following view:

```
test=# \d pg_available_extension_versions
View "pg_catalog.pg_available_extension_versions"
    Column    |  Type    | Modifiers
--------------+----------+------------
 name         | name     |
 version      | text     |
 installed    | boolean  |
 superuser    | boolean  |
 relocatable  | boolean  |
 schema       | name     |
 requires     | name[]   |
 comment      | text     |
```

Some more detailed information is available here as shown in the next listing:

```
test=# SELECT * FROM pg_available_extension_versions LIMIT 1;
-[ RECORD 1 ]------------------------------------------------------------
name        | earthdistance
version     | 1.1
installed   | t
superuser   | t
relocatable | t
schema      |
requires    | {cube}
comment     | calculate great-circle distances on the surface of the Earth
```

PostgreSQL will also tell you whether the extension can be relocated, which schema it has been deployed in, and what other extensions are needed. Then there is the comment describing the extension, which has already been shown previously.

The main question now is: where does PostgreSQL find all this information about extensions on the system? Assuming that you have deployed PostgreSQL 9.6 from the official PostgreSQL RPM repository, the /usr/pgsql-9.6/share/extension directory will contain a couple of files:

```
...
-bash-4.3$ ls -l citext*
-rw-r--r-- 1 root root  1028 Oct 26 13:28 citext--1.0--1.1.sql
-rw-r--r-- 1 root root  2748 Oct 26 13:28 citext--1.1--1.2.sql
-rw-r--r-- 1 root root   307 Oct 26 13:28 citext--1.2--1.3.sql
-rw-r--r-- 1 root root 12991 Oct 26 13:28 citext--1.3.sql
-rw-r--r-- 1 root root   158 Oct 26 13:28 citext.control
-rw-r--r-- 1 root root  9781 Oct 26 13:28 citext-unpackaged--1.0.sql
...
```

The default version of the citext (case-insensitive text) extension is 1.3, so there is a file called citext--1.3.sql. In addition to that there are files used to move from one version to the next (1.0 ◎ 1.1, 1.1 ◎ 1.2, and so on).

Then there is the .control file:

```
-bash-4.3$ cat citext.control
# citext extension
comment = 'data type for case-insensitive character strings'
default_version = '1.3'
module_pathname = '$libdir/citext'
relocatable = true
```

It contains all the metadata related to this extension; the first entry contains the comment. Note that this content is what will be shown in the system views just discussed. When you access those views, PostgreSQL will go to this directory and read all the .control files. Then there is the default version and the path to the binaries. If you are installing a typical extension from RPM, the directory is going to be $libdir, which is inside your PostgreSQL binary directory. However, if you have written your own commercial extension, it might very well reside somewhere else.

The last setting will tell PostgreSQL whether the extension can reside in any schema or whether it has to be in a fixed, predefined schema.

Finally, there is the unpackaged file. Here is an extract:

```
. . .
ALTER EXTENSION citext ADD type citext;
ALTER EXTENSION citext ADD function citextin(cstring);
ALTER EXTENSION citext ADD function citextout(citext);
ALTER EXTENSION citext ADD function citextrecv(internal);
. . .
```

The unpackaged file will turn existing code into an extension. It is therefore important to consolidate existing things in your database.

Making use of contrib modules

After this theoretical introduction to extensions, it is time to take a look at some of the most important extensions. In this section, you will learn about modules provided to you as part of the PostgreSQL `contrib` module. When you install PostgreSQL, I recommend that you always install those `contrib` modules as they contain vital extensions that can really make your life easier.

In this section, you will be guided through some of the ones I find most interesting.

Using the adminpack

The idea behind the `adminpack` module is to give administrators a way to access the filesystem without SSH access. The package contains a couple of functions to make that possible.

To load the module into the database, run the following command:

```
test=# CREATE EXTENSION adminpack;
CREATE EXTENSION
```

One of the most interesting features of `adminpack` module is the ability to inspect log files. The `pg_logdir_ls` function checks out the log directory and returns a list of log files:

```
test=# SELECT * FROM pg_catalog.pg_logdir_ls() AS (a timestamp, b text);
ERROR:  the log_filename parameter must
     equal 'postgresql-%Y-%m-%d_%H%M%S.log'
```

The important thing here is that the `log_filename` parameter has to be adjusted to `adminspack` module's needs. If you happen to run RPMs downloaded from the PostgreSQL repositories, the `log_filename` parameter is defined as `postgresql-%a`, which has to be changed in this case to avoid the error.

After the change, a list of log filenames are returned:

```
test=# SELECT * FROM pg_catalog.pg_logdir_ls() AS (a timestamp, b text);
          a          |                      b
---------------------+---------------------------------------------
 2017-03-03 16:32:58 | pg_log/postgresql-2017-03-03_163258.log
(1 row)
```

It is also possible to determine the size of a file on disk. Here is an example:

```
test=# SELECT b, pg_catalog.pg_file_length(b)
     FROM pg_catalog.pg_logdir_ls() AS (a timestamp, b text);
                    b                    | pg_file_length
-----------------------------------------+----------------
 pg_log/postgresql-2017-03-03_163258.log |           1525
(1 row)
```

In addition to those features, there are some more functions provided by the module:

```
test=# SELECT proname FROM pg_proc WHERE proname ~ 'pg_file_.*';
    proname
----------------
 pg_file_write
 pg_file_rename
 pg_file_unlink
 pg_file_read
 pg_file_length
(5 rows)
```

You can read, write, rename, or simply delete files.

> Note that those functions can, of course, only be called by superusers.

Applying bloom filters

Since PostgreSQL 9.6, it is possible to add index types on the fly using extensions. The new CREATE ACCESS METHOD command as well as some additional features made it possible to create fully functional and transaction logged indexes types on the fly.

The bloom extension provides PostgreSQL users with bloom filters, which are a pre-filter, which helps to efficiently reduce the amount of data as soon as possible . The idea behind a bloom filter is to calculate a bit mask and to compare the bit mask to the query. The bloom filter might produce some false positives but still reduce the amount of data dramatically.

It is especially useful when a table consists of hundreds of columns and millions of rows. It is not possible to index hundreds of columns with B-trees so a bloom filter is a good alternative because it allows indexing everything at once.

To show you how things work, I have installed the extension:

```
test=# CREATE EXTENSION bloom;
CREATE EXTENSION
```

In the next step, a table containing various columns is created:

```
test=# CREATE TABLE t_bloom
(
        id              serial,
        col1            int4 DEFAULT random() * 1000,
        col2            int4 DEFAULT random() * 1000,
        col3            int4 DEFAULT random() * 1000,
        col4            int4 DEFAULT random() * 1000,
        col5            int4 DEFAULT random() * 1000,
        col6            int4 DEFAULT random() * 1000,
        col7            int4 DEFAULT random() * 1000,
        col8            int4 DEFAULT random() * 1000,
        col9            int4 DEFAULT random() * 1000
);
CREATE TABLE
```

To make it easier, those columns have a default value so that data can easily be added using a simple SELECT clause:

```
test=# INSERT INTO t_bloom (id) SELECT *
    FROM    generate_series(1, 1000000);
INSERT 0 1000000
```

The query adds 1 million rows to the table. Now the table can be indexed:

```
test=# CREATE INDEX idx_bloom ON t_bloom
     USING bloom(col1, col2, col3, col4, col5, col6, col7, col8, col9);
CREATE INDEX
```

Not that the index contains nine columns at a time. In contrast to a B-tree, the order of those columns does not really make a difference. Note that the table I just created is around 65 MB without indexes.

The index adds another 15 MB to the storage footprint:

```
test=# \di+ idx_bloom
                        List of relations
 Schema |    Name    | Type  | Owner |  Table   | Size  | Description
--------+------------+-------+-------+----------+-------+-------------
 public | idx_bloom  | index | hs    | t_bloom  | 15 MB |
(1 row)
```

The beauty of the bloom filter is that it is possible to look for any combination of columns:

```
test=# explain SELECT count(*)
     FROM     t_bloom
     WHERE    col4 = 454
              AND col3 = 354
              AND col9 = 423;
                                  QUERY PLAN
-----------------------------------------------------------------------------
-------
 Aggregate  (cost=20352.02..20352.03 rows=1 width=8)
   ->  Bitmap Heap Scan on t_bloom   (cost=20348.00..20352.02
                                              rows=1 width=0)
         Recheck Cond: ((col3 = 354) AND (col4 = 454) AND (col9 = 423))
         ->  Bitmap Index Scan on idx_bloom
               (cost=0.00..20348.00 rows=1 width=0)
                 Index Cond: ((col3 = 354) AND (col4 = 454) AND (col9 = 423))
(5 rows)
```

What you have seen so far feels exceptional. A natural question that might arise is: why not always use a bloom filter? The reason is simple--the database has to read the entire bloom filter in order to use it. In the case of a, say, B-tree, this is not necessary.

In future, more index types will most likely be added to ensure that even more use cases can be covered with PostgreSQL.

If you want to read more about bloom filters, consider reading our blog: `http://www.cyber tec.at/trying-out-postgres-bloom-indexes/`.

Deploying btree_gist and btree_gin

After this brief section about indexes, there are more indexing-related features that can be added. In PostgreSQL, there is the concept of operator classes, which has already been discussed in one of the earlier chapters. `contrib` module offers two extensions (namely, `btree_gist` and `btree_gin`) to add B-tree functionality to GiST and GIN indexes.

Why is that so useful? GiST indexes offer various features that are not supported by B-trees. One of those features is the ability to perform **k-nearest neighbor** (**KNN**) search.

Why is that relevant? Imagine somebody is looking for data that was added yesterday around noon. So when is that? In some cases, it might be hard to come up with boundaries. Or somebody is looking for a product that costs around 70 Euros. KNN might come to the rescue. Here is an example:

```
test=# CREATE TABLE t_test (id int);
CREATE TABLE
```

In the next step, some simple data is added:

```
test=# INSERT INTO t_test SELECT * FROM generate_series(1, 100000);
INSERT 0 100000
```

Now the extension can be added:

```
test=# CREATE EXTENSION btree_gist;
CREATE EXTENSION
```

Adding a GiST index to the column is easy. Just use the `USING gist` clause. Note that adding a GiST index on an integer column works only if the extension is around. Otherwise, PostgreSQL will report that there is no suitable operator class:

```
test=# CREATE INDEX idx_id ON t_test USING gist(id);
CREATE INDEX
```

Once the index has been deployed, it is possible to order by distance already:

```
test=# SELECT * FROM t_test ORDER BY id <-> 100 LIMIT 6;
 id
-----
 100
 101
  99
 102
  98
  97
(6 rows)
```

As you can see, the first row is an exact match. The next matches are already less precise and are getting worse. The query will always return a fixed number of rows.

The important thing is the execution plan:

```
test=# explain SELECT * FROM t_test ORDER BY id <-> 100 LIMIT 6;
                                  QUERY PLAN
------------------------------------------------------------------------------
--------------
 Limit  (cost=0.28..0.64 rows=6 width=8)
   ->  Index Only Scan using idx_id on t_test
             (cost=0.28..5968.28 rows=100000 width=8)
         Order By: (id <-> 100)
(3 rows)
```

As you can see, PostgreSQL goes straight for an index scan, which speeds up the query significantly.

In future versions of PostgreSQL, B-trees will most likely also support KNN search. A patch to add this feature has already floated around on the development mailing list. Maybe, it will eventually make it to the core. Having KNN as a B-tree feature could eventually lead to fewer GiST indexes on standard datatypes.

Dblink - consider phasing out

The desire to use database links has been around for many years already. However, around the turn of the century PostgreSQL foreign data wrappers were not even on the horizon and a traditional database link implementation was definitely not in sight either. Around this time, a PostgreSQL developer from California (Joe Conway) pioneered the work on database connectivity by introducing the concept of dblink into PostgreSQL. While dblink served people well over the years, it is no longer state-of-the-art.

Therefore, it is recommended to move from dblink to the more modern SQL/MED implementation (which is a specification that defines the way external data can be integrated in a relational database). The `postgres_fdw` extension has been built on top of SQL/MED and will offer more than just database connectivity as it allows to connect to basically any data source.

Fetching files with file_fdw

In some cases, it can make sense to read a file from disk and expose it to PostgreSQL as a table. This is exactly what you can achieve with `file_fdw` extension. The idea is to have a module which allows you to read data from disk and query it using SQL.

Installing the module works as expected:

```
CREATE EXTENSION file_fdw;
```

In the next step, we create a virtual server:

```
CREATE SERVER file_server FOREIGN DATA WRAPPER file_fdw;
```

The `file_server` is based on the `file_fdw` extension foreign data wrapper, which tells PostgreSQL how to access the file.

To expose a file as a table, the following command can be used:

```
CREATE FOREIGN TABLE t_passwd
(
    username text,
    passwd          text,
    uid             int,
    gid             int,
    gecos           text,
    dir             text,
    shell           text
) SERVER file_server
OPTIONS (format 'text', filename '/etc/passwd', header 'false', delimiter
':');
```

In my example, the /etc/passwd file will be exposed. All fields have to be listed and data types have to be mapped accordingly. All the additional important information is passed to the module using options. In this example, PostgreSQL has to know the type of file (text), the name and the path of the file as well as the delimiter. It is also possible to tell PostgreSQL whether there is a header. If the setting is true, the first line will be skipped and not important. Skipping headers is especially important if you happen to load a CSV file.

Once the table has been created, it is already possible to read data:

```
SELECT * FROM t_passwd;
```

Unsurprisingly, PostgreSQL returns the content of /etc/passwd:

```
test=# \x
Expanded display is on.
test=# SELECT * FROM t_passwd LIMIT 1;
-[ RECORD 1 ]-------
username | root
passwd   | x
uid      | 0
gid      | 0
gecos    | root
dir      | /root
shell    | /bin/bash
```

When looking at the execution plan, you will see that PostgreSQL uses a foreign scan to fetch the data from the file:

```
test=# explain (verbose true, analyze true)
    SELECT * FROM t_passwd;
                                                    QUERY PLAN
------------------------------------------------------------------------------------------
--------------------------------
  Foreign Scan on public.t_passwd  (cost=0.00..2.80 rows=18 width=168)
             (actual time=0.022..0.072 rows=61 loops=1)
    Output: username, passwd, uid, gid, gecos, dir, shell
    Foreign File: /etc/passwd
    Foreign File Size: 3484
 Planning time: 0.058 ms
 Execution time: 0.138 ms
(6 rows)
```

The execution plan also tells us about the file size and so on. Since we're talking about the planner, there is a side note which is worth mentioning. PostgreSQL will even fetch statistics for the file. The planner checks the file size and assigns the same costs to the file as it would to a normal PostgreSQL table of the same size.

Inspecting storage using pageinspect

If you are facing storage corruption or some other storage-related problem that might be related to bad blocks in a table, the pageinspect extension might be the module you are looking for:

```
test=# CREATE EXTENSION pageinspect;
CREATE EXTENSION
```

The idea behind pageinspect is to provide you with a module which allows you to inspect a table on the binary level.

When using the module, the most important thing to do is to fetch a block:

```
test=# SELECT * FROM get_raw_page('pg_class', 0);
...
```

The function will return a single block. In the preceding example, it is the first block in pg_class parameter, which is a system table (of course, you can use any other table you want).

In the next step, you can extract the page header:

```
test=# \x
Expanded display is on.
test=# SELECT * FROM page_header(get_raw_page('pg_class', 0));
-[ RECORD 1 ]---------
lsn        | 1/35CAE5B8
checksum   | 0
flags      | 1
lower      | 240
upper      | 1288
special    | 8192
pagesize   | 8192
version    | 4
prune_xid  | 606562
```

It already contains a lot of information about the page. If you want to know even more, you can call the `heap_page_items` function, which dissects the page and returns one row per tuple:

```
test=# SELECT   *
       FROM    heap_page_items(get_raw_page('pg_class', 0))
       LIMIT 1;
-[ RECORD 1 ]---
lp            | 1
lp_off        | 49
lp_flags      | 2
lp_len        | 0
t_xmin        |
t_xmax        |
t_field3      |
t_ctid        |
t_infomask2   |
t_infomask    |
t_hoff        |
t_bits        |
t_oid         |
t_data        |  ...
```

You can also split the data into various tuples:

```
test=# SELECT tuple_data_split('pg_class'::regclass,
                               t_data, t_infomask, t_infomask2, t_bits)
       FROM heap_page_items(get_raw_page('pg_class', 0))
       LIMIT 2;
-[ RECORD 1 ]----+------------------------------------
tuple_data_split |
-[ RECORD 2 ]----+------------------------------------
tuple_data_split |
{"\\x6100000000000000000000000000000000000000000000000000000000000000
000000000000000000000000000000000000000000000000000000000000", "\\x98080000", "
\\x50ac0c00", "\\x00000000", "\\x01400000", "\\x00000000", "\\x4eac0c00", "\\x00
000000", "\\xbb010000", "\\x0050c347", "\\x00000000", "\\x00000000", "\\x01", "\\
x00", "\\x70", "\\x72", "\\x0100", "\\x0000", "\\x00", "\\x00", "\\x00", "\\x00", "\
\x00", "\\x00", "\\x00", "\\x01", "\\x64", "\\xc3400900", "\\x01000000", NULL, NULL
}
```

To read the data, you have to familiarize yourself with the on-disk format of PostgreSQL. Otherwise, the data might appear to be pretty obscure.

`pageinspect` provides functions for all access methods (tables, indexes, and so on) and allows dissecting storage in detail.

Investigating caching with pg_buffercache

After this brief introduction to the `pageinspect` extension, I want to focus your attention on the `pg_buffercache` extension, which allows you to take a deep look at the content of your I/O cache:

```
test=# CREATE EXTENSION pg_buffercache;
CREATE EXTENSION
```

The `pg_buffercache` extension provides you with a view containing a couple of fields:

```
test=# \d pg_buffercache
        View "public.pg_buffercache"
      Column       |    Type    | Modifiers
-------------------+----------+-----------
 bufferid          | integer    |
 relfilenode       | oid        |
 reltablespace     | oid        |
 reldatabase       | oid        |
 relforknumber     | smallint   |
 relblocknumber    | bigint     |
 isdirty           | boolean    |
 usagecount        | smallint   |
 pinning_backends  | integer    |
```

The `bufferid` field is just a number; it identifies the buffer. Then comes the `relfilenode` field, which points to the file on disk. If you want to look up which table a file belongs to, you can check out the `pg_class` module, which also contains a field, `relfilenode`. Then there are the `reldatabase` and the `reltablespace` fields. Note that all fields are defined as `oid` type, so to extract data in a more useful way, it is necessary to join system tables together.

The `relforknumber` field tells us which part of the table is cached. It could be the heap, the free space map, or some other component such as the visibility map. In the future there will surely be more types of relation forks.

The next, `relblocknumber`, tells us which block is cached. Finally, there is the `isdirty` flag, which indicates that a block has been modified, the usage counter, and the number of backends pinning the block.

If you want to make sense out of the pg_buffercache extension, it is important to add additional information. Suppose you want to figure out which database uses the cache the most. The following query might help:

```
test=# SELECT datname, count(*),
                      count(*) FILTER (WHERE isdirty = true) AS dirty
    FROM    pg_buffercache AS b, pg_database AS d
    WHERE    d.oid = b.reldatabase
    GROUP BY ROLLUP (1);
 datname   | count | dirty
-----------+-------+-------
 abc       |   132 |     1
 postgres  |    30 |     0
 test      | 11975 |    53
           | 12137 |    54
(4 rows)
```

In this case, the pg_database extension has to be joined. As you can see the oid is the join criteria, which might not be obvious to people who are new to PostgreSQL.

Sometimes you might want to know which blocks in the database you are connected to are cached:

```
test=# SELECT    relname, relkind,
       count(*),
       count(*) FILTER (WHERE isdirty = true) AS dirty
    FROM     pg_buffercache AS b, pg_database AS d, pg_class AS c
    WHERE    d.oid = b.reldatabase
             AND c.relfilenode = b.relfilenode
             AND datname = 'test'
    GROUP BY 1, 2
    ORDER BY 3 DESC
    LIMIT 7;
          relname           | relkind | count | dirty
----------------------------+---------+-------+-------
 t_bloom                    | r       |  8338 |     0
 idx_bloom                  | i       |  1962 |     0
 idx_id                     | i       |   549 |     0
 t_test                     | r       |   445 |     0
 pg_statistic               | r       |    90 |     0
 pg_depend                  | r       |    60 |     0
 pg_depend_reference_index  | i       |    34 |     0
(7 rows)
```

In this case, I filtered the current database and joined with the pg_class module, which contains the list of objects. The relkind column is especially noteworthy: r refers to table (relation) and i refers to index. It will tell you which object you are looking at.

Encrypting data with pgcrypto

One of the most powerful modules in the entire `contrib` module section is `pgcrypto`. It was originally written by one of the Skype sysadmins and offers countless functions to encrypt and decrypt data.

It offers functions for symmetric as well as for asymmetric encryption. Due to the large number of functions, it is definitely recommended to check out the documentation page: `https://www.postgresql.org/docs/current/static/pgcrypto.html`.

Due to the limited scope of this chapter, it is impossible to dig into all the details of the `pgcrypto` module.

Prewarming caches with pg_prewarm

When PostgreSQL operates normally, it tries to cache important data. The `shared_buffers` variable is important as it defines the size of the cache managed by PostgreSQL. The problem now is this: if you restart the database server, all the cache managed by PostgreSQL will be lost. Maybe the operating system will still have some data to reduce the impact on disk wait but in many cases this won't be enough.

The solution to the problem is called the `pg_prewarm` extension:

```
test=# CREATE EXTENSION pg_prewarm;
CREATE EXTENSION
```

The extension deploys a function that allows us to explicitly prewarm the cache whenever it is needed:

```
test=# \x
Expanded display is on.
test=# \df *prewa*
List of functions
-[ RECORD 1 ]-------+--------------------------------------------------------------
--
Schema              | public
Name                | pg_prewarm
Result data type    | bigint
Argument data types | regclass, mode text DEFAULT 'buffer'::text,
                                fork text DEFAULT 'main'::text,
                                first_block bigint DEFAULT NULL::bigint,
                                last_block bigint DEFAULT NULL::bigint
Type                | normal
```

The easiest and most common way to call `pg_prewarm` extension is to ask it to cache an entire object:

```
test=# SELECT pg_prewarm('t_test');
 pg_prewarm
------------
        443
(1 row)
```

Note that if the table is so large that it does not fit into the cache, only parts of the table will stay in cache, which is fine in most cases.

The function returns the number of 8,000 blocks processed by the function call.

If you don't want to cache all blocks of an object, you can also select a specific range inside the table. In the next example, you can see that blocks 10 to 30 are cached in the `main` fork:

```
test=# SELECT pg_prewarm('t_test', 'buffer', 'main', 10, 30);
pg_prewarm
------------
21
(1 row)
```

As you can see, 21 blocks were cached.

Inspecting performance with pg_stat_statements

`pg_stat_statements` is the most important module available in the `contrib` modules. It should always be enabled and is there to provide you with superior performance data. Without the `pg_stat_statements` module, it is really hard to track down performance problems.

Due to its importance, `pg_stat_statements` has already been discussed earlier in this book.

Inspecting storage with pgstattuple

Sometimes it can happen that tables in PostgreSQL grow out of proportion. The technical term for a table that has grown too much is **table bloat**. The question arising now is: which tables have bloated and how much bloat is there? The pgstattuple extension will help to answer those questions:

```
test=# CREATE EXTENSION pgstattuple;
CREATE EXTENSION
```

The module again deploys a couple of functions. In the case of the pgstattuple extension, those functions return a row consisting of a composite type. Therefore, the function has to be called in the FROM clause to ensure a readable result:

```
test=# \x
Expanded display is on.
test=# SELECT * FROM pgstattuple('t_test');
-[ RECORD 1 ]------+---------
table_len          | 3629056
tuple_count        | 100000
tuple_len          | 2800000
tuple_percent      | 77.16
dead_tuple_count   | 0
dead_tuple_len     | 0
dead_tuple_percent | 0
free_space         | 16652
free_percent       | 0.46
```

In my example, the table I used for testing seems to be in a pretty good state; the table is 3.6 MB in size and does not contain any dead rows. Free space is also limited. If you are suffering from table bloat, the number of dead rows and the amount of free space has grown out of proportion. Some free space and a handful of dead rows are normal--however, if the table has grown so much that it mostly consists of dead rows and free space, decisive action is needed to bring the situation under control again.

The pgstattuple extension also provides a function to inspect indexes:

```
test=# CREATE INDEX idx_id ON t_test (id);
CREATE INDEX
```

The `pgstattindex` function returns a lot of information about the index you want to inspect:

```
test=# SELECT * FROM pgstatindex('idx_id');
-[ RECORD 1 ]------+--------
version            | 2
tree_level         | 1
index_size         | 2260992
root_block_no      | 3
internal_pages     | 1
leaf_pages         | 274
empty_pages        | 0
deleted_pages      | 0
avg_leaf_density   | 89.83
leaf_fragmentation | 0
```

Our index is pretty dense (89%). This is a good sign. The default FILLFACTOR setting for an index is 90% so a value close to 90% indicates that the index is very good.

Sometimes you don't want to check a simple table but check all of them or just all tables in a schema. How can this be achieved? Normally, the list of objects you want to process is in the FROM clause. However, in my example, the function is already in the FROM clause so how can we make PostgreSQL loop over a list of tables? The answer is a LATERAL join. Here is an example:

```
test=# \x
Expanded display is on.
test=# SELECT tablename, (x).*
    FROM pg_tables,
        LATERAL (SELECT *
                FROM pgstattuple(tablename)) AS x
    WHERE schemaname = 'public';
-[ RECORD 1 ]------+-----------
tablename          | t_ort
table_len          | 114688
tuple_count        | 2354
tuple_len          | 88686
tuple_percent      | 77.33
dead_tuple_count   | 0
dead_tuple_len     | 0
dead_tuple_percent | 0
free_space         | 7732
free_percent       | 6.74
```

The first part of the FROM clause finds the table we are looking for. Each of the tables returned is then sent to the LATERAL join. A LATERAL join can be seen as a for each statement.

Keep in mind that pgstattuple has to read the entire objects. If your database is large it can take quite long to process. Therefore, it can be a good idea to store the results of the query you have just seen so that you can inspect it thoroughly without having to rerun the query again and again.

Fuzzy searches with pg_trgm

pg_trgm is a module that allows you to perform fuzzy searching. The module has already been discussed in Chapter 3, *Making Use of Indexes*.

Connecting to remote servers using postgres_fdw

Data is not always in one location only. More often than not, data is spread all over the infrastructure and it can happen that data residing in various places has to be integrated. The solution to the problem is a foreign data wrapper as defined by the SQL/MED standard.

In this section, the postgres_fdw extension will be discussed. It is a module that allows you to dynamically fetch data from a PostgreSQL data source. The first thing is to deploy the foreign data wrapper:

```
test=# \h CREATE FOREIGN DATA WRAPPER
Command:     CREATE FOREIGN DATA WRAPPER
Description: define a new foreign-data wrapper
Syntax:
CREATE FOREIGN DATA WRAPPER name
    [ HANDLER handler_function | NO HANDLER ]
    [ VALIDATOR validator_function | NO VALIDATOR ]
    [ OPTIONS ( option 'value' [, ... ] ) ]
```

Fortunately, the CREATE FOREIGN DATA WRAPPER command is hidden inside an extension; it can easily be installed using the normal process:

```
test=# CREATE EXTENSION postgres_fdw;
CREATE EXTENSION
```

In the next step, a virtual server has to be defined. It will point to the other host and tell PostgreSQL where to get the data. At the end of the data, PostgreSQL has to build a complete connect string--the server data is the first kind of thing PostgreSQL has to know. User information will be added later on. The server will only contain host, port, and so on:

```
test=# \h CREATE SERVER
Command:     CREATE SERVER
Description: define a new foreign server
Syntax:
CREATE SERVER server_name [ TYPE 'server_type' ] [ VERSION 'server_version'
]
    FOREIGN DATA WRAPPER fdw_name
    [ OPTIONS ( option 'value' [, ... ] ) ]
```

To show you how this works, I created a second database on the same host and created a server:

```
[hs@zenbook ~]$ createdb customer
[hs@zenbook ~]$ psql customer
customer=# CREATE TABLE t_customer (id int, name text);
CREATE TABLE
customer=# CREATE TABLE t_company (country text, name text, active text);
CREATE TABLE
customer=# \d
          List of relations
 Schema |    Name     | Type  | Owner
--------+-------------+-------+-------
 public | t_company   | table | hs
 public | t_customer  | table | hs
(2 rows)
```

Now the server should be added to the standard test database:

```
test=# CREATE SERVER customer_server
    FOREIGN DATA WRAPPER postgres_fdw
    OPTIONS (host 'localhost', dbname 'customer', port '5432');
CREATE SERVER
```

Note that all the important information is stored as OPTIONS clause. That is somewhat important because it gives a lot of flexibility to users. There are many different foreign data wrappers and each of them will need different options.

Once the server has been defined it is time to map users. If you connect from one server to the other, you might not be the same user in both locations. Therefore, foreign data wrappers require people to define the actual user mapping:

```
test=# \h CREATE USER MAPPING
Command:    CREATE USER MAPPING
Description: define a new mapping of a user to a foreign server
Syntax:
CREATE USER MAPPING FOR { user_name | USER | CURRENT_USER | PUBLIC }
    SERVER server_name
    [ OPTIONS ( option 'value' [ , ... ] ) ]
```

The syntax is pretty simple and it can be used easily:

```
test=# CREATE USER MAPPING FOR CURRENT_USER
    SERVER customer_server
    OPTIONS (user 'hs', password 'abc');
CREATE USER MAPPING
```

Again, all of the important information is hidden in the OPTIONS clause. Depending on the type of foreign data wrapper, the list of options will again differ.

Once the infrastructure is in place, you can create foreign tables. The syntax to create a foreign table is pretty similar to how one would create a normal local table. All the columns have to listed, including their datatypes:

```
test=# CREATE FOREIGN TABLE f_customer
    (
            id      int,
            name    text
    )
SERVER customer_server
OPTIONS (schema_name 'public', table_name 't_customer');
CREATE FOREIGN TABLE
```

All columns are listed just like in case of a normal CREATE TABLE clause. The special thing is just that the foreign table points to a table on a remote side. The name of the schema and the name of the table have to be specified in the OPTIONS clause.

Once it has been created, the table can be used:

```
test=# SELECT * FROM f_customer ;
 id | name
----+------
(0 rows)
```

To check what PostgreSQL does internally, it is a good idea to run the EXPLAIN clause with the analyze parameter. It will reveal some information about what is really going on in the server:

```
test=# EXPLAIN (analyze true, verbose true)
    SELECT * FROM f_customer ;
                                       QUERY PLAN
-----------------------------------------------------------------------------
------------------
 Foreign Scan on public.f_customer
     (cost=100.00..150.95 rows=1365 width=36)
     (actual time=0.221..0.221 rows=0 loops=1)
   Output: id, name
   Remote SQL: SELECT id, name FROM public.t_customer
 Planning time: 0.067 ms
 Execution time: 0.451 ms
(5 rows)
```

The important part here is Remote SQL. The foreign data wrapper will send a query to the other side and fetch as little data as possible. As many restrictions as possible are executed on the remote side to ensure that not much data has to be processed locally. Filter conditions, joins, and even aggregates can be performed remotely (as of PostgreSQL 10.0).

While the CREATE FOREIGN TABLE clause is surely a nice thing to use, it can be quite cumbersome to list all those columns over and over again.

The solution to the problem is called the IMPORT clause. It allows you to quickly and easily import entire schemas into your local database and to create foreign tables:

```
test=# \h IMPORT
Command:      IMPORT FOREIGN SCHEMA
Description: import table definitions from a foreign server
Syntax:
IMPORT FOREIGN SCHEMA remote_schema
    [ { LIMIT TO | EXCEPT } ( table_name [, ...] ) ]
    FROM SERVER server_name
    INTO local_schema
    [ OPTIONS ( option 'value' [, ... ] ) ]
```

IMPORT allows you to easily link large sets of tables easily. It also reduces the odds of typos and mistakes as all the information is directly fetched from the remote data source.

Here is how it works:

```
test=# IMPORT FOREIGN SCHEMA public
    FROM SERVER customer_server
    INTO public;
IMPORT FOREIGN SCHEMA
```

In this case, all tables previously created in the public schema are linked directly. As you can see, all remote tables are now available:

```
test=# \det
        List of foreign tables
 Schema |    Table    |      Server
--------+-------------+------------------
 public | f_customer  | customer_server
 public | t_company   | customer_server
 public | t_customer  | customer_server
(3 rows)
```

Handling mistakes and typos

Creating foreign tables is not really hard--however, it sometimes happens that people make mistakes, or maybe the passwords used simply change. To handle such issues, PostgreSQL offers two commands.

ALTER SERVER allows you to modify a server:

```
test=# \h ALTER SERVER
Command:     ALTER SERVER
Description: change the definition of a foreign server
Syntax:
ALTER SERVER name [ VERSION 'new_version' ]
    [ OPTIONS ( [ ADD | SET | DROP ] option ['value'] [, ... ] ) ]
ALTER SERVER name OWNER TO { new_owner | CURRENT_USER | SESSION_USER }
ALTER SERVER name RENAME TO new_name
```

You can use this command to add and remove options for a specific server, which is a good thing in case you have forgotten something.

If you want to modify user information, you can alter the user mapping as well:

```
test=# \h ALTER USER MAPPING
Command:     ALTER USER MAPPING
Description: change the definition of a user mapping
Syntax:
ALTER USER MAPPING FOR { user_name | USER | CURRENT_USER | SESSION_USER |
PUBLIC }
    SERVER server_name
    OPTIONS ( [ ADD | SET | DROP ] option ['value'] [, ... ] )
```

The SQL/MED interface is regularly improved and features are added as we speak. In future, even more optimizations will make it to the core, making the SQL/MED interface a good choice to improve scalability.

Other useful extensions

The extensions described so far are all part of the PostgreSQL `contrib` package, which is shipped as part of the PostgreSQL source code. However, the packages you have seen are not the only ones available in the PostgreSQL community. There are many more packages that allow you to do all kinds of things.

Unfortunately, this chapter is too short to dig into all the stuff which is currently out there. The number of modules is growing day by day and it is impossible to cover them all. Therefore, I only want to point to the ones I find most important.

PostGIS (`http://postgis.net/`) is the **geographical information systems** (**GIS**) database interface in the open source world. It has been adopted around the globe and is one of the de facto standards in the relational open source database world. It is a professional an extremely powerful solution.

If you are looking for geospatial routing, pgRouting is what you might be looking for. It offers various algorithms to find the best connections between locations and works on top of PostgreSQL.

In this chapter, you have already learned about the `postgres_fdw` extension, which allows you to connect to some other PostgreSQL database. There are many more foreign data wrappers around. One of the most famous and most professional ones is the `oracle_fdw` extension. It allows you to integrate with Oracle and fetch data over the wire just like it can be done with `postgres_fdw` extension.

Summary

In this chapter, you learned about some of the most promising modules shipped with the PostgreSQL standard distribution. These modules are pretty diverse and offer everything from database connectivity to case-insensitive text and modules to inspect your server.

After dealing with extensions, I want to shift your attention to migration. You will learn how you can move to PostgreSQL in the most simplistic way.

12
Troubleshooting PostgreSQL

In the previous chapter of this book, you learned about some useful extensions that are widely adopted and which can give your deployment a real boost. Following up, you will now be introduced to PostgreSQL troubleshooting. The idea is to give you a systematic approach to inspect and fix your system.

The following topics will be of interest:

- Approaching an unknown database
- Gaining a brief overview
- Identifying the key bottlenecks
- Handling storage corruption
- Inspecting broken replicas

Keep in mind that many things go wrong, so it is important to professionally monitor the database.

Approaching an unknown database

If you happen to administer a large-scale system, you might not know what the system is actually doing. Managing hundreds of systems implies that you won't know what is going on with each of them.

The most important thing, when it comes to troubleshooting, boils down to a single word-- data. If there is not enough data, there is no way to fix things. Therefore, the first step to troubleshooting is always to set up a monitoring tool such as pgwatch2 (`http://www.cyber tec.at/en/products/pgwatch2-next-generation-postgresql-monitoring-tool/`) that gives you some insights into your database server.

Once the reporting has told you about a situation worth checking, it means it has proven useful to approach the system in an organized way.

Inspecting pg_stat_activity

The first thing I recommend is checking out `pg_stat_statements`. Answer the following questions:

How many concurrent queries are currently executed on your system?

- Do you see similar types of queries showing up in the `query` column all the time?
- Do you see queries that have been running for a long time?
- Are there any locks that have not been granted?
- Do you see connections from suspicious hosts?

The `pg_stat_activity` view should always be checked first because it will give you an idea of what is happening on the system. Of course, graphical monitoring is supposed to give you a first impression of the system. However, at the end of the day, it really boils down to the queries actually running on the server. Therefore, a good overview of the system provided by `pg_stat_activity` is more than vital for tracking down issues.

To make it easier for you, I have compiled a couple of queries that I find useful to spot problems as fast as possible.

Querying pg_stat_activity

The following query shows how many queries are currently executed on your database:

```
test=# SELECT   datname,
        count(*) AS open,
        count(*) FILTER (WHERE state = 'active') AS active,
        count(*) FILTER (WHERE state = 'idle') AS idle,
        count(*) FILTER (WHERE state = 'idle in transaction') AS
idle_in_trans
FROM     pg_stat_activity
GROUP BY ROLLUP(1);
 datname | open | active | idle | idle_in_trans
---------+------+--------+------+---------------
 dev     |    1 |      1 |    0 |            0
 test    |    2 |      1 |    0 |            1
         |    3 |      2 |    0 |            1
(3 rows)
```

To show as much information as possible on the same screen, partial aggregates are used. You can see `active`, `idle`, as well as `idle in transaction` queries. If you see a high number of `idle in transaction` queries, it is definitely important to dig deeper to figure out how long those transactions have been kept open:

```
test=# SELECT pid, xact_start, now() - xact_start AS duration
    FROM   pg_stat_activity
    WHERE state LIKE '%transaction%'
    ORDER BY 3 DESC;
  pid  |           xact_start           |     duration
-------+--------------------------------+------------------
 22503 | 2017-03-15 13:13:08.368974+01  | 22:14:12.126463
(1 row)
```

The transaction in the listing has been open for more than 22 hours. The main question now is: how can a transaction be open for that long? In most applications, a transaction that takes so long is highly suspicious and potentially highly dangerous. Where does the danger come from? As you have learned earlier in this book already, the VACUUM clause can only clean up dead rows if no transaction can see that anymore. Now, if a transaction stays open for hours or even days, the VACUUM clause cannot produce useful results, which will lead to table bloat.

It is therefore highly recommended to ensure that long transactions are monitored, or killed in case they are too long. From version 9.6 on, PostgreSQL has a feature called **snapshot too old**, which allows you to terminate long transactions if snapshots are around for too long.

It is also a good idea to check whether there are any long queries going on:

```
test=# SELECT now() - query_start AS duration, datname, query
   FROM  pg_stat_activity
   WHERE       state = 'active'
   ORDER BY 1 DESC;
   duration      | datname | query
------------------+---------+--------------------------
 00:00:38.814526 | dev     | SELECT pg_sleep(10000);
 00:00:00         | test    | SELECT now() - query_start AS duration,
                             datname, query FROM pg_stat_activity WHERE
                             state = 'active' ORDER BY 1 DESC;
(2 rows)
```

In this case, all active queries are taken and the statements calculate how long a query has already been active. Often you see similar queries coming out on top, which can give you some valuable clues about what is happening on your system.

Treating Hibernate statements

Many ORMs such as Hibernate generate insanely long SQL statements. The trouble is this: pg_stat_activity will store only the first 1024 bytes of the query in the system view. The rest is truncated. In case of a long query generated by an ORM such as Hibernate, the query is cut off before the interesting parts (the FROM clause and so on) actually start.

The solution to the problem is to set a config parameter in the postgresql.conf file:

```
test=# SHOW track_activity_query_size;
track_activity_query_size
---------------------------
 1024
(1 row)
```

Increase this parameter to a reasonably high value (maybe 32,768) and restart PostgreSQL. You will then be able to see a lot longer queries and be able to detect issues more easily.

Figuring out where queries come from

When inspecting pg_stat_activity, there are some fields that will tell you where a query comes from:

```
 client_addr      | inet                              |
 client_hostname  | text                              |
 client_port      | integer                           |
```

Those fields will contain IP addresses and hostnames (if configured). But what happens if all applications send their requests from the very same IP because all applications reside on the same application server? It will be very hard for you to see which application generated a certain query.

The solution to the problem is to ask the developers to set an `application_name` variable:

```
test=# SHOW application_name ;
 application_name
------------------
 psql
(1 row)

test=# SET application_name TO 'some_name';
SET
test=# SHOW application_name ;
 application_name
------------------
 some_name
(1 row)
```

If people are cooperative, the `application_name` variable will show up in the system view and make it a lot easier to see where a query comes from. The `application_name` variable can also be set as part of the connect string.

Checking for slow queries

After inspecting `pg_stat_activity`, it makes sense to take a look at slow, time-consuming queries. Basically, there are two ways to approach the problem:

- Look for individual slow queries in the log
- Look for types of queries that take too much time

Finding single, slow queries is the classical approach to performance tuning. By setting the `log_min_duration_statement` variable to a desired threshold, PostgreSQL will start to write a log line for each query exceeding this threshold. By default, the slow query log is off:

```
test=# SHOW log_min_duration_statement;
 log_min_duration_statement
----------------------------
 -1
(1 row)
```

However, setting this variable to a reasonable good value makes perfect sense. Depending on your workload, the desired time might of course vary.

In many cases, the desired value might differ from database to database. Therefore, it is also possible to use the variable in a more fine-grained way:

```
test=# ALTER DATABASE test
    SET log_min_duration_statement TO 10000;
ALTER DATABASE
```

Setting the parameter only for a certain database makes perfect sense if your databases face different workloads.

When using the slow query log, it is important to consider one important factor--many smaller queries might cause more load than a handful of slow-running queries. Of course, it always makes sense to be aware of individual slow queries, but sometimes those queries are not the problem. Consider the following example: on your system, 1 million queries taking 500 milliseconds are executed along with some analytical queries running for minutes. Clearly, the real problem will never show up in the slow query log while every data export, every index creation, and every bulk load (which cannot be avoided in most cases anyway) will spam the log and point you to the wrong direction.

My personal recommendation, therefore, is to use a slow query log but to use it carefully, with caution. And most importantly, be aware of what you are really measuring.

The better approach in my opinion is to work more intensively with the pg_stat_statements variable. It will offer aggregated information and not just information about single queries. The pg_stat_statements variable has already been discussed earlier in this book. However, the importance of the module cannot be stressed more.

Inspecting individual queries

Sometimes, slow queries are identified but you still don't have a clue of what is really going on. The next step is, of course, to inspect the execution plan of the query and see what happens. Identifying those key operations in the plan that are responsible for bad runtime is fairly simple. Try to use the following checklist:

- Try to see where in the plan, time starts to skyrocket
- Check for missing indexes (one of the main reasons for bad performance)
- Use the EXPLAIN clause (buffers true, analyze true, and so on) to see if your query uses too many buffers

- Turn on the `track_io_timing` parameter to figure out whether there is an I/O problem or a CPU problem (explicitly check if there is random I/O going on)
- Look for wrong estimates and try to fix them
- Look for stored procedures that are executed too frequently
- Try to figure out whether some of them can be marked as `STABLE` or `IMMUTABLE`, provided this is possible

Note that `pg_stat_statements` does not account for parse time, so if your queries are very long (query string), `pg_stat_statements` might be slightly misleading.

Digging deeper with perf

In most cases, working through this tiny checklist will help you to track down the majority of problems in a pretty fast and efficient way. However, even the information extracted from the database engine is sometimes not enough.

perf is an analysis tool for Linux that allows you to directly see which C functions cause problems on your system. Usually perf is not installed by default, so it is recommended to install it. To use perf on your server, just log in to a root and run:

```
perf top
```

The screen will refresh itself every couple of seconds and you will have a chance to see what is going on live. The next listing shows what a standard read-only benchmark might look like:

```
Samples: 164K of event 'cycles:ppp', Event count (approx.): 109789128766
Overhead   Shared Object                Symbol
   3.10%   postgres                     [.] AllocSetAlloc
   1.99%   postgres                     [.] SearchCatCache
   1.51%   postgres                     [.] base_yyparse
   1.42%   postgres                     [.]
hash_search_with_hash_value
   1.27%   libc-2.22.so                 [.] vfprintf
   1.13%   libc-2.22.so                 [.] _int_malloc
   0.87%   postgres                     [.] palloc
   0.74%   postgres                     [.]
MemoryContextAllocZeroAligned
   0.66%   libc-2.22.so                 [.] __strcmp_sse2_unaligned
   0.66%   [kernel]                     [k] _raw_spin_lock_irqsave
   0.66%   postgres                     [.] _bt_compare
   0.63%   [kernel]                     [k] __fget_light
   0.62%   libc-2.22.so                 [.] strlen
```

You can see that no single function takes too much CPU time in our sample, which tells us that the system is just fine.

However, this may not always be the case. There is a problem, one that is quite common, called **spinlock contention**. What is that? Spinlocks (`https://en.wikipedia.org/wiki/Sp inlock`) are used by the PostgreSQL core to synchronize things such as buffer access. A spinlock is a feature provided by modern CPUs to avoid operating system interaction for small operations (such as incrementing a number). It is a good thing, but in some very special cases, spinlocks can go crazy. If you are facing spinlock contention, the symptoms are as follows:

- Really high CPU load
- Incredibly low throughput (queries that usually take milliseconds suddenly take seconds)
- I/O is usually low because the CPU is busy trading locks

In many cases, spinlock contention happens suddenly. Your system is just fine, and all of a sudden, load goes up and throughput drops like a stone. The `perf top` command will reveal that most of the time is spent in a C function called `s_lock`. If this is the case, you should try to do the following:

```
huge_pages = try                        # on, off, or try
```

Change `huge_pages` from `try` to `off`. It can be a good idea to turn off huge pages altogether on the operating system level. In general, it seems that some kernels are more prone to producing these kinds of problems than others. The Red Hat 2.6.32 series seems to be especially bad (note that I have used the word *seems* here).

perf is also interesting if you are using PostGIS. If the top functions in the list are all GIS-related (some underlying library), you know that the problem is not most likely not coming from bad PostgreSQL tuning but is simply related to expensive operations that take time to complete.

Inspecting the log

If your system smells trouble, it makes sense to inspect the log to see what is going on. The important point is this: not all log entries are created equal. PostgreSQL has a hierarchy of log entries that ranges from DEBUG messages to PANIC.

To the administrator, the following three error levels are of great importance:

- ERROR
- FATAL
- PANIC

ERROR is used for problems such as syntax errors, permission-related problems, and so on. Your log will always contain error messages. The critical factor is: how often does a certain type of error show up? Producing millions of syntax errors is certainly not the ideal strategy to run a database server.

FATAL is more scary than ERROR; you will see messages such as could not allocate memory for shared memory name or unexpected walreceiver state. In other words, those error messages are already really scary and will tell you that things are going wrong.

Finally there is PANIC. If you hit this kind of message, you know that something is really, really wrong. Classic examples of PANIC are lock table corrupted or too many semaphores created. It will result in a shutdown.

Checking for missing indexes

Once you are done with the first three steps, it is important to take a look at performance in general. As I kept stating throughout this book, missing indexes are super important to achieve super bad performance. So, whenever you are facing a slow system, is it recommended to check for missing indexes and deploy whatever is needed.

Usually customers ask you to optimize the RAID level, tune the kernel, or some other fancy stuff. In reality, those complicated requests often boil down to a handful of missing indexes. By my judgment, it always makes sense to spend some extra time on just checking whether all desired indexes are there. Checking for missing indexes is neither hard nor time consuming, so it should be done all the time regardless of the kind of performance problem you are facing.

Here is my favorite query to get an impression of where an index might be missing:

```
SELECT    schemaname, relname, seq_scan, seq_tup_read,
          idx_scan, seq_tup_read / seq_scan AS avg
FROM      pg_stat_user_tables
WHERE     seq_scan > 0
ORDER BY seq_tup_read DESC
LIMIT 20;
```

Try to find large tables (high `avg`) that are scanned often. Those tables will typically come on top.

Checking for memory and I/O

Once you are done finding missing indexes, you can inspect memory and I/O. To figure out what is going on, it makes sense to activate `track_io_timing`. If it is on, PostgreSQL will collect information about disk wait and present it to you.

Often the main question asked by a customer is: if we add more disks, is it going to be faster? It is possible to guess what will happen, but in general, measuring is the better and more useful strategy. Enabling `track_io_timing` will help you to gather the data to really figure it out.

PostgreSQL exposes disk wait in various ways. One way to inspect things is to take a look at `pg_stat_database`:

```
test=# d pg_stat_database
          View "pg_catalog.pg_stat_database"
     Column      |          Type          | Modifiers
-----------------+------------------------+-----------
 datid           | oid                    |
 datname         | name                   |
 . . .
 conflicts       | bigint                 |
 temp_files      | bigint                 |
 temp_bytes      | bigint                 |
 . . .
 blk_read_time   | double precision       |
 blk_write_time  | double precision       |
```

Note that there are two fields towards the end: `blk_read_time` and `blk_write_time`. It will tell you about the amount of time PostgreSQL has spent on waiting for the OS to respond. Note that we are not really measuring disk wait here but rather the time the operating system needed to return data. If the operating system produces cache hits, this time will be fairly low. If the OS has to do really nasty random I/O, you will see that a single block can even take a couple of milliseconds.

In many cases, high `blk_read_time` and `blk_write_time` happen when `temp_files` and `temp_bytes` show high numbers. Also in many cases, this points to a bad `work_mem` or bad `maintenance_work_mem` setting. Remember this: if PostgreSQL cannot do things in memory, it has to spill to disk. `temp_files` is the way to detect that. Whenever there are `temp_files`, there is a chance for nasty disk wait.

While a global view on a per database level makes sense, it does not yield in-depth information about the real source of trouble. Often, only a few queries are to blame for bad performance. The way to spot those is to use `pg_stat_statements`:

```
test=# d pg_stat_statements
          View "public.pg_stat_statements"
        Column          |        Type        | Modifiers
------------------------+--------------------+-----------
. . .
 query                  | text               |
 calls                  | bigint             |
 total_time             | double precision   |
. . .
 temp_blks_read         | bigint             |
 temp_blks_written      | bigint             |
 blk_read_time          | double precision   |
 blk_write_time         | double precision   |
```

You will be able to see on a per query basis, whether there is disk wait or not. The important part is to see the `blk_` time in combination with `total_time`. The ratio is what counts. In general, a query that shows more than 30% of disk wait can be seen as heavily I/O bound.

Once you are done checking the PostgreSQL system tables, it makes sense to inspect what the `vmstat` command on Linux tells you. Alternatively, you can use the `iostat` command:

```
[hs@zenbook ~]$ vmstat 2
procs -----------memory---------- ---swap-- -----io---- -system-- ------
cpu-----
 r  b   swpd   free   buff  cache   si   so    bi    bo   in   cs us sy id
wa st
 0  0 367088 199488     96 2320388    0    2    83    96  106  156 16  6 78
 0  0
 0  0 367088 198140     96 2320504    0    0     0    10  595 2624  3  1 96
 0  0
 0  0 367088 191448     96 2320964    0    0     0     8  920 2957  8  2 90
 0  0
```

When doing database work, you should focus your attention on three fields: bi, bo, and wa. The bi field tells you about the number of blocks read; 1000 is the equivalent to 1 MB/second. The bo field is about blocks out. It tells us about the amount of data written to disk. In a way, bi and bo are the raw throughput. I would not consider a number to be harmful. What is a problem is a high wa value. Low values for bi and bo fields combined with a high wa value tell you about a potential disk bottleneck, which is most likely related to a lot of random I/O taking place on your system. The higher the wa value, the slower your queries, because you are waiting on the disk to respond.

> Good raw throughput is a good thing; it can also point to a problem. If high throughput is needed on an OLTP system, it can tell you that there is not enough RAM to cache things or that indexes are missing and PostgreSQL has to read too much data. Keep in mind that things are interconnected and data should not be seen as isolated.

Understanding noteworthy error scenarios

After a basic guideline to hunt down the most common issues, this section will discuss some of the most common error scenarios happening in the PostgreSQL world.

Facing clog corruption

PostgreSQL has a thing called **commit log**, also called **clog**. It tracks the state of every transaction on the system and helps PostgreSQL determine whether a row can be seen or not. In general, a transaction can be in four states:

```
#define TRANSACTION_STATUS_IN_PROGRESS     0x00
#define TRANSACTION_STATUS_COMMITTED       0x01
#define TRANSACTION_STATUS_ABORTED         0x02
#define TRANSACTION_STATUS_SUB_COMMITTED   0x03
```

The clog has a separate directory in the PostgreSQL database instance.

In the past, people have reported something called **clog corruption**, which can be caused by faulty disks or bugs in PostgreSQL that have been fixed over the years. A corrupted commit log is a pretty nasty thing to have because all your data is there but PostgreSQL does not know whether things are valid or not anymore. Corruption in this area is nothing short of a total disaster.

How does the administrator figure out that the commit log is broken? Here is what you normally see:

```
ERROR:  could not access status of transaction 118831
```

If PostgreSQL cannot access the status of a transaction, trouble is certain. The main question is: how can this be fixed? To put it straight, there is no way to really fix the problem--you can only try to rescue as much data as possible.

As stated already, the commit log keeps two bits per transaction. This means that we have four transactions per bytes, leaving us with 32,768 transactions per block. Once you have figured out which block it is, you can fake the transaction log:

```
dd if=/dev/zero of=<data directory location>/pg_clog/0001
    bs=256K count=1
```

You can use dd to fake the transaction log and set the commit status to the desired value. The core question is really: which transaction state should be used? The answer is that *any state* is actually wrong because you really don't know, how those transactions ended. However, usually it is a good idea to just set them to committed in order to lose less data. It really depends on your workload and your data when deciding what is less disruptive.

When you have to do that, you should fake as little clog as necessary. Remember, you are essentially faking the commit status, which is not a nice thing to do to a database engine.

Once you are done faking the clog, you should try to create a backup as fast as you can and recreate the database instance from scratch. The system you are working with is not too trustworthy anymore so you should try to extract data as fast as you can. Keep this in mind: the data you are about to extract can be contradictory and wrong, so make sure that some quality checks are imposed on whatever you are able to rescue from your database server.

Understanding checkpoint messages

Checkpoints are essential to data integrity as well as performance. The further checkpoints are apart, the better performance usually is. In PostgreSQL, the default configuration is usually fairly conservative and checkpoints are therefore comparatively fast. If a lot of data is changed in the database core at the same time, it can happen that PostgreSQL tells us that it considers checkpoints to be too frequent. The log file will show the following entries:

```
LOG:  checkpoints are occurring too frequently (2 seconds apart)
LOG:  checkpoints are occurring too frequently (3 seconds apart)
```

During heavy writing due to dump/restore or due to some other large operation, PostgreSQL might notice that the configuration parameters are too low. A message is sent to the log to tell us exactly that.

If you see this kind of message, it is strongly recommended for performance reasons to increase checkpoint distances by increasing the `max_wal_size` parameter dramatically (in older versions the setting was called `checkpoint_segments`). In recent versions of PostgreSQL, the default configuration is already a lot better than it used to be. However, writing data too frequently can still happen easily.

When you see a message about checkpoints, there is one thing you have to keep in mind... Checkpointing too frequently is not dangerous at all--it just happens to lead to bad performance. Writing is simply a lot slower than it could be but your data is not in danger. Increasing the distance between two checkpoints sufficiently will make the error go away and speed up your database instance at the same time.

Managing corrupted data pages

PostgreSQL is a very stable database system. It protects data as much as possible and has proven its worth over the years. However, PostgreSQL relies on hardware and a properly working filesystem. If storage breaks, so will PostgreSQL--there is not much you can do about it apart from adding replicas to make things more fail-safe.

Once in a while, it happens that the filesystem or the disk fails. But in many cases, the entire thing will not go south; just a couple of blocks are corrupted for whatever reason. Recently, we have seen that happening in virtual environments. Some virtual machines don't flush to disk by default, which means that PostgreSQL cannot rely on things being written to disk. This kind of behavior can lead to random problems which are hard to predict.

When a block cannot be read anymore, you might face an error message like the following one:

```
"could not read block %u in file "%s": %m"
```

The query you are about to run will error out and stop working.

Fortunately, PostgreSQL has means to deal with these things:

```
test=# SET zero_damaged_pages TO on;
SET
test=# SHOW zero_damaged_pages;
 zero_damaged_pages
--------------------
 on
(1 row)
```

`zero_damaged_pages` is a config variable that allows you to deal with broken pages. Instead of throwing an error, PostgreSQL will take the block and simply fill it with zeros.

Note that this will definitely lead to data loss. But remember, data was broken or lost before anyway so this is simply a way to deal with corruption caused by bad things happening in your storage system.

I would advise everybody to handle the `zero_damaged_pages` variable with care--be aware of what you are doing when you call it.

Careless connection management

In PostgreSQL, every database connection is a separate process. All those processes are synchronized using shared memory (technically in most cases, it is mapped memory but for this example, that makes no difference). This shared memory contains the I/O cache, the list of active database connections, locks, and more vital stuff which makes the system function properly.

When a connection is closed, it will remove all relevant entries from shared memory and leave the system in a sane state. However, what happens when a database connection simply crashes for whatever reason?

The postmaster (the main process) will detect that one of the child processes is missing. Then, all other connections will be terminated and a roll-forward process will be initialized. Why is that necessary? When a process crashes it might very well happen that the shared memory area is edited by the process. In other words, a crashing process might leave shared memory in a corrupted state. Therefore, the postmaster reacts and kicks everybody out before the corruption can spread in the system. All memory is cleaned and everybody has to reconnect.

From an end user point of view, this feels like PostgreSQL has crashed and restarted, which is not the case. As a process cannot react on its own crash (segmentation fault) or on some other signals, cleaning out everything is absolutely essential to protect your data.

The same happens if you use `kill -9` command on a database connection. The connection cannot catch the signal (-9 cannot be caught by definition), and therefore the postmaster has to react again.

Fighting table bloat

Table bloat is one of the most important issues when dealing with PostgreSQL. When you are facing bad performance, it is always a good idea to figure out whether there are objects that need a lot more space than they are supposed to.

How can you figure out where table bloat is happening? Consider checking out the `pg_stat_user_tables` parameter:

```
test=# d pg_stat_user_tables
           View "pg_catalog.pg_stat_user_tables"
          Column          |             Type             | Modifiers
--------------------------+------------------------------+-----------
 relid                    | oid                          |
 schemaname               | name                         |
 relname                  | name                         |
 . . .
 n_live_tup               | bigint                       |
 n_dead_tup               | bigint                       |
```

The `n_live_tup` and `n_dead_tup` fields will give you an impression of what is going on. You can also use `pgstattuple` as outlined in an earlier chapter.

What can you do if there is serious table bloat? The first option is to run VACUUM FULL clause. The trouble is that the VACUUM FULL clause needs a table lock. On a large table, this can be a real problem because users cannot write to the table while is is rewritten.

If you are using at least PostgreSQL 9.6, you can use a tool called `pg_squeeze`. It organizes a table behind the scenes without blocking: `http://www.cybertec.at/introducing-pg_sq` `ueeze-a-postgresql-extension-to-auto-rebuild-bloated-tables/`.

> This is especially useful if you are reorganizing a very large table.

Summary

In this chapter, you learned to systematically approach a database system and detect the most common issues people face with PostgreSQL. You learned about some important system tables as well as some other important factors that decide whether you will succeed or fail.

In the final chapter of this book, we will focus our attention on migrating to PostgreSQL. If you are using Oracle or some other database system, you might be willing to check out PostgreSQL. The next chapter will tell you how to do that.

13
Migrating to PostgreSQL

In the previous chapter of this book, I showed you how to approach the most common issues related to PostgreSQL troubleshooting. The important thing is to have a systematic approach to tracking down problems, which is exactly what I tried to provide.

The final chapter of this book is about moving to PostgreSQL. Many readers might still be suffering from the pain caused by commercial database license costs. I want to give all those users out there a way out and show how data can be moved from some proprietary system to PostgreSQL. Moving to PostgreSQL not only makes sense from a financial point of view, but also makes sense if you are looking for more advanced features and more flexibility. PostgreSQL has so much to offer and new features are added as we speak.

The following things will be covered in this chapter:

- Migrating SQL statements to PostgreSQL
- Moving from Oracle to PostgreSQL
- Moving MySQL to PostgreSQL

At the end of the chapter, you should be able to move a basic database from some other system to PostgreSQL.

Migrating SQL statements to PostgreSQL

When moving from a database to PostgreSQL it makes sense to take a look and figure out which database engine provides which kind of functionality. Moving the data and the structure itself is usually fairly easy. However, rewriting SQL might not be. Therefore I decided to include a section which explicitly focuses on various advanced features of SQL and their availability in today's database engines.

In this section of this chapter, the most important stuff will be covered. To successfully move a database, it makes sense to understand which features are supported by which database. For the following sections, I have selected the most common database engines and compiled a comparison.

Using lateral joins

In SQL, a lateral join can basically be seen as some sort of loop. It basically allows us to parameterize a join and execute everything inside the LATERAL clause more than once. Here is a simple example:

```
test=# SELECT *
    FROM generate_series(1, 4) AS x,
        LATERAL (SELECT array_agg(y)
                    FROM generate_series(1, x) AS y
                ) AS z;
 x | array_agg
---+-----------
 1 | {1}
 2 | {1,2}
 3 | {1,2,3}
 4 | {1,2,3,4}
(4 rows)
```

The LATERAL clause will be called for each x. To the end user, it is basically some sort of loop.

Supporting lateral

In this chapter, you will learn a lot about various databases and figure out which features are supported in which engine. One important SQL feature is lateral join. The following list shows which engines support lateral join and which don't:

- MariaDB: Not supported
- MySQL: Not supported
- PostgreSQL: Since PostgreSQL 9.3
- SQLite: Not supported
- DB2 LUW: Since version 9.1 (2005)
- Oracle: Since 12c
- MS SQL Server: Since 2005 but when using with different syntax

Using grouping sets

Grouping sets are very useful if you want to run more than one aggregate at the same time. Using grouping sets can speed up aggregation because you don't have to process the data more than once.

Here is an example:

```
test=# SELECT x % 2, array_agg(x)
          FROM  generate_series(1, 4) AS x
          GROUP BY ROLLUP (1);
 ?column? | array_agg
----------+-----------
        0 | {2,4}
        1 | {1,3}
          | {2,4,1,3}
(3 rows)
```

PostgreSQL offers more than just the ROLLUP clause. The CUBE and GROUPING SETS clause are also supported.

Supporting grouping sets

Grouping sets are essential to generate more than just one aggregation in a single query. The following list shows which engines support grouping sets and which don't:

- MariaDB: Only ROLLUP clause is supported since 5.1 (incomplete support)
- MySQL: Only ROLLUP clause since 5.0 (incomplete support)
- PostgreSQL: Since PostgreSQL 9.5
- SQLite: Not supported
- DB2 LUW: Since at least 1999
- Oracle: Since 9iR1 (around 2000)
- MS SQL Server: Since 2008

Using WITH clause - common table expressions

Common table expressions are a nice way to execute things inside an SQL statement only once. PostgreSQL will execute all WITH clauses and allows you to use the results all over the query.

Here is a simplified example:

```
test=# WITH x AS (SELECT avg(id)
                  FROM generate_series(1, 10) AS id)
   SELECT  *, y - (SELECT avg FROM x) AS diff
   FROM    generate_series(1, 10) AS y
   WHERE   y > (SELECT avg FROM x);
  y  |         diff
----+--------------------
  6  | 0.5000000000000000
  7  | 1.5000000000000000
  8  | 2.5000000000000000
  9  | 3.5000000000000000
 10  | 4.5000000000000000
(5 rows)
```

In this example, the `WITH` clause **common table extension** (**CTE**) calculates the average value of the time series generated by `generate_series` function. The resulting x can be used just like a table all over the query. In my example x is used twice.

Supporting WITH clause

The following table shows which engines support `WITH` clause and which don't:

- MariaDB: Not supported
- MySQL: Not supported
- PostgreSQL: Since PostgreSQL 8.4
- SQLite: Since 3.8.3
- DB2 LUW: Since 8 (year 2000)
- Oracle: Since 9iR2
- MS SQL Server: Since 2005

Note that, in PostgreSQL, a CTE can even support writes (`INSERT`, `UPDATE`, and `DELETE` clause).

Using WITH RECURSIVE clause

The `WITH` clause comes in two forms:

- Standard CTEs as shown in the previous section (Using `WITH` clause)
- A method to run recursions in SQL

The simple form of a CTE has already been covered in the previous section. In this section, the recursive version will be covered.

Supporting WITH RECURSIVE clause

The following table shows which engines support WITH RECURSIVE clause and which don't:

- MariaDB: Not supported
- MySQL: Not supported
- PostgreSQL: Since PostgreSQL 8.4
- SQLite: Since 3.8.3
- DB2 LUW: Since 7 (year 2000)
- Oracle: Since 11gR2 (in Oracle, it is usually more common to use CONNECT BY clause instead of WITH RECURSIVE clause)
- MS SQL Server: Since 2005

Using FILTER clause

When looking at the SQL standard itself, you will notice that the FILTER clause has already been around with SQL (2003). However, not many systems actually support this highly useful syntax element.

Here is an example:

```
test=# SELECT  count(*),
               count(*) FILTER (WHERE id < 5),
               count(*) FILTER (WHERE id > 2)
       FROM    generate_series(1, 10) AS id;
 count | count | count
-------+-------+-------
    10 |     4 |     8
(1 row)
```

The FILTER clause is useful if a condition cannot be used inside a normal WHERE clause because some other aggregate is in need of the data.

Before the introduction of the FILTER clause, the same could be achieved using a more cumbersome syntax:

```
SELECT sum(CASE WHEN .. THEN 1 ELSE 0 END) AS whatever
  FROM some_table;
```

Supporting FILTER clause

The following table shows which engines support FILTER clause and which don't:

- MariaDB: Not supported
- MySQL: Not supported
- PostgreSQL: Since PostgreSQL 9.4
- SQLite: Not supported
- DB2 LUW: Not supported
- Oracle: Not supported
- MS SQL server: Not supported

Using windowing functions

Windowing and analytics have already been discussed extensively in this book. Therefore, we can jump straight to the SQL compliance part.

Supporting windowing and analytics

The following table shows which engines support window functions and which don't:

- MariaDB: Not supported
- MySQL: Not supported
- PostgreSQL: Since PostgreSQL 8.4
- SQLite: Not supported
- DB2 LUW: Since version 7
- Oracle: Since version 8i
- MS SQL server: Since 2005

Some other databases such as Hive, Impala, Spark, and NuoDB also
support analytics.

Using ordered sets - WITHIN GROUP clause

Ordered sets are fairly new to PostgreSQL. The difference between an ordered set and
normal aggregate is that in the case of an ordered set, the way data is fed to the aggregate
does make a difference. Suppose you want to find a trend in your data—the order of data is
relevant.

Here is a simple example of calculating a median value:

```
test=# SELECT id % 2,
        percentile_disc(0.5) WITHIN GROUP (ORDER BY id)
  FROM generate_series(1, 123) AS id
  GROUP BY 1;
 ?column? | percentile_disc
----------+-----------------
        0 |              62
        1 |              61
(2 rows)
```

The median can be determined only if there is sorted input.

Supporting WITHIN GROUP clause

This list shows which engines support windows functions and which don't:

- MariaDB: Not supported
- MySQL: Not supported
- PostgreSQL: Since PostgreSQL 9.4
- SQLite: Not supported
- DB2 LUW: Not supported
- Oracle: Since version 9iR1
- MS SQL Server: The query has to be remodeled using the windowing function

Using TABLESAMPLE clause

Table sampling has long been the real strength of commercial database vendors. Traditional database systems have provided sampling for many years. However, the monopoly has been broken. Since PostgreSQL 9.5, we also have a solution to the problem of sampling.

Here is how it works:

```
test=# CREATE TABLE t_test (id int);
CREATE TABLE
test=# INSERT INTO t_test
    SELECT * FROM generate_series(1, 1000000);
INSERT 0 1000000
```

First a table containing 1 million rows is created. Then tests can be executed:

```
test=# SELECT count(*), avg(id)
         FROM t_test TABLESAMPLE BERNOULLI (1);
 count |         avg
-------+---------------------
  9802 | 502453.220873291165
(1 row)
test=# SELECT count(*), avg(id)
         FROM t_test TABLESAMPLE BERNOULLI (1);
 count |         avg
-------+---------------------
 10082 | 497514.321959928586
(1 row)
```

In this example, a 1% sample is taken from the data. The average value is pretty close to 5 million so the result is pretty good from a statistical point of view.

Supporting TABLESAMPLE clause

The following list shows which engines support TABLESAMPLE clause and which don't:

- MariaDB: Not supported
- MySQL: Not supported
- PostgreSQL: Since PostgreSQL 9.5
- SQLite: Not supported
- DB2 LUW: Since version 8.2
- Oracle: Since version 8
- MS SQL Server: Since 2005

Using limit/offset

Limiting a result in SQL is a somewhat sad story. To make it short, every database does things somewhat differently. Although there is actually an SQL standard on limiting results, not everybody fully supports the way things are supposed to be. The correct way to limit data is to actually use the following syntax:

```
test=# SELECT * FROM t_test FETCH FIRST 3 ROWS ONLY;
 id
----
  1
  2
  3
(3 rows)
```

If you have never seen this syntax before, don't worry. You are definitely not alone.

Supporting FETCH FIRST clause

The following list shows which engines support FETCH FIRST clause and which don't:

- MariaDB: Since 5.1 (usually, limit/offset is used)
- MySQL: Since 3.19.3 (usually, limit/offset is used)
- PostgreSQL: Since PostgreSQL 8.4 (usually, limit/offset is used)
- SQLite: Since version 2.1.0
- DB2 LUW: Since version 7
- Oracle: Since version 12c (used subselects with row_num finction)
- MS SQL Server: Since 2012 (traditionally top-*N* is used)

As you can see, limiting result sets is quite tricky, and when you are porting a commercial database to PostgreSQL, you will most likely always be confronted with some proprietary syntax.

Using OFFSET

The OFFSET clause is a similar drama as the FETCH FIRST clause . It is easy to use but it has not been widely adopted early on. It is not as bad as in the the FETCH FIRST clause case, but it still tends to be an issue.

Supporting OFFSET clause

The following list shows which engines support OFFSET clause and which don't:

- MariaDB: Since 5.1
- MySQL: Since 4.0.6
- PostgreSQL: Since PostgreSQL 6.5
- SQLite: Since version 2.1.0
- DB2 LUW: Since version 11.1
- Oracle: Since version 12c
- MS SQL Server: Since 2012

As you can see, limiting result sets is quite tricky and, when you are porting a commercial database to PostgreSQL, you will most likely always be confronted with some proprietary syntax.

Using temporal tables

Temporal tables are provided by some database engines to handle versioning. Unfortunately, there is no such thing as out-of-the-box versioning in PostgreSQL. So, if you are moving from DB2 or Oracle, there is some work ahead of you to port the desired functionality to PostgreSQL. Basically changing the code a bit on the PostgreSQL side is not hard. However, it does need some manual intervention—it is not a straight copy and paste thing anymore.

Supporting temporal tables

The following list shows which engines support temporal tables and which don't:

- MariaDB: Not supported
- MySQL: Not supported
- PostgreSQL: Not supported
- SQLite: Not supported
- DB2 LUW: Since version 10.1
- Oracle: Since version 12cR1
- MS SQL server: Since 2016

Matching patterns in time series

The most recent SQL standard I am aware of (SQL 2016) provides a feature designed to find matches in time series. So far, only Oracle has implemented this functionality into their latest version of the product.

At this point, no other database vendor has followed and added similar functionality. If you want to model this state-of-the-art technology in PostgreSQL, you have to work with windowing function and subselects. Matching time series patterns in Oracle is pretty powerful; there is not just one type of query to achieve the same in PostgreSQL.

Moving from Oracle to PostgreSQL

So far, you have seen how the most important advanced SQL features can be ported or used in PostgreSQL. After this introduction, it is time to take a look at migrating Oracle database systems in particular.

These days, migrating from Oracle to PostgreSQL has become really popular due to Oracle's new license and business policy. Around the world, people are moving away from Oracle and adopting PostgreSQL. To help people make Oracle a thing of the past, I have included a special section here. Many people are already moving to PostgreSQL to seriously reduce license costs.

Using the oracle_fdw extension to move data

One of my preferred methods to move people from Oracle to PostgreSQL is Laurenz Albe's `oracle_fdw` extension (`https://github.com/laurenz/oracle_fdw`). It is a **foreign data wrapper** (**FDW**), which allows you to represent a table in Oracle as table in PostgreSQL. `oracle_fdw` extension is one of the most sophisticated FDWs and is rock solid, well documented, free, and open source.

Installing the `oracle_fdw` extension requires you to install the Oracle client library. Fortunately, there are already RPM packages which can be used out of the box (`http://www.oracle.com/technetwork/topics/linuxx86-64soft-092277.html`). The `oracle_fdw` extension needs the OCI driver to talk to Oracle. In addition to ready-made Oracle client drivers, there is also an RPM package for the `oracle_fdw` extension itself, which is provided by the community. If you are not using an RPM based system, you might have to compile things on your own, which is clearly possible but a bit more labor intensive.

Once the software has been installed, it can be enabled easily:

```
test=# CREATE EXTENSION oracle_fdw;
```

The CREATE EXTENSION clause loads the extension into your desired database. In the next step, a server can be created and users can be mapped to their counterparts on Oracle side:

```
test=# CREATE SERVER oraserver FOREIGN DATA WRAPPER oracle_fdw
        OPTIONS (dbserver '//dbserver.example.com/ORADB');
test=# CREATE USER MAPPING FOR postgres SERVER oradb
        OPTIONS (user 'orauser', password 'orapass');
```

Then it is time to fetch some data. My preferred way is to use the IMPORT FOREIGN SCHEMA clause to import the data definitions. The IMPORT FOREIGN SCHEMA clause will create a foreign table for each table in a remote schema and expose the data on the Oracle side, which can then be read easily.

The easiest way to make use of the schema import is to create separate schemas on PostgreSQL, which just hold the database schema. Then data can be sucked into PostgreSQL easily using the FDW. The last section of this book about migrating from MySQL shows an example of how this can be done with MySQL/MariaDB. Keep in mind that the IMPORT FOREIGN SCHEMA clause is part of the SQL/MED standard and therefore the process is the same as witty MySQL/MariaDB. This applies to pretty much every FDW which supports the IMPORT FOREIGN SCHEMA clause.

While oracle_fdw extension does most of the work for you, it still makes sense to see how datatypes are mapped. Oracle and PostgreSQL don't provide the exact same datatypes so some mapping is either done by oracle_fdw extension or by you manually. The following list gives you an overview of how types are mapped. The left column shows the Oracle types and the right side presents the potential PostgreSQL counterparts:

Oracle types	PostgreSQL types
CHAR	char, varchar, and text
NCHAR	char, varchar, and text
VARCHAR	char, varchar, and text
VARCHAR2	char, varchar, and text
NVARCHAR2	char, varchar, and text
CLOB	char, varchar, and text
LONG	char, varchar, and text

RAW	uuid and bytea
BLOB	bytea
BFILE	bytea (read-only)
LONG RAW	bytea
NUMBER	numeric, float4, float8, char, varchar, and text
NUMBER(n,m) with m<=0	numeric, float4, float8, int2, int4, int8, boolean, char, varchar, and text
FLOAT	numeric, float4, float8, char, varchar, and text
BINARY_FLOAT	numeric, float4, float8, char, varchar, and text
BINARY_DOUBLE	numeric, float4, float8, char, varchar, and text
DATE	date, timestamp, timestamptz, char, varchar, and text
TIMESTAMP	date, timestamp, timestamptz, char, varchar, and text
TIMESTAMP WITH TIME ZONE	date, timestamp, timestamptz, char, varchar, and text
TIMESTAMP WITH LOCAL TIME ZONE	date, timestamp, timestamptz, char, varchar, and text
INTERVAL YEAR TO MONTH	interval, char, varchar, and text
INTERVAL DAY TO SECOND	interval, char, varchar, and text
MDSYS.SDO_GEOMETRY	geometry

If you want to use geometries, make sure that PostGIS is installed on your database server.

The downside of oracle_fdw extension is definitely that it cannot migrate procedures out of the box. Stored procedures are a somewhat special thing and need some manual intervention.

Using ora2pg to migrate from Oracle

People migrated from Oracle to PostgreSQL long before foreign data wrappers existed. High license costs have plagued people for a long time, and so moving to PostgreSQL has been a natural thing to do for many years.

The alternative to `oracle_fdw` extension is something called ora2pg, which has been around for many years and which can be downloaded freely from `https://github.com/darold/ora2pg`. Ora2pg has been written in Perl and has a long tradition of new releases.

The features provided by ora2pg are stunning:

- Migration of the full database schema including tables, views, sequences, and indexes (unique, primary, foreign key, and check constraints).
- Migration of privileges for users and groups.
- Migration of partitioned tables.
- Export predefined functions, triggers, procedures, packages, and package bodies.
- Migration of full or partial data (using a `WHERE` clause).
- Full support of Oracle `BLOB` object as PostgreSQL `bytea`.
- Export Oracle views as PostgreSQL tables.
- Export Oracle user defined types.
- Basic automatic conversion of PL/SQL code to PL/pgSQL code. Note that a fully automated conversion of everything is not possible. However, a lot of stuff can be transformed automatically.
- Export Oracle tables as foreign data wrapper tables.
- Export materialized view.
- Display of detailed reports of an Oracle database content.
- Assessment of the complexity of the migration process of an Oracle database.
- Migration cost assessment of PL/SQL code from a file.
- Ability to generate XML files to be used with Pentaho data integrator (Kettle).
- Export Oracle locator and spatial geometries into PostGIS.
- Export database links as Oracle FDW.
- Export synonyms as views.
- Export directory as an external table or directory for `external_file` extension.
- Dispatch a list of SQL orders over multiple PostgreSQL connections.
- Perform a diff between Oracle and PostgreSQL database for test purpose.

Using ora2pg looks hard at first glance. However, it is actually a lot easier than it seems. The basic concept is as follows:

```
/usr/local/bin/ora2pg -c /some_path/new_ora2pg.conf
```

ora2pg needs a config file to run. The config file contains all the information needed to handle the process. Basically, the default config file is already really nice and it is a good start for most migrations. In ora2pg language a migration is a project.

The configuration will drive the entire project. When you run the thing, ora2pg will create a couple of directories with all the data extracted from Oracle:

```
ora2pg --project_base /app/migration/ --init_project test_project
Creating project test_project.
/app/migration/test_project/
                schema/
                        dblinks/
                        directories/
                        functions/
                        grants/
                        mviews/
                        packages/
                        partitions/
                        procedures/
                        sequences/
                        synonyms/
                        tables/
                        tablespaces/
                        triggers/
                        types/
                        views/
                sources/
                        functions/
                        mviews/
                        packages/
                        partitions/
                        procedures/
                        triggers/
                        types/
                        views/
                data/
                config/
                reports/

Generating generic configuration file
Creating script export_schema.sh to automate all exports.
Creating script import_all.sh to automate all imports.
```

As you can see, scripts are generated which can just be executed. The resulting data can then be imported in PostgreSQL nicely. Be prepared to change procedures here and there. Not everything can be migrated automatically, so manual intervention is usually expected.

Common pitfalls

There are some very basic syntax elements that work in Oracle but might not work in PostgreSQL. This section lists some of the most important things. Of course, this list is not complete by far, but it should point you into the right direction.

In Oracle, you might find the following statement:

```
DELETE mytable;
```

In PostgreSQL, this statement is wrong as PostgreSQL requires you to use a FROM clause in the DELETE statement. The good news is that this kind of statement is easy to fix.

The next thing you might find is:

```
SELECT sysdate FROM dual;
```

PostgreSQL neither has sysdate function nor dual function. The dual function part is easy to fix as you can simply create a view returning one line. In Oracle, dual function works like this:

```
SQL> desc dual
Name Null? Type
---------------------------------------- -------- -
DUMMY VARCHAR2(1)

SQL> select * from dual;

D
-
X
```

In PostgreSQL, the same can be achieved by creating the view:

```
CREATE VIEW dual AS SELECT 'X' AS dummy;
```

The `sysdate` function is also easy to fix. It can be replaced with `clock_timestamp()` function.

Another common problem is the lack of datatypes such as `varchar2` as well as the lack of special functions only supported by Oracle. A good way to get around these issues is to install `orafce` extension, which provides most of the stuff typically needed. It certainly makes sense to check out `https://github.com/orafce/orafce` to learn more about `orafce` extension. It has been around for many years and is a solid piece of software. A study recently conducted shows that `orafce` extension helps to ensure that at 73% of all Oracle SQL can be executed on PostgreSQL without modifications if `orafce` extension is around (done by NTT).

One of the most common pitfalls is the way Oracle handles outer joins. Consider the following example:

```
SELECT employee_id, manager_id
   FROM employees
   WHERE employees.manager_id(+) = employees.employee_id;
```

This kind of syntax is not provided by PostgreSQL and never will be. Therefore the join has to be rewritten as a proper outer join. The + is highly Oracle specific and has to be removed.

Moving from MySQL or MariaDB to PostgreSQL

In this chapter, you have already learned some valuable lessons about how to move from databases such as Oracle to PostgreSQL. Migrating both database systems to PostgreSQL is fairly easy. The reason for that is that Oracle might be expensive and Oracle might be a bit cumbersome from time to time. The same applies to Informix. However, both Informix and Oracle have one important thing in common: CHECK constraints are honored properly and datatypes are properly handled. In general, you can safely assume that the data in those commercial systems is somewhat correct and doesn't violate the most basic rules of data integrity and common sense.

Our next candidate is different. Many things you know from commercial databases are not true in MySQL. NOT NULL does not mean much to MySQL (unless you explicitly use strict mode). In Oracle, Informix, DB2, and all other systems I am aware of NOT NULL is a law, which is obeyed under all circumstances. MySQL does not take those constraints that seriously by default. In case of migration, this causes some issues. What are you going to do with data which is technically wrong? If your NOT NULL column suddenly reveals countless null entries, how are you going to handle that? MySQL doesn't just insert null values in NOT NULL columns. It will insert an empty string or 0 based on the datatype. So, things can be pretty nasty.

Handling data in MySQL and MariaDB

As you might imagine and as you might have noticed already, I am far from unbiased when it comes to databases. However, I don't want to turn this into blind MySQL/MariaDB bashing. My goal is really to show you why MySQL and MariaDB can be such a pain in the long run. I am biased for a reason and I really want to point out why this is the case. All the things you are going to see are deeply scary and have serious implications on the migration process in general. I have pointed out already that MySQL is somewhat special, and this section will try to prove my point.

Let me get started by creating a simple table:

```
MariaDB [test]> CREATE TABLE data (
    id      integer NOT NULL,
    data    numeric(4, 2)
);
Query OK, 0 rows affected (0.02 sec)

MariaDB [test]> INSERT INTO data VALUES (1, 1234.5678);
Query OK, 1 row affected, 1 warning (0.01 sec)
```

So far, there is nothing special. I have created a table consisting of two columns. The first column is explicitly marked as NOT NULL. The second column is supposed to contain a numeric value, which is limited to four digits. Finally, I have added a simple row. Can you see a potential landmine about to blow up? Most likely not. However, check the following listing:

```
MariaDB [test]> SELECT * FROM data;
+----+--------+
| id | data   |
+----+--------+
|  1 | 99.99  |
+----+--------+
1 row in set (0.00 sec)
```

If I remember correctly, I have added a four digit number, which should not have worked in the first place. However, MariaDB has simply changed my data. Sure, a warning is issued but this is not supposed to happen as the content of the table does not reflect what I have actually inserted.

Let me try to do the same thing in PostgreSQL:

```
test=# CREATE TABLE data (
    id    integer NOT NULL,
    data  numeric(4, 2)
);
CREATE TABLE
test=# INSERT INTO data VALUES (1, 1234.5678);
ERROR:  numeric field overflow
DETAIL:  A field with precision 4, scale 2 must round to an absolute value
less than 10^2.
```

The table is created just like earlier, but in sharp contrast to MariaDB/MySQL, PostgreSQL will error out because we are trying to insert a value into the table, which is clearly not allowed. What is the point in clearly defining what we want if the database engine just does not care? Suppose you have won the lottery, but you might have just lost a couple of million just because the system has decided what is good for you.

I have been fighting commercial databases all my life, but I have never seen similar things in any of the expensive commercial systems (Oracle, DB2, MS SQL, and so on). They might have issues of their own but the data was just fine in general.

Changing column definitions

Let us see what happens if you want to modify the table definition:

```
MariaDB [test]> ALTER TABLE data MODIFY data numeric(3, 2);
Query OK, 1 row affected, 1 warning (0.06 sec)
Records: 1  Duplicates: 0  Warnings: 1
```

Do you see a problem here?

```
MariaDB [test]> SELECT * FROM data;
+----+------+
| id | data |
+----+------+
|  1 | 9.99 |
+----+------+
1 row in set (0.00 sec)
```

As you can see, the data has been modified again. It should not have been there in the first place and has been changed all over again. Remember, you might again have lost money or some other nice asset because MySQL tried to be clever.

What happens in PostgreSQL:

```
test=# INSERT INTO data VALUES (1, 34.5678);
INSERT 0 1
test=# SELECT * FROM data;
 id | data
----+-------
  1 | 34.57
(1 row)
```

Let us change the column definition now:

```
test=# ALTER TABLE data ALTER COLUMN data TYPE numeric(3, 2);
ERROR:  numeric field overflow
DETAIL:  A field with precision 3, scale 2 must round to an absolute value
less than 10^1.
```

Again, PostgreSQL will error out and it won't allow you to do nasty things to your data. The same is expected to happen in any important database. The rule is simple: PostgreSQL and others won't allow you to destroy your data.

However, PostgreSQL allows you to do one thing:

```
test=# ALTER TABLE data
    ALTER COLUMN data
         TYPE numeric(3, 2)
         USING (data / 10);
ALTER TABLE
```

You can explicitly tell the system how to behave. In this case, I explicitly told PostgreSQL to divide the content of the column by 10. Developers can explicitly provide the rules applied to the data. PostgreSQL won't try to be smart and it does so for good reason:

```
test=# SELECT * FROM data;
 id | data
----+------
  1 | 3.46
(1 row)
```

The data is exactly as expected.

Handling null values

I don't want to turn this into a *why MariaDB is bad chapter* but I wanted to add a final example here, which I consider to be of high importance:

```
MariaDB [test]> UPDATE data SET id = NULL WHERE id = 1;
Query OK, 1 row affected, 1 warning (0.01 sec)
Rows matched: 1  Changed: 1  Warnings: 1
```

Remember, the id column was explicitly marked as NOT NULL:

```
MariaDB [test]> SELECT * FROM data;
+----+------+
| id | data |
+----+------+
|  0 | 9.99 |
+----+------+
1 row in set (0.00 sec)
```

Obviously, MySQL and MariaDB think that null and zero are the same thing. Let me try to explain the problem with a simple parable: if you know your wallet is empty it is not the same as *I don't know how much I have*. As I am writing those lines, I don't know how much money I have with me (null = unknown), but I am 100% sure that it is way more than zero (I know with certainty that it is enough to refuel my beloved car on the way home from the airport, which is hard to do if you have nothing in your pocket).

Here is more scary news:

```
MariaDB [test]> DESCRIBE data;
+-------+--------------+------+-----+---------+-------+
| Field | Type         | Null | Key | Default | Extra |
+-------+--------------+------+-----+---------+-------+
| id    | int(11)      | NO   |     | NULL    |       |
| data  | decimal(3,2) | YES  |     | NULL    |       |
+-------+--------------+------+-----+---------+-------+
2 rows in set (0.00 sec)
```

MariaDB does remember that the column is supposed to be null. However, it simply modifies your data again.

Expecting problems

The main problem is that you might have trouble moving data to PostgreSQL. Just imagine you want to move some data and there is a NOT NULL constraint on the PostgreSQL side. We know MySQL does not care:

```
MariaDB [test]> SELECT CAST('2014-02-99 10:00:00' AS datetime) AS x,
    CAST('2014-02-09 10:00:00' AS datetime) AS y;
+------+---------------------+
| x    | y                   |
+------+---------------------+
| NULL | 2014-02-09 10:00:00 |
+------+---------------------+
1 row in set, 1 warning (0.00 sec)
```

PostgreSQL will definitely reject the 99 of February (for a good reason), but it might not accept the null value either if you have explicitly banned it (for a good reason). What you have to do in this case is to somehow fix the data to make sure that it honors the rules of your data models, which are in place for a reason. You should not take this lightly because you might have to change data, which is actually wrong in the first place.

Migrating data and schema

After trying to explain why moving to PostgreSQL is a good idea and after outlining some of the most important issues, it is time to take a look at some of the possible options you have to finally get rid of MySQL/MariaDB.

Using pg_chameleon

One way to move from MySQL/MariaDB to PostgreSQL is to use Federico Campoli's tool called pg_chameleon, which can be downloaded freely from GitHub: `https://github.com/the4thdoctor/pg_chameleon`. It has been explicitly designed to replicate data to PostgreSQL and does a lot of work such as converting the schema and so on for you.

Basically the tool performs the following four steps:

1. pg_chameleon reads the schema and data from MySQL and creates a schema in PostgreSQL.
2. Stores MySQL's master connection information in PostgreSQL.
3. Create primary keys and indices in PostgreSQL.
4. Replicates from MySQL / MariaDB to PostgreSQL.

pg_chameleon provides basic support for DDLs such as `CREATE`, `DROP`, `ALTER TABLE`, `DROP PRIMARY KEY`, and so on. However, due to the nature of MySQL/MariaDB, it does not support all DDLs. Instead it covers the most important features.

However, there is more to pg_chameleon. I have stated extensively already that data is not always the way it should be and expected to be. The way pg_chameleon approaches the problem is to discard rubbish data and store it in a table called `sch_chameleon.t_discarded_rows`. Of course, this is not a perfect solution but, given the fairly low quality input, it is the only sensible solution which comes to my mind. The idea is to let developers decide what to do with all the broken rows. There is really no way for pg_chameleon to decide on how to handle something which has been broken by somebody else.

Recently, a lot of development has taken place and a lot of work has gone into the tool. Therefore, it is really recommended to check out the GitHub page and read through all the documentation. Features and bug fixes are added as we speak. Given the limited scope of this chapter full coverage is therefore not possible.

> Stored procedures, triggers, and so on need special treatment and can only be handled manually. pg_chameleon cannot process those things automatically.

Using foreign data wrappers

If you want to move from MySQL/MariaDB to PostgreSQL there is more than one way to succeed. The use of foreign data wrappers is an alternative to pg_chameleon and offers a way to quickly fetch the schema as well as the data and import it into PostgreSQL. The ability to connect MySQL and PostgreSQL has been around for quite a while and therefore foreign data wrappers are definitely a field which can be exploited to your advantage.

Basically, the `mysql_fdw` extension works just like any other FDW out there. Compared to other less known FDWs the `mysql_fdw` extension is actually quite powerful and offers the following features:

- Writing to MySQL/MariaDB
- Connection pooling
- The `WHERE` clause push down (which means that filters applied on a table can actually be executed remotely for better performance)
- Column push down (only the columns needed are fetched from the remote side, older versions used to fetch all the columns, which leads to more network traffic)
- Prepared statements on the remote side

The way to use the `mysql_fdw` extension is to make use of the `IMPORT FOREIGN SCHEMA` statement, which allows moving data over to PostgreSQL.

Fortunately, this is fairly easy to do on a Unix system.

The first thing you have to do is to download the code from GitHub:

```
git clone https://github.com/EnterpriseDB/mysql_fdw.git
```

Then run the following commands to compile the FDW. Note that the paths might differ on your system. For this chapter, I have assumed that both MySQL and PostgreSQL are under `/usr/local` directory, which might not be the case on your system:

```
$ export PATH=/usr/local/pgsql/bin/:$PATH
$ export PATH=/usr/local/mysql/bin/:$PATH
$ make USE_PGXS=1
$ make USE_PGXS=1 install
```

Once the code has been compiled, the FDW can be added to your database:

```
CREATE EXTENSION mysql_fdw;
```

The next step is to the server you want to migrate:

```
CREATE SERVER migrate_me_server
    FOREIGN DATA WRAPPER mysql_fdw
    OPTIONS (host 'host.example.com', port '3306');
```

Once the server has been created you can create the desired user mappings:

```
CREATE USER MAPPING FOR postgres
    SERVER migrate_me_server
    OPTIONS (username 'joe', password 'public');
```

Finally, it is time to do the real migration. The first thing to do is to import the schema. I suggest creating a special schema for the linked tables first:

```
CREATE SCHEMA migration_schema;
```

When running IMPORT FOREIGN SCHEMA statement you can use this schema as the target schema, in which all the database links will be stored. The advantage is that you can delete it conveniently after the migration.

Once you are done with IMPORT FOREIGN SCHEMA statement you can already create real tables. The easiest way to do that is to use the LIKE keyword provided by CREATE TABLE clause. It allows you to copy the structure of a table and create a real local PostgreSQL table. Fortunately this also works if the table you are cloning is just a foreign data wrapper. Here is an example:

```
CREATE TABLE t_customer
    (LIKE migration_schema.t_customer);
```

Then you can already process the data:

```
INSERT INTO t_customer
    SELECT * FROM migration_schema.t_customer
```

This is actually the point where you can correct the data, eliminate chunk rows, or do a bit of processing of the data. Given the low quality origin of the data, it can be useful to apply constraints and so on after moving the data for the first time. It might be less painful. In proper databases, the reverse process might make sense.

Once the data has been imported, you are ready to deploy all the constraints, indexes, and so on. At this point you will actually start to see some nasty surprises because as I stated previously, don't expect the data to be rock solid.

Summary

In this chapter, you learned how to move to PostgreSQL. Migration is an important topic and more and more people are adopting PostgreSQL as we speak.

Index

R